68-26191

1/20/73

RELIGIOUS SYMBOLISM

RELIGION AND CIVILIZATION SERIES

RELIGIOUS
SYMBOLISM

EDITED BY

F. Ernest Johnson

PROFESSOR EMERITUS OF EDUCATION, TEACHERS
COLLEGE, COLUMBIA UNIVERSITY

KENNIKAT PRESS, INC./PORT WASHINGTON, N. Y.

THE INSTITUTE FOR RELIGIOUS AND SOCIAL STUDIES
RELIGIOUS SYMBOLISM

Copyright 1955 By The Institute For Religious And Social Studies
Reissued 1969 By Kennikat Press
By arrangement with Harper & Row, Publishers, Incorporated

Library of Congress Catalog Card No: 68-26191
Manufactured in the United States of America

ESSAY AND GENERAL LITERATURE INDEX REPRINT SERIES

This volume is based on lectures given at The Institute for Religious and Social Studies of The Jewish Theological Seminary of America during the winter of 1952–1953. Doctor Hugo Weisgall spoke on "The Use of Music in Religious Liturgy," but unfortunately could not prepare a chapter for publication.

Each chapter in this volume represents solely the individual opinion of the author. Neither the Institute nor the editor assumes responsibility for the views expressed. The contributors were invited to address the Institute because of the special contribution each could make to general knowledge of the subject.

This is a Jacob Ziskind Memorial publication.

FOREWORD

The series of addresses appearing in this volume represent one aspect of the current exploration of symbolism by scholars in many fields. They are in part a by-product of the Thirteenth Symposium of the Conference on Science, Philosophy and Religion, published early this year. A paragraph from the Foreword to the Symposium, written by R. M. MacIver, is highly relevant here. Speaking of the relation between art and religion, with respect to symbolism, he says:

No area of human communication depends more on symbolic expression than that of religious experience. This is a theme that deserves intensive study. The study would be not only illuminative, but also of practical import, for perhaps in no area so much as in the area of religion does consideration need to be given to the problem of adapting old symbols to new conditions and to minds trained in a very different way from those to which the old symbols were addressed.[1]

Along with that timely observation it is well to consider some sharply critical words of Susanne K. Langer:

As soon as religion becomes prosaic or perfunctory art appears somewhere else. Today the Church tolerates utterly bad painting and sculpture, and banal music, in the belief that saccharine Virgins and barbershop harmonies are "nearer to the people" than the "distanced," visionary Madonnas to which great artists gave (and still give) their souls and skills. . . . Indifference to art is the most serious sign of decay in any institution; nothing bespeaks its old age more eloquently than that art, under its patronage, becomes literal and self-imitating.[2]

[1] R. M. MacIver, *Symbols and Values: An Initial Study,* Conference on Science, Philosophy and Religion in Their Relation to the Democratic Way of Life, New York, 1954, p. xi.
[2] Suzanne K. Langer, *Feeling and Form,* Charles Scribner's Sons, New York, 1953, pp. 402–403.

The addresses which follow deal with religious symbols in a wide context. The reader will quickly sense both the difficulty which scholars are having in defining the word, "symbol," and the wide range of applicability which it inevitably has acquired. The role of symbols in achieving "awareness," the way they effectuate communication between cultures, their essential contribution to corporate worship, their indispensable function in theology and in the mediation of religious experience with its infinite variety—all these aspects of a fascinating subject are informingly reported on.

The bearing of the scientific analysis of symbolism on the understanding of religious symbols is impressively shown. Also, the reader is reminded of a danger that the legitimate and essential use of religious symbols may be vitiated by a "clamor for symbolism" which confuses a material symbol with what is symbolized.

The significance of myth in great literature is given original treatment. The rediscovery of religious drama, and the reinstatement of the religious dance—which might perhaps without irreverence be called a "resurrection of the body"—are strikingly described. Light is thrown on the rapidly developing field of religious architecture, which presents the problem of maintaining historic continuity in the integration of traditional forms with changing functional needs.

The series ends with a three-faith look into the future of religious symbolism. That future is as certain as the future of religion.

For the convenience of the reader the appended bibliographic material is presented under the relevant chapter headings, as submitted by the writers themselves. Because of the nature of some of the addresses bibliographies directly relevant to them are not available.

THE EDITOR

May, 1954

CONTENTS

RELIGIOUS SYMBOLISM

I

THE FOUNDATIONS OF CHRISTIAN SYMBOLISM

BY

CYRIL C. RICHARDSON, TH.D.

*Washburn Professor of Church History,
Union Theological Seminary*

My paper will be concerned with early Christian symbolism. In the first part I shall attempt to describe the nature of this symbolism, drawing various illustrations from the Roman catacombs. In the second part I shall deal with baptism, using the frescoes from Dura-Europos to indicate its meaning. Finally I shall treat the Eucharist especially in connection with the frescoes in the Crypts of the Sacraments in Rome. From these illustrations I hope to give a cursory but representative view of the way the early Christians thought of the central themes of their faith, and the way they depicted them in symbolic form.

The Nature of Symbolism

Let us then start by asking what symbolism is. Trained as we are in a highly rational and mechanical culture, where the control of nature and the dominance of rational thinking are primary concerns, we may have some initial difficulty in penetrating the mind of the Early Church. We are likely to think of symbolism as something essentially unnecessary. We deal in hard facts, which do not lend themselves to the symbolic. We think of a symbol as standing for something else, and we imagine that as soon as we grasp that something else, the symbol has served its turn and is no longer of use. It

I

is the something else, to which the symbol points, that is the reality; and hence we no longer need the symbol once we have passed beyond it to the truth it veils. That is why, as a culture, we have so few symbols. We do not instinctively think in symbolic terms, because we suppose we have outgrown them. We imagine that our control of nature, for instance, brings us into direct contact with reality, which we can manipulate for our own ends and which needs no symbolic expression. A symbol is a token of something else, and the more quickly we grasp that something else and do away with the symbol, the better.

The superficiality of this view is becoming clear as we penetrate the depths of our being through psychotherapy. We are discovering that symbols are the primary mode of our becoming aware of things. They are the way we register meanings in our depths. Far from being unnecessary, they are the first means we have of apprehending things; and the symbols, which the unconscious throws up, dominate our ways of acting. Dream analysis is showing us that our relations with other people and with ourselves are highly symbolic. We think, for instance, of so-and-so as a tiger; and without even being directly conscious of it, we form our pattern of conduct toward him on that presupposition. We are dominated by that symbol. While it certainly stands for such and such a person or type of person (for we react to types more often than to individuals), it does not stand for him in such a way that we can grasp his reality behind the symbol, and so do away with it. What we really know about him *is* the symbol. It is this that influences us. Nor can we easily be rid of it. When our symbols are distorted, it is a lengthy process of psychotherapy which is needed until we can alter them. But even when we are enabled to change them, we do not get beyond them. They are our way of becoming aware, of registering meanings. Indeed, most of reality is not accessible to us without symbols; for it is by symbols that we come into contact with it. What the symbol does is to give reality meaning, so that we can participate in it. As we uncover the actual symbols by which we live and which form the foundations of our patterns of conduct, we will be increasingly driven to see their dynamic importance.

Too long we have imagined that Church symbolism, for instance, has to do with making windows which no one can today understand. They are purely artificial, being dug up from a remote past with which we are out of contact. They have to be explained; and in the explaining they are surely finished: for as soon as a symbol is explained in other terms, it ceases to be a true symbol. It is a mere sign or token, artificial and lifeless, and its explanation, not itself, is the point of contact we have with reality: for a true symbol cannot be "explained" in the sense that the explanation is more important than the symbol, and makes it unnecessary. Rather is the symbol a sort of fountainhead from which a great many meanings and relationships flow; but without the symbol these could not be known. In knowing them, moreover, the symbol becomes heightened, not lessened, in significance. It is like a treasure chest, in which are discovered treasures new and old and which often seems inexhaustible.

The word, "symbol," is derived from the Greek verb, *symballō*. It is perhaps true that the noun, *"symbolon,"* takes its meaning as a sign by which one knows or infers something, from the extended sense of *symballō,* to compare, hence to conjecture or infer. In the medical world *symbolon* meant a symptom or distinctive mark. Yet the deeper significance of the word, "symbol," lies in the more original sense of the verb, *"to bring together."* In three most important ways the symbol "brings together."

First, it is the means by which something is made intelligible or accessible to us. For this to happen, events or truths must be brought together into a coherent pattern. A unity must be established, otherwise there is only a chaos of items. That is what the symbol does. It draws together events or truths so that they can be grasped by us in an intelligible unity. Let us illustrate this from one of the most frequent pictures on the sarcophagi of the Roman catacombs.

The question is asked, "Who is Peter?" The early Christian did not answer this by telling you the various events of Peter's life, where he was born and so on, or by painting his portrait as he actually was— tall or short, fat or thin, with this or that complexion. None of these things really answers the question in the deepest sense; and most of them are irrelevant to Peter's real meaning for Roman Christianity. And so the early Christian drew a symbolic picture—a naive one to be sure, and often one of surprising crudeness, yet nonetheless profound for all that. It was, too, a quite surprising picture, which has given literal-minded interpreters no little trouble. It is a picture of a bearded man striking a rock and water flowing from it. That is Peter in all important senses for the early Christian. But, you object, have you not misunderstood this? Surely that is Moses, striking the rock in the wilderness. No, it is not Moses, for the artist is careful to add the beard. When Moses is depicted he is beardless; and there is one fresco which brings this out very clearly. We see the beardless Moses taking off his shoes (the reference is, of course, to the story of the burning bush), and beside him the bearded Peter striking the rock. The two are together in other frescoes of the giving of the Law. Now what does this all mean? Is it not obvious? Peter is the new Moses; like Moses, he receives the new law from God, and like Moses, he strikes the rock and water issues from it. Is not Peter himself (as his very name, "Kepha," indicates) the rock of the Church, and did he not come to Rome for the very purpose of making available the waters of baptism? Peter, moreover, was responsible for baptizing the first Gentile convert, Cornelius—a point of particular interest to the Roman Church; and this is depicted on the sarcophagi by showing Roman legionaries, rather than Israelites, slaking their thirst in the waters from the rock. Thus in that picture is comprehended the very essence of Roman Christianity. It tells everything important about Peter—the new lawgiver; the rock of the Church, the waters of baptism, the conversion of Gentiles. What symbol could be more fitly chosen to answer the question, "Who is Peter?" Everything important is brought together into a coherent and intelligible whole.

But the symbol "brings together" in a second way. It is the cohesive factor in a society. It is its meaningful center. It gives shape and pattern to its belief and conduct. It is not the society which gives the symbol meaning, so much as the symbol which gives the society meaning. Not for nothing did the Latins speak of the *Credo* as *symbolum*. By this more is meant than that the Creed was the distinctive mark of Christians. It was the Creed as the comprehensive affirmation of the Faith, which bound the society together and gave it direction and substance. When, in the fifth century, the Eastern poet

Narsai describes the Liturgy, he mentions the fact that "at the time of the mysteries" the congregation "thunder forth with their faith, reciting it with mouth and heart without doubting." Here we catch a glimpse of what the *Credo* meant. It was the affirmation of truth, to which the Christian society gave unconditional allegiance. It was the core of their social being.

Yet in a third way the symbol "brings together." Perhaps its most marked characteristic is its capacity to comprehend an almost infinite variety of meanings and relationships. And the fact that these are brought together into a very simple, single whole, gives the symbol its fascination. Who has not noticed this in his own dreams? A single figure or incident will sum up a whole complicated series of patterns and relationships. The associations will be of many kinds. They will include color, names, puns, position—almost anything. And when the conscious mind begins to penetrate their significance, one often feels that there is something uncanny in the way the sub-conscious can join together so much into so simple a picture.

The two dominant symbols in the catacombs illustrate this with peculiar force; and we may dwell upon them for a moment. The first is the sacred fish. It is everywhere displayed in the catacombs, and references to it come again and again in early Christian literature. What does it mean and whence did it arise?

Over this latter question a great debate has been held, and it is not yet settled. Does the fish come from the Gospels or from paganism? Was it first suggested by the fact that the Greek letters, "i-ch-th-u-s," form an acrostic, being the initial letters of the words, "Jesus Christ, Son of God and Savior"? [1] I cannot here review this interminable debate. It must suffice to give my own view about the origin and meaning of the Christian fish, drawing upon sources which this debate has uncovered.

It cannot be disputed that there were two predisposing factors in the Christian environment, which certainly helped in the choice of this symbol. For one thing the Gospel had had its origin among the fisherfolk of Galilee. For another, the fish from time immemorial had appeared to man as a mysterious creature, fit to be venerated, for

[1] *Iesous Christos Theou (H)uios Sōter.*

its existence depended upon conditions which were the precise opposite of those favorable to man. The painstaking researches of Franz
Doelger and Robert Eisler have uncovered so much about the sacred
fish in pagan religion, that one gets the impression that everyone in
the first century was a devotee of the sacred fish, under one form or
another. Of course this is exaggeration; but the evidence, which
Doelger managed to spin out to four volumes, is certainly impressive.
Everywhere we seem to find fish. They form the fit sacrifice for the
gods of the underworld. They are the offering for the dead in the
cult of Adonis, and they are the symbol of luck and life in Syria and
Mesopotamia. They are the holy food of the priests of Atargatis in
Syro-Phrygia. They are the *coena pura* of the Jewish meal initiating
the Sabbath. And from remote ages the Babylonian priests of Oannes
dressed themselves up as fish. Add to this the astral connection with
the Pisces of the Zodiac, and we may say there was a good deal that
was "fishy" about ancient religion in more senses than one.

But these predisposing factors do not, by themselves, suffice to
explain the Christian symbol. The Early Church did not devise its
symbolism in such a haphazard and accidental fashion. Suggestions
certainly they took from their own environment and from paganism.
But not *any* suggestion. We must look for something at once more
simple and profound, if we are satisfactorily to account for the symbol.

For myself I cannot but think the acrostic was an afterthought. It
is possible that a scribe writing out "Jesus Christ, Son of God" in an
abbreviated form, might have hit upon the connection, but this is
doubtful. We are not too clear about the manner of these abbrevia-
tions in early manuscripts; and while puns and acrostics were the
order of the day in popular as well as sophisticated religion, I feel a
much more simple and obvious connection is to be found.

When we consider the high significance of adult baptism in the
Early Church, and the role that the baptism of Jesus played in the
imagination of the early Christian, we can find a ready clue to the
solution of our problem. Jesus was the God revealed in the water. In
the earliest strata of the Gospel the baptism of Jesus is the event
which determines His mission, gives Him the awareness of the Kingdom as now present in some sense in Himself, and, by the appearance

of the dove, is the first Epiphany. Indeed, the feast of Epiphany originally celebrated the baptism, and certainly antedated the feast of Christmas. What connection would be more obvious then than this: Jesus is the God revealed in the water, hence the sacred fish?

But, like all profound symbols, the fish caught up a great variety of meanings, and to these we must now address ourselves. If Jesus was the sacred fish because He was the God revealed in the water, then the baptized Christian is the little fish (*pisculus*). In consequence, the catacombs sometimes show Christ as a fisherman, fishing in the water from Peter's rock. But more than this. The waters of baptism are consecrated by the descent of the Christ-Logos into them, to purify them. And so in a double sense the Christ is the God in the water. Thus Serapion prays over the baptismal waters, "Let thine ineffable Logos come to be in them and transform their energy and cause them to be generative."

But the fish is also food. The tag of Augustine, *"piscis assus, Christus est passus"* (the fish which is eaten is the Christ Who suffered) gives us another connection. The same God revealed in the water, and descending again into the water at Christian baptism, is the heavenly food of the Eucharist. Hence the consecration of the bread and wine is often depicted by the consecration of the sacred fish. This, too, is related to the fish in the story of Tobit (Chapter 6). Tobias cooks and eats the fish, and it is also a charm against evil spirits and cures blindness. The idea, however, of the Christ as the sacred fish which is eaten in the Eucharist, is most clearly expressed in the famous inscriptions of Abercius and Pectorius. Abercius says, "(Faith) set before me for food the pure fish from the mighty spring, whom a spotless Virgin caught, and gave this to friends to eat, always having sweet wine and giving the mixed cup with bread." Similarly Pectorius: "Take from the Redeemer of the saints the food as sweet as honey; eat with joy and desire, holding the Fish in thy hands. I pray, give as food the Fish, Lord and Savior."

Yet the fish, as the sacrificial food, is also the food of the Heavenly Banquet. There is an eschatological note in the symbol. It looks toward the final consummation of the Kingdom in the Heavenly Banquet, and speaks also of the fact that this Kingdom is partly realized, though not fulfilled, in the Church. For the sacred fish is Leviathan, of Jewish apocalyptic; and Leviathan is the main course at the Heavenly Banquet. And yet a further connection. In Ezekiel 47, the hoped-for Kingdom involves the healing of the Dead Sea. We often forget to what extent the Jewish imagination was depressed by the arid desert and the fruitlessness of the Dead Sea. The healing of this barren waste, so that it flows with crystal water and is alive with fish, is Ezekiel's symbol of the good times to come, and cannot have been unknown to the early Christian who searched the Scriptures with more care than we are accustomed to.

But we are not yet done. The fish is the symbol of the resurrection. The sign of Jonah, which perpetually recurs in the catacombs, is the sign of Christ's resurrection, and of our own. So the sacred fish revealed in the waters of Jordan, descending on the baptismal water, eaten in the sacred mystery, to be eaten in the final Kingdom, is also the fish of the resurrection.

Often, too, the fish in the catacombs is in the form of a dolphin. And here we must go to the pagan connections to search out its meaning. The dolphin is the friend of man, the savior of the shipwrecked, the guide of souls to the underworld and the islands of the blest. All these meanings, of course, are applied to Christian baptism. Salvation comes from Christ, the dolphin. With Him one goes down to the underworld, being buried in baptism, and rises to enter the heavenly land. Finally (for there must be an end to this!) the dolphin is connected with music. It stands for the New Song, which Christianity brought to the world. It symbolizes the New Age now inaugurated by the heavenly music, upon which Clement of Alexandria expatiates in his *Protreptikos*.

The fish, then, means practically everything in the Early Christian faith. Baptism, Resurrection, Eucharist, and Kingdom are caught up into one central symbol. Through the fish the truths of the Faith are made a coherent whole.

The other example with which I wish to illustrate this comprehensive element in symbolism, is that of the Orante. It occurs with remarkable persistence in the catacombs; and because of the rich variety of its meaning it has been the center of as much debate as the fish.

The Orante is a figure, mostly feminine but sometimes masculine, which is employed with great frequency in the frescoes and on the sarcophagi. It is a figure in the attitude of prayer, with the arms extended upward and the elbows bent.

There can be little doubt that it stands, in the first place, for the soul of the dead person, for we are dealing in the catacombs with funerary art. The soul is regarded as feminine, even when the tomb is of a male. But for whom is the dead person praying? For those left behind, or for him or herself before God? Or does the figure represent the religious joy of the one now departed and living a glorified existence? We must never forget the striking element of joy that throbs through the catacombs. Death is not the final evil; but having been conquered by Christ, it is entrance into the land of light and peace. Hence early Christian funerals were anything but mournful. The day of death was the day of birth; and friends and relatives escorted the bier to the tomb with palm branches and cries of "Alleluia." For the funeral spoke about the resurrection, and the victory over death.

It would, I think, be artificial to claim any one of these interpretations for the Orante. Probably all are intended—and others, too. There are many instances in the frescoes where the Orante does not refer directly to the deceased, but stands for the Kingdom. This is especially the case when it bears a direct relation to the picture of the Good Shepherd, of which I shall say more later. Then, again, the Orante means the Church. In a fresco depicting the consecration of the sacred fish on a tripod by a man in a *pallium,* an Orante is seen standing before the table. This is the Church in prayer. Finally, the Orante means the communion of the saints. The votive inscriptions around these figures are twofold. On the one hand, wishes are expressed *for* the dead, and on the other, the prayers of the dead are asked for the living. Thus the Orante unites heaven and earth, and speaks of the Church which transcends space and time, and of that fellowship which reaches across the boundary of death.

The extension of the arms in prayer was the customary pagan

mode of petition to God. But the Christian saw in it special significance, because this was the form of the cross. It is interesting in this
connection that the early pictures of the crucifixion (a theme purposely avoided in the catacombs, as the Christ as risen rather than as
crucified is the center of their attention) show the Savior crucified in
this attitude of prayer, where the arms are not fully extended, but the
elbows bent.

This, then, must suffice to illustrate the three ways in which symbols
"bring together." The symbol forms our contact with different aspects
of reality, because it makes of them an intelligible whole. It brings
together a society, knitting it into a cohesive group. And, finally, the
symbol comprehends a great number of meanings and relationships,
bringing them together into a single unit so that their intimate connection with each other may not be lost.

Baptism

In order to grasp the full significance of Christian baptism, let us
now take a look at the frescoes recently discovered in the earliest
Christian church which has been unearthed, the building at Dura-
Europos on the middle Euphrates. Dura formed a Roman military
camp on the outskirts of the Syrian desert, and was finally swept into
oblivion when the Sassanians captured and sacked it around 256 A.D.
It was left for the expedition from Yale University to recover it for
the world; and the Mithraeum and the Christian baptistry have been
reconstructed in the Art Museum at New Haven.

The Christian church is an unpretentious middle class dwelling
house by the west wall of the city. It stands, as it were, on Church
Street, for various temples along with the Mithraeum and the Jewish
synagogue are on the same street. Outwardly the church looks just
like any of the smaller houses in the area. It was, indeed, originally
one of them, and was built in 232 A.D. Soon afterward it was converted into a church. Two rooms on the north were knocked together
to constitute the main assembly hall, and a small room on the south
was transformed into a baptistry. This was decorated with frescoes,
which tell in a striking way the meaning of baptism.

It is well to recall that this church was in operation during the period of the first great persecution of the Church under Decius (249–251 A. D.). Thus, as we take ourselves in imagination to Christian baptism in Dura, we would do well to remember the dangers that surround the new convert.

The regular time for baptism is the Paschal Vigil; for as baptism essentially means dying and rising with Christ, it is appropriately held at Eastertide. Saturday evening we go as inconspicuously as possible up the little alley that leads to the front door. There we find deacons guarding our entrance. Satisfied that we are believers, they let us through; and we give them a little loaf with a decussated cross and a vial of wine. These we have brought with us for the first time as our offering for the Eucharist, because we shall now be privileged to attend it after our baptism.

We have already undergone a long period of instruction. How long in Dura it is not certain. In Rome it lasted three years. Joining the Church was a more serious step, and one more carefully prepared for, than it is today; and while infant baptism was practised as early as the second century, adult baptism was naturally the most usual.

All night we spend the time in prayer, Scripture reading, and instruction. The reading is from the Old Testament primarily, and the lessons are lengthy. They have as their central theme God's acts of redemption. Consequently we hear the stories of Adam and Eve, of Noah, Isaac, the Exodus, the Passover, the valley of dry bones in Ezekiel, Jonah, and the three children in the fiery furnace. These are the ancient Roman lections, and those in Dura were doubtless similar. Toward dawn—the dawn on which the Savior rose—comes our actual baptism, to which we have been looking forward perhaps for three whole years.

We are taken across the central court of the house and enter the baptistry. We have never seen it before, and the frescoes strike us at once. It is still dark, and the little chamber is lit with torches which play upon the painted walls. There, as we go in, we notice, first, on the upper part of the opposing wall, the healing of the paralytic. It is in two brief scenes. We see the sick man on his bed and Christ stretching out His hand to him, and alongside we see the paralytic carrying his bed on his shoulder. They are simple pictures, but full of motion and life—something like a child's drawing, free and realistic. They mean, of course, "Thy sins are forgiven thee." We are sick, and the root cause of it is sin. Yet baptism will be the healing of both sin and sickness. The picture, moreover, is associated with baptism because the story in Mark 2 has become connected in our minds with the healing of the impotent man at the pool of Bethzatha (John 5). Next we make out from the flickering torches a ship on the sea. And there is Peter sinking in the waves (as we shall soon be sinking in the waters of baptism); and there, too, is the Christ standing on the water and ready to raise up both him and us.

Underneath these pictures, we see the most striking one of all, running the whole length of the wall. There is a massive sarcophagus, sealed tight. In the darkness, indicated by the two stars on either side of the tomb, are coming the two Marys and Salome. Slowly, with rhythmic movements they approach the grave, bearing torches and bowls of spices for the anointing. Their classical movements are purposely meant to contrast with the lively pictures above, and to indicate the solemn nature of the mystery here portrayed. The imagination which created this picture can only be appreciated when we see it in relation to the Paschal Vigil. Our baptism occurs at exactly the moment that the Marys came in the darkness. The Christ is not yet risen. He is still in the grave. Thither we, too, will descend at baptism; and only then will He arise and we with Him. That is the significance of having this as the leading picture on the wall as we enter. It speaks to us of death and anticipated resurrection. The vases of ointment, moreover, are intended to refer to the anointing we will undergo after baptism. The Church, symbolized by the Marys, brings the gift of the Spirit through the holy chrism with which the bishop will anoint us.

When we are fully in the room we look at the other walls. The opposite one is decorated with a picture of David slaying Goliath. The symbolism is plain: it refers to redemption through the Son of David, the giant Goliath standing for the apparently overwhelming forces of sin and paganism. The baptismal connection, however, must not be forgotten. David finds his stones in the brook: the means of salvation comes by water. We also observe the woman of Samaria, drawing from the well the living waters of baptism.

The picture on the small east wall has been so destroyed that all that survives is the feet of five women. It is possible that, like the Marys, these are more myrrhophores. In any case what is notable is the dominant feminine element in the symbolism of this baptistry. It may perhaps be connected with the fact that women probably formed the larger part of an early Christian congregation. We recall, too, the significance of the Orante, of which we have already spoken; and it may well be that the themes of the soul, the Church, and the Kingdom (all feminine ideas) were here portrayed in some way.

The west end of the baptistry is the most colorful. There is an *aedicula,* a sort of little chapel which contains the font. Overarching the font is a canopy supported on colored columns. The inside roof of the canopy is painted blue with stars—to indicate, perhaps, the Valley of the Shadow, through which one passes in baptism. Baptism is, of course, total immersion and in the nude. On the west wall, immediately over the font, is the picture of the Good Shepherd, surrounded by a flock of sheep and carrying a large ram on his shoulders. Below, on a smaller scale, are Adam and Eve, the tree and the snake.

Here the symbolism, in general, is too obvious to need comment. Baptism means that what was lost in Eden is now recovered in the new creation and the new birth. That is why we are baptized nude, as we came from the mother's womb and are now brought forth from the womb of the Church. We may pause, however, to ask why the Good Shepherd, rather than the baptized Christ, should be the central picture. We might have thought it more appropriate to find such a picture as T. S. Eliot describes thus:

> A painter of the Umbrian school
> Designed upon a gesso ground
> The nimbus of a Baptized God.
> The wilderness is cracked and browned
>
> But through the water pale and thin
> Still shine the unoffending feet

> And there above the painter set
> The Father and the Paraclete.[2]

The reason why the Good Shepherd was preferred is not only because this was a favorite symbol of the Early Church, but also because it had a wide variety of connections, many of them being directly baptismal. It told far more than a picture of the baptized Christ could tell. Like all the great symbols, that of the Good Shepherd was comprehensive.

The Good Shepherd is the Teacher, because he shows the sheep the right pastures. He is the King, as Agamemnon or Jahweh is a Shepherd-King. He is the Logos assuming human nature, for the lamb or ram on his shoulders refers to this, as well as to the individual Christian, whom he rescues as a wounded sheep. Then again, like Orpheus and Hermes, he is the Guide of Souls to heaven. The Christian form of the Good Shepherd, indeed, is directly taken from similar statues of Orpheus Boukolos (The Herdsman) or Hermes Kriophoros (Ram-bearer). That is where the ram or the kid on his shoulders (instead of the lamb) comes from. We should not be astonished at the readiness of Christian artists to employ pagan forms as models. There are many examples in the Roman catacombs. Jonah's fish, for instance, is the dragon of Andromeda; Noah's ark is the chest of Deucalion and of Danaë and Perseus; while Jonah sleeping under his gourd is Endymion. We even find Christ directly pictured as Orpheus (lyre, cap, and all) charming wild beasts. The reference, of course, is to Isaiah 11:1–6, and to the restoration of nature by the Shepherd-God. In all these instances the point is not that Christianity was syncretic in blending paganism with itself, but that, quite careless of form, it used the pagan models to express a new meaning; just as it utilized pagan ideas to suggest a message which was essentially different. One cannot identify Orpheus and Christ. The way in which they were Saviors of Souls is far from the same. Thus, when the Christian Good Shepherd is surrounded by the seven planets, this means that he conducts the soul through all the hazards of celestial enemies; but it does not mean that either the hazards or

---

[2] T. S. Eliot, "Mr. Eliot's Sunday Morning Service," *Collected Poems, 1909–1935*, Harcourt, Brace & Company, New York, 1936, p. 63.

the redemption are conceived from the same point of view as a pagan cult.

The Good Shepherd has many connections with baptism, and they are most clearly seen in reference to the Twenty-third Psalm. "He leadeth me beside the still waters"—the waters of baptism which are "still" because the Logos descends upon them. "Yea, though I walk through the valley of the shadow of death, I will fear no evil." Baptism is just such a valley with its simulation of drowning and its dying with Christ. "Thou anointest my head with oil": here is the holy chrism. "Thou preparest a table before me . . . my cup runneth over": here is the baptismal Eucharist. Is it any wonder that the Good Shepherd was chosen as the central symbol of baptism, when it was expressive of so much?

Such, then, is the symbolism of the Dura baptistry. The pictures are bound together by the ideas of the saving water and the holy chrism. One dies and rises with Christ, and passing through the Paschal Vigil, one is brought to the joy of the resurrection and the heavenly pastures of the Good Shepherd.

The Eucharist

After baptism comes the Paschal Eucharist; and to illustrate its meaning let us transport ourselves from Dura to the Crypts of the Sacraments in the cemetery of Callixtus in Rome.

There is no symbolism more gripping than that of eating and drinking. It expresses in the deepest way the idea of participation. One becomes what one eats, and food is the very source of one's existence. It is for these reasons that feasting has always played a large role in cult practices. It is the bond which unites a fellowship with the closest ties; and the sacrificial imagery implied in the slaying of animals finds its consummation in the banquet that follows.

In the Christian frescoes the first important point to note is the close connection of the feast with baptism. Every Eucharist was a recalling of that event when the new convert was born anew and added to the fellowship of Christ. Hence Justin Martyr observes, after describing the Paschal ceremonies, "Henceforward we constantly remind one another of these things" (1 Apol. 67). By this he means that the Sunday Eucharist is a reenacting of the events of initiation, just as Sunday is the weekly celebration of the annual Pascha. With the growth of infant baptism, of course, the depth of this symbolism has long been lost. It is hard for us to recapture what it meant to be converted in later years and to undergo Christian initiation as an adult.

The arrangement of the frescoes in the Crypts of the Sacraments brings out very clearly this intimate association of baptism with the Eucharist. First we see the typical pictures of baptism: the man striking the rock, the man fishing, someone being baptized, and the paralytic with his bed. Then, on the principal wall, we observe the symbols of the Eucharist. First we see a three legged table bearing a loaf and a fish. A man wearing a *pallium* stretches his hands over these, to consecrate them. Beside the table stands the Orante, symbolizing the Church in prayer. The picture has a double meaning. It refers, in the first place, to the *missa pro defunctis* (of which we first hear in Tertullian); for we must not forget that catacomb art is funerary art in the first instance. But it also stands for the baptismal Eucharist and for every Sunday Eucharist which is so closely bound up with the recalling of baptism. Next we have a fresco depicting a banquet. Seven men are reclining at a banquet table in the usual form of a Sigma. Bread and fish are on the table, and six baskets of loaves are on either side of it. What does this mean?

First it means the Heavenly Banquet, at which the departed are now the guests. This is the celestial aspect of the Eucharist which unites earth and heaven. From Jewish Apocalyptic, as we have already observed, as well as from Gospel sayings such as Luke 22, 30, we know that Paradise was viewed in terms of eating and drinking.[3] The baskets of loaves, furthermore, symbolize the heavenly food, and refer, of course, to the miracle of the multiplication, at which the Christ anticipated the redemption of nature and the feast of the Kingdom.

But the banquet in our fresco has a second sense. It refers to the

[3] There is an interesting fresco in the cemetery of Domitilla showing a Christian, Veranda, being introduced to Paradise by St. Petronilla, Paradise being symbolized by a table with loaves and fish.

funeral *agape,* held in honor of the deceased. These feasts were not celebrated in the catacombs themselves as a rule, though it is possible this was the case in larger chapels such as the Capella Graeca. More usually, however, they took place in halls constructed above the catacombs,[4] Christians receiving some immunity for this—at any rate during years when persecution was not intense—as a funeral *collegium.* Such banquets were customary in the pagan world, and, indeed, we have a remarkable confirmation of this in a syncretistic fresco which has found its way into the Christian catacombs by some accident. In part of the cemetery of Praetextatus (which originally was not Christian at all, but added later) we see a tomb of a certain priest Vincentius. The frescoes depict the death of his wife, Vibia. She is shown carried off by Pluto in his chariot, then standing before his tribunal for judgment. Pluto's wife Proserpina is there, and the Fates are to the left. Then Vibia is introduced by a "good angel" to the celestial banquet, and takes her place, crowned with laurel, at the table. Then, to the side, is shown the funeral banquet given in her honor by her surviving husband, Vincentius. Seven "pious priests" (as the inscription reads) of the cult of Sebasis, are shown at the feast. The syncretistic nature of this cult is clear from the introduction of the sacred fish on the heavenly table, and the close affinity in other ways, with definitely Christian frescoes. However this may be, the picture indicates the typical pagan funeral banquet.

It may be remarked that the literary evidence for the funeral banquets of Christians is late (fourth century); but these catacomb frescoes, of which there are quite a few (the famous second century *Fractio Panis* [5] in the Capella Graeca of the cemetery of Priscilla being the earliest), would lead us to suppose that funeral *agapai* were considerably earlier, and that Christian churches were sometimes registered as burial societies. From the fourth century, when, under the peace of the Church, converts were flocking to the new faith, these

---

[4] The Liberian catalogue indicates that Pope Fabian built a number of such halls in the third century.

[5] This picture also has the double meaning of the Heavenly Banquet and the funeral *agape.* It is unfortunate that scholars still debate which of these two are intended. The answer surely is both. We have already said enough about the comprehensive nature of symbolism to make this clear.

agapai for the dead became scenes of debauchery and were gradually suppressed. Too much of the heathen element of the *Parentalia* was associated with them.

But to return to the Crypts of the Sacraments. Following the picture of the banquet is one of Abraham about to sacrifice Isaac, and (in the second crypt) another of the raising of Lazarus. These frescoes are of great significance; for they give us the interpretation of the Eucharist. It is at once sacrificial and the food of the resurrection. These are the two dominant themes in the symbolism of the Eucharist, as it was developed in the course of the centuries; and we may pause to say something about them.

It will be well, first to emphasize that sacrifice and resurrection apply to the Heavenly Banquet and the *agape,* as much as to the Eucharist. They form a single whole; and while the *agape* declined in sacramental importance and the chief emphasis fell upon the mystery of the Eucharist, the original identity of the rites was never completely lost. The fact, indeed, that Hippolytus in his *Apostolic Tradition* has to emphasize their difference, distinguishing between the "blessed bread" of the *agape* and "Eucharist" (26), sufficiently indicates the popular confusion which long survived.

Sacrifice and resurrection, then, are the meaning of the Christian banquet, in all its aspects, whether this is the heavenly one, or the Eucharistic one, or the funeral *agape.*

The ways in which the Eucharistic feast was sacrificial were many. The bread and wine which each contributed to the feast represented both the gifts of God and the labor of man's hands. Thus they were the pure sacrifice foretold by Malachai: a wheaten offering, for instance, for sin to replace the similar Levitical offering for cleansing from leprosy; and they were also the self, with its labor and possessions, offered to God. But in the deepest meaning the feast recalled the Christ as sacrificed for the sins of the world. Only in union with His sacrifice, could the Christians be complete. This recalling was more realistically conceived than in most current Protestantism. An image, a symbol, or a dramatic re-presentation was more than a sign or token. It implied that the image or "type" shared in the reality to which it pointed and which it conveyed. What we have already said about the dynamic power of symbols, applies with peculiar force to the sacraments. They are the way by which the heavenly reality is made accessible. They participate in it, making it intelligible and bringing it within our reach. In its fullest development this sacrificial aspect is most clearly seen in the Roman Mass which is dominated by this motif. On the altar the Christ, the pure victim, is sacrificed for the sin of the world. It would be wrong to claim that early Christianity, before Cyprian at any rate, was quite so realistic in its conception. But there can be no question that the Eucharist enacted the drama of the Passion in such a way that what was once and for all done on Calvary was made available in a moment of time to the Christian.

But the resurrection was the dominant note of the Christian celebration; and this is particularly the case in the context of the catacombs. It is interesting that the crucifixion is never depicted there. There is only one solitary fresco of Jesus being beaten and mocked, and it may well be that the reference here is also to some martyr. Death, to the early Christian, pointed at once to the joy of resurrection; and the earliest commentaries we have on the Eucharist (by Theodore of Mopsuestia and Narsai of Nisibis) give the theme of the resurrection the central place in this mystery. The offertory procession signifies the Passion and entombing: the consecration is the resurrection. As Theodore says: "We think of him on the altar as if he were placed in the sepulchre." And again, at the Epiclesis, "It is necessary, therefore, that our Lord should now rise from the dead by the power of the things that are taking place." This has always been the central motif of the Eastern rite; and, indeed, the symbolism of the Passion came to be confined to the preparatory service of the *Prothesis,* during which, with reference to Isaiah 53, the cutting of the loaves to be used at the Liturgy, was interpreted as the slaying of the Lamb of God. The fresco of the raising of Lazarus reminds us that to the early Christian the note of resurrection was the climactic one in the Eucharist. Sacrifice finds its culmination in the New Life: out of death life is born. While the symbolism was far from as fully developed as it became in the Eastern rites, where the original prayers do not always correspond to the interpretation along these lines, it is nonetheless clear that to the early Christian the consecrated bread and

wine were (as Ignatius says) "the drug of immortality." The gift
was resurrection and eternal life.

The banquet is also the Heavenly Banquet. The Eucharist unites
heaven and earth, and is a pledge of the Kingdom to come. That is
the meaning of the frescoes (in other cemeteries) of the marriage
in Cana of Galilee, which points to the marriage feast of the Lamb
with His Bride, the Church. It is the point, too, of the solitary fresco
of the raining of manna in the wilderness, manna being the food
brought by the Messiah for the messianic banquet of Jewish Apocalyptic, and referred to in John 6. And it is also the sense (as we have
already said) in which the miracle of the multiplication of the loaves
was taken.

A symbol which unites all these meanings in a very simple and
comprehensive way is that of a fish bearing on its back a basket of
bread and wine. Another is the curious one of a lamb carrying a milk
pail. The milk stands for the milk and honey received by the newly
baptized, along with the bread and wine, in the Paschal Eucharist, a
custom to which Hippolytus refers. This was the food first given
to infants in the ancient world. The new convert is as a little child,
having been born again. It stands, too, for the milk and honey of the
Promised Land, and also for the Eucharist itself, which is viewed
as the milk from the breast of the Savior or of the Church, by which
the convert is perpetually fed.

Thus, under terms of feasting, there are again brought together
the central themes of the Christian faith. Sacrifice, new birth, resurrection, and the heavenly Kingdom are united in a single, intelligible
whole.

Summary

Our cursory survey of Early Christian symbolism has, I hope, given
a representative view of the way the early Church conceived of its
faith, and sought to express its inner meanings and connections in
dynamic and striking pictures. The art is often crude, always naive.
Pagan influences, as we have seen, are frequently present in the forms
adopted. Yet one cannot but sense the presence of lively imagination

and creative genius. Something new had been born in the world. Especially is this evident in the funerary art. Here, in the very presence of death, a joy and a hope shine forth which are unconquerable.

Bibliography

Franz Doelger, *Ichthus,* Aschendorff, Muenster, 1922–1928, 4 vols. (For discussion of the symbolism of the fish.)

Robert Eisler, *Orpheus the Fisher,* J. M. Watkins, London, 1921. (For discussion of the symbolism of the fish.)

C. Hopkins and P. V. C. Baur, *The Christian Church at Dura-Europos,* Yale University Press, New Haven, 1934. (The frescoes in the Dura-Europos baptistry are here described in detail, but without an appreciation of their baptismal symbolism, in this reprint from the fifth report of the Yale excavations. A number of photographs and restorations are included.)

Dictionnaire d'Archeologie chrétienne et de Liturgie, article by L. Leclercq, Vol. 7, Cols. 1990–2086, 1927.

W. Lowrie, *Art in the Early Church,* Pantheon, New York, 1947. (An accessible, useful survey, which includes many photographs.)

W. Weidle, *The Baptism of Art,* Dacre Press, Westminster (London), 1950. (An illuminating pamphlet on the catacomb art.)

Josef Wilpert, *Die Malereien der Katacomben Roms,* Herder, Freiburg, 1903, 2 vols. (An indispensable book for the study of the art of the catacombs.)

II

THE LITURGICAL REVIVAL IN PROTESTANTISM

BY

MARVIN P. HALVERSON, B.D.

*Executive Director, Department of Worship and the Fine Arts,
The National Council of the Churches of Christ in the United
States of America*

Striking changes in the corporate worship of Protestant churches
are evident on every hand. Increased formalism and ceremonial can
be found in virtually every denominational expression of Protestantism. What these developments constitute and what they imply with
respect to the self-consciousness of the churches are questions for
which there are no simple responses. The title "The Liturgical Revival of Protestantism" itself involves certain presuppositions which
must be scrutinized before an adequate statement of the present situation can be made. There are those who would contend, for instance,
that "The Recent Discovery of Liturgy by Protestantism" would be
more descriptive of the actual situation. The present interest in worship is a new awareness within Protestantism which has no lively
antecedents but rather represents a dimension of the Church's life
which was lost in the Reformation. This argument has a certain
plausibility, for the patterns of worship and ceremonial today represent a sharp break with the practices of only a few decades ago. Yet
it is my conviction that this interpretation, though immediately appealing, has no support as one explores the formative periods of
Protestantism.

Manifestly, one cannot scrutinize Protestantism in its entirety. One
may rightly consider the Lutheran, Anglican, and Reformed churches

23

as representative of the main line of Protestantism. The Reformed branch, with a certain amount of historical elasticity, may be considered to include Presbyterians, Congregationalists, Methodists, Baptists, and Disciples of Christ. The topic must be defined even further by considering the word, "liturgical," for in its common usage it is somewhat tangential to its basic meaning. According to its etymology, liturgy signifies a "public work." It is that which concerns and involves the entire religious community. Liturgy is the structure through which the Church shows forth its faith before the world and it is on this basis that the Church's worship can properly be called "public worship." Liturgy in terms of its fundamental meaning, then, is not primarily a matter of greater or lesser ceremonial, elaborate or simple clerical attire, highly decorated or barren churches. Liturgical worship is that which enables the Christian community to show forth with fitness before the world the praises of the God Who in His mighty historical acts has made them His people. It is a communal reality and an activity on the part of God's people gathered in a particular place. The discussion of the liturgical revival in Protestantism is an assessment of a heritage, the decay of that heritage, and its renewal or revival. For when liturgy is conceived in this way, the Reformation is seen to have been, among other things, a liturgical movement. That awareness came upon me as a surprise because, like so many other Protestants, I had thought of Protestantism in terms of a later individualism which religiously is closer to pre-Reformation and late medieval individualism. I thought in terms of the religious atomization which has taken place in the centuries subsequent to the Reformation. Yet an exploration of the sixteenth century discloses that the Reformation was a liturgical movement.

The Reformation was grounded first of all in the belief that the Eucharist, the Lord's Supper, was the norm of worship if not the normal weekly service of the Christian community. Second, it was rooted in the belief that worship is a corporate act. And third, it was based on the Scriptures as the disclosure of that activity of God which calls forth worship.

Luther, Calvin, the Anglican Reformation, the early English Baptists and Congregationalists, the Methodists, and the Disciples of

Christ, despite their different nuances and varying testimonies, are all rooted in a liturgical movement. They were one in their concern that the Lord's Supper be recovered as the chief service of the Church's weekly worship. This constituted a radical demand. At the time of the Reformation very few Christians partook of Communion more often than once a year. Many explanations for the decline and the eventual neglect of the practises of the early Church may be made. However that may be, at the time of the Reformation the Mass was celebrated daily but it had ceased to be a communal act in the sense in which the Roman Catholic Church seeks to encourage participation today. The Mass was largely a thing to be observed and with the elevation of the Host the worshiper felt his "duty" had concluded. It was in order to restore a purified "Mass" to the people that Luther and Calvin soon dealt with the question of worship. Luther, for instance, took the Mass as it was then known and recast it in the German language, removing those elements which he thought were offensive to the new understanding of the Gospel through the Scriptures. It constituted a restoration of the Lord's Supper with communion by the people, together with preaching, as the chief act of worship.

Calvin desired to have the Eucharist celebrated in each church every Sunday morning as the chief service. He was thwarted by the magistrates in Geneva who feared a return to Roman Catholic practises, as well as thwarted by the indolence of the people for whom this was a new venture involving the responsibility of preparing to receive Communion weekly. Calvin was prevented from carrying out his liturgical reforms and accordingly made adjustments. He arranged to have the Lord's Supper celebrated in at least one church in Geneva each Sunday morning and, by this staggering of Communion, to insure its observance each Sunday and its availability to the Christian community weekly. In addition, Calvin established a pattern of worship which had the structure of the Eucharist, what is sometimes called a "dry Communion." Although the "elements" of the Communion were absent, the structure of worship pointed to a fulfilment in the breaking of the bread and the sharing of the cup.

In the Anglican Reformation the Eucharist was restored to centrality through the *Book of Common Prayer* in which the "Order of Holy Communion" was made the chief service. It should be noted that the order for Holy Communion was the only service in the Prayer Book which made specific provision for a sermon. Morning Prayer and Evening Prayer were the "reformed" versions of the canonical offices. Scrutiny of their structure and historical inquiry reveal them to be daily services. They were never intended to constitute the weekly worship of a Christian congregation. Holy Communion on Sunday was preceded often by Morning Prayer and the Litany, but the Lord's Supper was basic to worship. In the absence of communicants, the service was truncated as with Calvin's suggestions, thereby becoming an ante-Communion which still preserved the structure and focus of the Eucharist.

The same concern for the centrality of the Lord's Supper can be found in the later manifestations of the continuing Reformation. Contrary to popular opinion, the English ancestors of the present-day Baptists and Congregationalists believed firmly in the importance of weekly observance of the Lord's Supper. By the time these movements arose, the habits of worship in the Church of England had lost the initial impetus and it was the Baptists and Congregationalists who represented a concern for frequent if not weekly celebration of the Lord's Supper.

Among the early Methodists the concern of John Wesley for frequent attendance at Holy Communion exerted influence. *The Eucharistic Hymns of John and Charles Wesley,* published recently, has made vivid Wesley's concern with the Eucharist in terms which emphasize the corporate nature of the Holy Communion and the congregation's identification with its Lord Who is both Priest and Victim. Apart from his seemingly "high church" attitude, in contrast to "high clerical" views, Wesley's preaching heightened interest in participation at the Lord's Table to such an extent that parish priests in the Church of England were hard put. It has been suggested that the denial of Communion to masses of people who responded to the evangelical and eucharistic preaching prompted the ordination of ministers who might preside at the Table. It is intriguing to think that Methodism as a distinct denominational entity arose in some measure from the demand of Christian people to receive the Communion denied them at the altars of local parish churches.

The illustration of the eucharistic concern in Protestantism can be extended to the United States. The Disciples of Christ is a group indigenous to America, although it is represented in Great Britain. Arising out of Thomas and Alexander Campbell's dismay that all Christians could not gather around the Table of a common Lord, the movement displayed a concern for the Eucharist and Christian unity. Although frustrated in part of its purpose, since the movement became a new denomination, its witness to the Eucharist is manifested in each Disciples of Christ church where the Lord's Supper is celebrated every Sunday as an integral part of the congregation's worship.

This heritage has been lost in some instances and obscured or blunted in virtually every branch of the Reformation. Because of the infidelities of the children of the Reformation this heritage of a Eucharist-centered worship has disappeared to such an extent that its recovery in our day is not recognized as such but as an unjustified intrusion upon Protestant principles. Renewed historical interest, however, is making Protestants aware of traditions and roots which can be the source of new life in worship.

Secondly, the Reformation not only saw the Eucharist as the service or the norm of worship, but it emphasized the corporate nature of worship. To be sure, there was varying emphasis on this aspect in the different branches of the Reformation. Luther, for instance, inherited the strain of individualism in late Roman Catholicism. His own religious experience made for a subjectivity which was the mark of medieval piety. But his subjectivity was not completely individualistic, for it was rooted in the Gospel to such an extent that it became personal and thereby social. The community of believers offering up their thanksgiving for salvation through God's free gift of faith is a genuine community. Its orientation, however, is somewhat different from that of Calvin. Calvin's concern for membership in the elect made for an emphasis on the corporate aspect of worship, the intimate and organic involvement of one member with another in the offering to God of obedience and praise. The cohesion which explicit Calvinism throughout Europe demonstrated in succeeding centuries is an instance of that corporateness which the early Reformed worship vividly expressed.

It is to other groups in Protestantism, however, that we need to look for some of the most interesting manifestations of the corporate aspect of worship. Today the Sunday morning service is expected to carry the entire load of Christian life, communion, and witness. People gather from many parts of a city into a church, not knowing one another, possessing no communal experience of face-to-face relationships. This is unquestionably a sociological problem with peculiar urgency in an urban, commercial, and technological culture. In the early Church the weekly offering of worship was that of a community of persons known to one another as persons. The intimacy of many New Testament letters is rarely found in a contemporary communication of a church official. However, in the chapter meetings of the democratically governed monasteries, the early Church's experience of fellowship was continued. Early Baptists and Congregationalists in their weekly church meetings and Methodists in their class meeting displayed an understanding of the Christian life and its relationship to worship which contributes to our understanding of the problem today. These groups recognized the necessity of several organs for the full expression and nurture of the Christian corporate life. In the weekly meeting of the Church the faithful gathered and witnessed to one another, sharing in understanding the Christian faith, making confession and declaring forgiveness within the context of the Christian community. In this development, I believe, the Protestant concern for the corporateness of worship found its proper ground and the only adequate basis for full participation of the community of belief in the celebration of its rites and mysteries.

For all of Protestantism, corporate worship was enabled by the use of the vernacular and the development of orders which gave a role to the congregation. The hymnody of Protestantism afforded the congregation a vehicle for its vocal expression of liturgical activity. The metrical versions of the Psalms, which the Jesuits called "the siren of Calvinism," and the chorales of Lutheranism strengthened the feeling and vocation of the Protestants in a continually threatened existence. But primarily they united congregations for corporate worship in a way not possible in the former Roman Mass.

The third aspect of the Protestant heritage in worship is the basis which the rediscovered Scriptures afforded. While some included the witness of the undivided Church as authority, all of Protestantism was one in its adherence to Scripture as the ground of faith and the authority for Christian life and worship. There is a distinction which must be observed between the Lutheran and Calvinist expressions of the Reformation. The consequences for worship, ritual, ceremony, and art have continued to the present. While Luther understood worship, like faith, to be determined by the Scriptures, his understanding of the Bible was such that anything in Christian worship was permissible which was not explicitly prohibited. Thus Luther was able to justify continuance of vestments, candles, incense, and anything that helped a believer toward faith and a response of love. Thus one can find in Lutheran churches use of eucharistic vestments and ceremonial customarily associated with Roman Catholicism.

For Calvin, however, the situation was contrary. Only that which was specifically authorized or had precedent in Scripture was valid for Christian worship. For that reason the greater changes in worship occurred in Calvinist churches. The cries of outrage at Calvinist destruction of images, windows, and altars have echoed in our day, but for esthetic rather than religious reasons. Calvin's followers did not always employ the possibilities found in Scriptural precedent, for it was only sects like the Shakers that dared follow the biblical example of dancing with joy before the Lord!

The liturgical revival of Protestantism must be assessed in terms of this inheritance. But alas, it is a heritage which is not often understood or known. We have been historically derelict and we have oftentimes misread the past or failed to read the past. Tremendous changes have taken place in Protestant worship during the centuries since the Reformation. Except for the Episcopalians—and the Lutherans in some degree—it is virtually impossible to go into a Protestant church and discover by attending a service what was the nature of worship in the founding years of that particular tradition. Our contemporary patterns of worship, for the most part, are fragmented, distorted, and vestigial forms. It is in terms of this loss of coherence and integrity that Protestantism is engaged in liturgical discovery.

Much has been lost. Not only have the respective liturgical traditions become obscured and confused, but there has been loss of the corporateness of worship and decline of the Scriptural basis for worship. The subjectivity of the Gospel which was a mark of early Protestant worship has become oftentimes the subjectivity of individualism. This decline is evident in hymnody. The great hymns of the past were Scriptural in imagery and language. Even when Watts broke with the metrical psalms in writing new hymns, he believed he was "baptizing the Psalms in Christ." The chorales were steeped in the symbolism of the Bible and the experience of salvation through God's historic acts. An examination of a hymnal published in the first half of the twentieth century, however, would reveal countless hymns with no reference to Scripture or the imagery of Christianity whatsoever. They dealt sometimes with psychological disorders, sometimes with sunset vistas, sometimes with erotic overtones, and the biblical imagery and language vanished from the hymnals.

What has happened in Protestantism is illustrated in the story of a New England meeting house. This is only one instance, yet it suggests the inner transformation of Protestantism and its unhappy accommodation to a changing culture. I know rather well a beautiful meeting house built for a church in 1790. It was built by simple artisans without benefit of an architect, yet they were so possessed of a sense of proportion and grace that it is a building of dignity and beauty to this day. When erected, the meeting house had a large pulpit in the center, as was true in the eighteenth century of Episcopalian churches in Virginia, Lutheran churches in Pennsylvania, Presbyterian churches in New Jersey, and Congregational churches in New England. As with all these churches, the pulpit was not designed merely to enable a minister to be heard, but was a symbol of the primacy of the Word. The pulpit was the "throne of the Word of God" and the sermon was the "monstrance of the Gospel."

In front of the pulpit was a table. It was a table for the meal of God's people and it was placed in that location in order that all might see the symbolic action of breaking bread and pouring the cup in the Lord's Supper. The restoration of the table-altar to the "basilican" position of the early Christian churches was undertaken by the Calvinist Reformation, and it extended to the Church of England as well as some Lutheran churches. What was significant in the ethos of Protestantism was not so much the bread and the wine, as the "breaking" of the bread and the "sharing" of the cup. This action was integrally related to the sermon in which the minister was expected to "rightly divide the Word." Although the church building was lacking in color, images, pictures, and many ritual objects, it possessed an intensity by the concentration on the pulpit, the table, and the Bible. In fact the emptiness became filled with meaning, for as Paul Tillich has pointed out, space can be one of the most meaningful religious symbols.

The 1790 meeting house embodied these principles of worship. But changes were made. About 1830, when the revival movements were influencing New England religious life, the pulpit was removed and a new one built with reduced elevation so that the minister was closer to the people. The most significant architectural changes took place around 1880 and indicate the rapid transformation in the Congregational expression of Protestantism. The pulpit was removed altogether. Instead there was installed a platform as one might find in a lecture hall, and a spindly Victorian Gothic lectern. The church building was now transformed into a lecture hall with a platform across which a " 'pulpit' personality" might stride and display his personality and his learning by occasional reference to the notes on the lectern. The throne of the Word of God and the sermon as the monstrance of the Gospel and the Table of noble dimensions for the banquet of the Lord—they were gone. The organic unity of the preaching and the administering of the Word was lost with the disappearance of the mighty pulpit and table.

What is the point of all this? It seems to me that this architectural devolution is symbolic of the change which had taken place in Protestantism. What Protestants are now reacting against is not the tradition of the Reformation, which had cogency and coherence and integrity. Protestants are reacting against a disintegrated and fragmented expression of a once vital tradition of worship. This sterility of a withered tradition constitutes one of the motivating factors for liturgical change in Protestantism.

Another factor of great significance is the ecumenical movement which arose partially out of the feeling that the differences which divided Protestants were not sufficiently important as to divide the churches in perpetuity. Out of the desire to "get together," out of the conviction that our differences were not great nor significant, and out of a belief that a common allegiance united them, Protestants commenced to associate themselves together in conferences and cooperative activity. As they confronted one another in conferences and in worship, Protestants discovered that there were differences of tradition, distinctions in ways of worship, and varying styles of life which separated them. Communication between persons of different communions proved difficult as the superficial differences were discovered to have deep roots. Out of the ecumenical movement, which at first assumed an identity of interest, there has arisen an awareness of distinctions and differences. Self-consciousness among the churches with respect to their traditions of worship is one of the consequences of the ecumenical movement.

Another dominant motivation for the contemporary liturgical interest is in the renewed theological concern of Protestantism. Karl Barth, whose work has been termed the "theological watershed" of theological development, is reputedly "anti-liturgical." Yet from the renewed emphasis upon the Scriptures and a theology rooted in the biblical disclosure there flow implications for the church's interior life and its worship. Among Barth's young followers in Europe, for example, there is concern that the new theological insights influence worship and overcome the liberal concern for individual worship experiences.

Out of the inheritance of Protestantism and the motivations of recent decades, there have arisen liturgical changes in contemporary Protestantism. These changes are exceedingly varied but three patterns can be observed.

The most obvious and the most widespread change has taken place during the past forty years. While change was evident before that time, the new patterns of church architecture commenced to influence Protestant liturgical interests with the work of Ralph Adams Cram. The Episcopalians had been constructing churches in the Gothic spirit ever since the Oxford movement a century ago sought a return to pre-Reformation liturgical and ritual practises. Their appropriation of an architectural style and interior arrangement was an attempt to recover the centrality of the Eucharist in the medieval manner. Chancels, which had been cleared of monks' stalls so that the communicants might gather around the altar-table for the service of the Lord's Supper, were now restored fully equipped with stalls into which vested choirs were placed. Although initiated by the nineteenth century "high church" wing of Anglicanism, these architectural arrangements and attendant ceremonial and ritual practises gradually spread throughout the Episcopal Church. Shortly after the beginning of the twentieth century, non-Episcopal Protestant churches commenced to build churches after the manner of English parish churches or cathedrals. This practise arose in part from the successful prosecution of the claim that Gothic architecture was the most "religious" form of architecture. The protagonist of this view was primarily Ralph Adams Cram, who was retained by Presbyterian and Congregational as well as Episcopal churches as an architect. He and his disciples were eminently successful in presenting this view of architecture. Protestant traditions had disintegrated to the point where the Gothic claim was appealing. It filled a void or it answered the confusion of Protestant church architecture.

Protestant churches and ministers emulated the Episcopalians not only in architecture but in patterns of worship and ceremonial. Today it is possible to enter a Methodist or Baptist or Congregational church and believe oneself to be in an Episcopal church. The service has been made more elaborate in the attempt to "enrich worship." Altars, candles, vestments, choir processions, and sometimes kneeling for prayer can be found in churches which two centuries ago were marked by the absence of such objects and practises. Worship came to be thought of as an "experience" which would be given a congregation. Thus the choir was given an increasing role in making musical introductions and responses at appropriate places in the service. One result has been the development of a dialogue between the minister and the choir and a gradual silencing of the congregation. In so far as the congregation's role has been reduced to that of an audience or spectators, Protestant churches are dangerously close to the situation which gave rise to the Reformation.

The dangers in the "enriched worship" of Protestantism are increasingly apparent. The liturgical changes in this movement represented the theological expression of the untheological. But the basis on which worship and ceremonial have been ordered in many Protestant churches is one of eclecticism and syncretism. The psychology of worship rather than the theology of worship has been dominant. Esthetic canons have often replaced Scriptural norms. Churches have attempted to worship God more fitly, but often in the belief that it should be done by "worshiping the Lord in the holiness of beauty" rather than "the beauty of holiness."

As a corrective to many of the present liturgical expressions there are two developments—the ecumenical concern, with its theological and historical inquiries, and the new expressions of the Church's vitality, as for instance in the Iona Community. The work of the Commission on Ways of Worship of the World Council of Churches will have great meaning for the liturgical life of Protestantism. The mutual exchange of theological and historical reflection in the conversations of the ecumenical movement enables the various traditions to see themselves more clearly. The sharpness of theological inquiry counters the sentimentality which has injured much of contemporary Protestant liturgical expressions. Paul Claudel has said that the modern Roman Catholic in response to the question, "If the salt hath lost its savor, wherewith shall it be salted?" replies, "With sugar." This commentary on the saccharine in much of the Church's life is especially appropriate to much Protestant worship. But through the work of theologians and liturgical scholars, fresh approaches are being introduced. The work of numerous liturgical scholars during the past two decades makes it clear how confused has been our apprehension of the Church's worship in the past. Dom Gregory Dix, the Anglican monk, William D. Maxwell, the Church of Scotland scholar, and Horton Davies, the English Congregational theologian, have opened new insights into our past. Furthermore, an underlying unity in the Church's worship of God is discovered, despite differences. So one discovers Dom Gregory appreciating a celebration of the Lord's Supper which an early Congregationalist would find more comfortable than some present-day Congregational appropriations of nineteenth century Episcopalianism.

What seems to me to be most promising is neither the concern for "enriched worship" nor a purely historical or archeological approach to worship. Liturgy is the vehicle for the Church to offer its worship to God in terms of the age in which it lives and works and to which it has a charge to fulfil. Among the churches which recognize their poverty in liturgy there is opportunity of appropriating the past in such a way that it is expressed in fresh ways. We cannot return to the past, for such "returns" are illusory. Neither can the church ignore its past, for the Christian community is nourished not only by hope but by historical memory as well. With some degree of achievement, the Iona Community in Scotland has attempted this. Its celebration of Holy Communion, for instance, gathers up many elements of ancient and early Scottish worship, relating these to the task which confronts the Church of declaring its Lord before today's world. Therefore, prettiness and sentimentality have been eliminated by a functionalism which relates worship to the vocation of the Church. For it is only as the Church discovers its vocation in the modern world that its liturgical life will be brought under the scrutiny of the contemporary and the judgment and renewal of the eternal. In the United States, the East Harlem Protestant Parish represents such an attempt to relate work and worship. Unquestionably the liturgical rediscovery in Protestantism is only beginning. But the foretaste of what a revitalized Church can do in its worship suggests that extensive changes will take place within the next two decades. Already disquiet regarding the imitative and derivative patterns of church architecture point to fundamental questions which have not been answered by Protestant liturgical practice today. All of this is related to the basic problem of communicating the Gospel in the contemporary world. The brokenness of communication in society is to be found in the Church, but as conversation is renewed between the different branches of the

Church and the best voices outside the Church, there is possible a liturgical revival of significance. In writing on the problem of contemporary Protestantism, Denis de Rougemont states that liturgical rediscovery is the basic task not only for the Church's life but in fulfilling its responsibility to contemporary culture:

The true problem of the century is that of the community. It is bound up with the problem of a common language. Liturgy can contribute toward recreating and authenticating this language; but only under two equally determinative conditions: it must remain biblical at its source, and it must find a contemporaneous form. It is only in a creative effort, surpassing both our riches and our poverties, through a general forward movement, that our present divisions will be able to transform themselves into converging diversities.[1]

Bibliography

G. W. O. Addleshaw and Frederick Etchells, *The Architectural Setting of Anglican Worship,* Faber & Faber, Ltd., London, 1948.

John C. Bowmer, *The Sacrament of the Lord's Supper in Methodism,* Dacre Press, Westminster (London), 1951.

Yngve Brilioth, *Eucharistic Faith and Practice,* A. G. Hebert, translater, Society for Promoting Christian Knowledge, London, The Macmillan Company, New York and Toronto, 1930.

W. K. L. Clarke and C. Harris, *Liturgy and Worship,* Society for Promoting Christian Knowledge, London, 1933.

H. S. Coffin, *The Public Worship of God,* The Westminster Press, Philadelphia, 1946.

Horton Davies, *The Worship of the English Puritans,* Dacre Press, Westminster (London), 1948.

Father Gregory Dix, *The Shape of the Liturgy,* Dacre Press, Westminster (London), 1945.

Pehr Edwall, Eric Hayman and William D. Maxwell, editors, *Ways of Worship,* Harper & Brothers, New York, 1951.

A. G. Hebert, *Liturgy and Society,* Faber & Faber, Ltd., London, 1936.

[1] Denis de Rougemont, *"A Common Language,"* Christ, Vol. 12, No. 3, 1947.

Bernard L. Manning, *The Hymns of Wesley and Watts,* Epworth Press, London, 1942.

W. D. Maxwell, *Outline of Christian Worship,* Oxford University Press, Humphrey Milford, London, 1936.

—— *John Knox's Genevan Service Book,* Oliver & Boyd, 1931.

Nathaniel Micklem, *Christian Worship,* The Clarendon Press, Oxford, 1936.

J. Ernest Rattenbury, *The Eucharistic Hymns of John and Charles Wesley,* Epworth Press, London, 1948.

Erik Routley, *The Church and Music,* Duckworth, London, 1950.

Massey H. Shepherd, Jr., *The Oxford American Prayer Book Commentary,* Oxford University Press, New York, 1950.

III

SYMBOLISM IN CATHOLIC WORSHIP

DANIEL J. SULLIVAN, M.A.

Assistant Professor of Philosophy,
School of Education, Fordham University

Catholic worship is centered on the official prayer of the Church, the Liturgy, or the Common Act—preeminently the Mass, but also the Canonical Hours, the sacraments and the sacramentals. In a broader interpretation, Catholic worship means the realization of the specifically Christian world view through our lives and actions.[1]

Christianity has always given full recognition to the ambivalence of man as a creature composed of both body and soul. Man, even though he is endowed with a spiritual soul, has to act in a material universe. The liturgy, therefore, works on two levels, signifying in the material and natural orders the reality of the spiritual and supernatural orders.

The official worship of the Church is thus embedded in sensible signs symbolic of hidden realities. The fullness of the Christian revelation is too rich to be grasped all at once by mortal man. This is given only to the Blessed in the beatific vision. For us in this life the mysteries are disclosed fragmentarily and under the veil of symbols. To illustrate this breadth of symbolic disclosure, let us consider the symbolism of the liturgical cycles, where the very rhythm of the

---

[1] *Cf.* Dom Theodore Wesseling, *Liturgy and Life,* Longmans, Green & Company, London, 1938, p. 42; also *cf.* Dom Illtyd Trethowan, *Christ in the Liturgy,* Sheed & Ward, London, 1952, p. 4.

changing seasons is utilized to represent the organic rhythm of the divine plan for the salvation of man.[2]

The two great anniversaries of the life of Our Lord which the liturgy celebrates are Christmas and Easter. The lesser cycle of Christmas-Epiphany brings to our minds the mystery of the Incarnation; the greater Easter-Pentecost cycle commemorates the mystery of the Redemption.

The Advent season with which the Christmas cycle begins reminds us of the time of the Patriarchs and Prophets, with their thirst for the coming of the Messiah. The Scriptural texts of the Mass, and of the Divine Office of this period, stress the Fall of man and his need of redemption. The prophetic symbols of Advent focus on Christ as the central Fact of all time. Each year, with the coming of Advent, we are prepared anew not only for the First Coming of Christ, but also for His Second Coming at the end of time.

The Christmas season celebrates, of course, the birth of Our Lord, Who by uniting human nature to His Divine Nature causes mankind itself to be born again to the Divine Life. The Feast of Christmas coincides with the old pagan feast which celebrated the rebirth of the sun with the first lengthening of the days of the new year. (We find frequently this link of the liturgical symbol with the cosmic symbolism of earlier periods.) At the moment when the sun has reached its lowest point we are reminded each year of the birth of the Sun of Justice. Symbolized, too, is the birth of Christ in our souls.

The Nativity shows us God made man; the Epiphany shows us the divinity of the man-god.

The Feast of Easter, the great peak at the center of the second liturgical cycle, gives this second cycle of the liturgy its basic solemnity and importance. The Christmas cycle, itself dependent on the Easter cycle, emphasizes those aspects of the life of Christ which reveal His divinity; the Easter cycle accents Christ as Man and Savior.

Preparatory and purificatory for the great Feast of Easter are the seasons of Septuagesima and Lent. During the season of Lent the convergence of different orders of symbolism is well illustrated, for

---

[2] *Cf.* Jean Daniélou, *Bible et Liturgie*, Les Editions du Cerf, Paris, 1951, II, for a treatment of the symbolic meaning of the weekly and yearly cycles of the Liturgy.

the ceremonies of this time still echo that period when catechumens were prepared for the solemn reception of baptism and public penitents for the reception of the Sacrament of Penance. The period of Lent is the time when, by dying to sin and uniting our sufferings to those of Christ we prepare to take up the new life which Our Lord brings to the earth through His Resurrection.

The liturgy of Passiontide and Eastertime abounds with symbols surcharged with many layers of significance: symbols of joy and sorrow; the tree of death and the tree of life; the prince of life and the prince of death; oldness and newness; burial and resurrection; symbols of night and day, fire, light, and the sun.

The symbols of joy and triumph predominate during the Eastertide and the garment of the Church changes to white, the color of innocence and joy. Fasting is forbidden during the forty days of the Eastertide; certain prayers are said standing as expressive of triumph, and the threefold Alleluia is woven through the liturgy. The Paschal candle, symbolic of Our Lord's presence on earth before His Ascension, is lighted.

The day of the Ascension, the ultimate triumph of Our Lord, sees the extinction of the Paschal candle, after the reading of the Gospel of the day which relates the story of the Ascension.

Pentecost, the final aspect of the Paschal mystery, commemorates the full communication of the new life of the Gospel, through the sending of the Holy Spirit into our souls. The visible life of Christ on earth is at an end, and now begins the secret life of God within the faithful of His Church, the Mystical Body.

After Pentecost the liturgical garb changes to green to suggest the life and growth of the Holy Spirit within us. (Green, too, is the symbol of hope and of immortality.)

The last Sunday after Pentecost is prophetic, both of the return of Advent in the liturgical cycle, and of the Second Advent of the Savior at the end of the world.

The temporal cycle as a whole manifests the great mystery of the Trinity. The season of Advent recalls the reign of God the Father over His people, the season from Christmas to the Ascension the reign of the Son, and the season from Pentecost through the remainder of the temporal cycle manifests the rule of the Holy Spirit in the Church until the time of the Second Coming.

Besides the Mass and the Divine Office, the final mode of participation in the divine life through the liturgy is by way of the Sacraments and the Sacramentals. And here, too, the symbolism is rich, spread through many levels of signification. Think only, for example, of the multiple layers of symbols implied in the immersion of the neophyte in the waters of baptism: Adam and Paradise, creation and deluge, the flight out of Egypt and the passage of the Red Sea, Joshua's crossing of the Jordan, the general theme of death and resurrection, and so on.

There is no question then, as to the fact of the wide use of symbolism in Catholic worship. But do these symbols have any more than a superficial, vaguely illustrative value? Is the meaning attached to symbols an arbitrary, conventional, imposed assignment, as in the case, for example, of words, of signal flags, of traffic signs, or does the liturgical symbol have something in itself of the meaning it conveys?

Let us first see what the history of philosophy and theology has to tell us on this point.

Christian philosophers and theologians from the beginning have held that there is a real revelation of God in the things of the created universe, which are material signs of God. St. Augustine, for example, held that material things are more than just a mirrored reflection of the eternal types: they reveal something of God Himself. The maker puts his mark on what he makes. Not that the universe is a direct image of God Himself; rather there are resemblances which lie deeper, so to speak, than a surface resemblance. The portrait painter gives us images of his different subjects, but all the different portraits bear the unmistakable stamp of the portrait painter himself. So, too, for St. Augustine, God is revealed in His creation, and Augustine saw everywhere the stamp of the divine Trinity: things are composed of measure, number and weight; unity, species and order; being, form and movement.[3]

[3] *Cf.* Étienne Gilson, *Introduction à l'étude de Saint Augustin*, J. Vrin, Paris, 1931, p. 275.

Even more do rational and spiritual beings, created in the image and likeness of God, mirror the triune nature of God. In the *Book on the Trinity,* St. Augustine gives us the memory, understanding, and will as constituting in the mind the image of the Trinity. The external senses mirror the Trinity; there is, for example, the triad of the thing sensed, the act of sensing, and the will to sense. Internal sensation gives us the trinity of sense memory, internal vision, and will.[4] And so on, for page after page, vestiges and images of the Trinity are seen in the powers and activities of man.

The symbolic interpretation of the universe is taken up with even greater zest by the philosophers, theologians, and artists of the following centuries. The early Middle Ages saw the earth as "a sort of Bible, with things for words," says Étienne Gilson. "Bestiaries, mirrors of the world, stained glass, cathedral porches, each in its own way expressed a symbolic universe in which things taken in their very essence are merely so many expressions of God."[5]

The symbolism of earlier centuries emphasized the reality of God by stressing the shadowiness of creatures. We turn to creatures only to be turned by them to God. This tendency to dissolve the creature in the clouds of symbolism seems a characteristic of Augustinianism in general, though we read in St. Bonaventure, one of the most prolific of all the symbol detectives, that "creatures may be considered either as things or as signs."[6]

Philosophers such as Thomas Aquinas, Robert Grosseteste, Roger Bacon, subordinate the symbolic aspects of creation to rational interpretation. They do not deny the validity of the imaginative symbolism of the earlier centuries, but they endeavor to put it within rational limits. St. Thomas sees in the worth and dignity of the created order an even deeper stamp of the Divinity, whose creative power radiates through the very structure of being itself. "God, like a good teacher,"

[4] Aurelius Augustinus, *On the Trinity, Basic Writings of St. Augustine,* II, Random House, New York, 1948, X, 12, 19; XI, 2, 3, 6.

[5] Étienne Gilson, *Spirit of Medieval Philosophy,* Charles Scribner's Sons, New York, 1936, p. 100.

[6] St. Bonaventura, "Commentary on the Four Books of Sentences of Peter Lombard," I, 3, 3, reply to objection 2; *Selections from Mediaeval Philosophers,* II, Richard McKeon, editor, Charles Scribner's Sons, New York, 1930.

St. Thomas says, "has taken care to compose most excellent writings that we may be instructed in all perfection. 'All that is written,' says the Apostle, 'is written for our instruction.' And these writings are in two books: the book of the creation and the book of the Holy Scriptures. In the former are so many creatures, so many excellent writings that deliver the truth without falsehood. And so Aristotle, when asked whence it was that he had his admirable learning, replied: 'From things, which do not know how to lie.' " [7]

But whether we consider the Augustinians or the Aristotelians, the artists or the theologians, behind all the differences of approach and emphasis it remains true for all of them that the universe declares the glory of God because it bears His likeness. "The heavens show forth the glory of God, and the firmament declareth the work of his hands" (Psalm XVIII, 2).

This deep conviction that the realm of the material is a symbol of profound, inner spiritual realities is the source of what is called the sacramental view of the universe. The physical world is a very real world for the Christian, and if he is faithful to his tradition he will stress its proper worth and dignity. But the physical world is also revelatory of deeper realities—of metaphysical and spiritual depths which may, again in the words of Gilson, be read no longer in terms of "force, energy and law," but in terms of "participations and analogies of the divine Being. . . . For whoever understands this, the Christian world takes on the character of a sacred world, with a relation to God inscribed in its very being and in every law that rules its functioning." [8]

This revelation of the inner spiritual reality by the outward, visible, material sign is preeminently exemplified in the case of man. Man, literally spirit in flesh, is above all creatures truly sacramental.

Things then, for these philosophers, are meaning-bearing, just as are words. But although words have their meanings assigned to them in arbitrary fashion, things carry their meaning within their very nature. In the case of natural signs, smoke, for example, as the sign

[7] Jean Mouroux, *The Meaning of Man*, Sheed & Ward, New York, 1948, p. 20, quoting *Sermo* V, in *Dom. 2 de Adventu-Vives*, XXIX, 194.
[8] Gilson, *Spirit of Medieval Philosophy, op. cit.*, p. 100.

of fire, the relationship of sign to thing signified is a real relationship, not one that exists only in thought. The doctrine of St. Thomas as expounded by John of St. Thomas and interpreted by Jacques Maritain [9] holds that the relationship of sign and thing signified is the relationship of formal rather than of efficient causality. In the case of knowing, the sign (the concept or the sense image) causes knowledge because it causes the re-presence in the knowing power of the thing signified. The thing signified is there in the knower in another mode of existence, in its formal being. When I know Socrates, for example, man exists in me through the formal causality of the concept, though in a universal rather than a material and individuated mode of existence.[10]

Again, when I recall a thing through the form preserved in memory, what is known is the thing or event remembered *by means of* the form preserved in memory. Even in the case of purely instrumental signs, such as a statue or a portrait, the thing signified is in the sign under another mode of existence. "What may be that element of the thing signified which is joined to the sign and present in it, as distinct from the sign itself and its own entity?" asks John of St. Thomas. And he answers, "No other element than the very signified itself in another mode of existence." [11]

Research in the field of comparative religion seems to add confirmatory detail to the contention that there is a natural aptitude of physical realities to signify one thing or group of things rather than another. Mircea Eliade, for example, in his *Traité d'Histoire des Religions* [12] points out repeated and independent appearances in ancient religions of the same symbols to express the manifestations of the divine through nature. Thus, the sun universally expresses the notion of creation, of life, and fecundity; the heavens signify transcendence;

[9] *Cf.* Jacques Maritain, *Redeeming the Time,* G. Bles, The Centenary Press, London, 1946, p. 192.

[10] *Cf.* Thomas Aquinas, *On Being and Essence,* St. Michael's College Philosophical Texts, Toronto, 1934, Chapter 3, p. 35. In the *Marietta* text, Turin, 1932, the reference is Chapter 4: *Patet ergo quod natura hominis absolute considerata abstrahit a quolibet esse, ita quod non fiat praecisio alicujus eorum.*

[11] Maritain, *op. cit.,* p. 193, quoting John of St. Thomas, *Log.,* P. II, q. 21, a. 6.

[12] Mircea Eliade, *Traité d'Histoire des Religions,* Payot, Paris, 1949.

the moon signifies both fertility and death; water signifies both beneficence and destruction, death and resurrection; and so on for many other natural symbols. An examination of a vast accumulation of fact leads Eliade to believe that there are a few dominant, recurrent hierophanies in natural religion. These hierophanies or manifestations of the divine are fluid in meaning, but their flexibility is within very definite limits. The basic community of significance they display over a wide area of space and time is indicative, Eliade thinks, of an objective reference, of a fundamental natural aptitude of physical things to signify one thing rather than another. (This explanation would, of course, rule out the position which explains the similarity of symbols in the different religions of man as due to the influence of one on the other in such a way that all the related meanings are ultimately borrowed; or again the position which holds that the likeness can be explained as the heritage of a common tradition.)

The work of some psychologists, notably Jung, has tended to show that certain uses of symbols are tied in with deep subconscious drives of the psyche, so that the repeated pattern of symbolic use throughout mankind is a reverberation from the biologic depths of man. The net result of these investigations again indicates a community and constancy of content in the basic symbols man uses. The psychologist tends, however, to deny that these symbols have any epistemological value. He sees them only as a sublimation of instinctive drives or a mythical expression of the biological sensitivity to the rhythms of the physical world.

Granted the profound insights of the psychologist into the interconnection between the subconscious and the conscious use of symbols, particularly the role of the "inverse" symbol, it still remains true that beyond this relationship the symbol may have a true value as an instrument of knowledge, signifying for us realities otherwise inaccessible. (And, indeed, does not the psychologist employ the symbol in that very fashion when he uses it to interpret the secret recesses of the soul?)

It is readily apparent that there is a connection between the symbols employed in the liturgy and those used in older religions. How is the Christian to interpret this wide correspondence and borrowing from other religions? The Christian sees in the revelation of the divine through nature the foundation of natural religion, the precursor of the revealed religions. "Natural religion," says Father Daniélou, "consists in the knowledge of the fidelity of God as it is known through the regularity of the cosmic cycles." [13] And he reminds us of the saying of St. Paul: "For the invisible things of him, from the creation of the world, are clearly seen, being understood by the things that are made" (Romans I, 20). And again from St. Paul: "Who in times past suffered all nations to walk in their own ways. Nevertheless he left not himself without testimony, doing good from heaven, giving rains and fruitful seasons, filling our hearts with food and gladness" (Acts XIV, 15, 16).

Father Daniélou sees in the myth the degradation of natural religion. Instead of adoring God through his faithfulness in the cosmic cycles, the pagans came to adore not God, but the sun, the moon, the stars, and the other objects which should have served rather to reveal God. Quoting St. Paul again: "When they knew God, they have not glorified him as God, or given thanks, but become vain in their thought . . . and they changed the glory of the incorruptible God into the likeness of the image of a corruptible man, and of birds, and of four-footed beasts, and of creeping things" (Romans I, 21, 23).

Natural religion, then, when it becomes corrupt, issues in myth, which, failing to rise above the horizon of physical nature, becomes blind to the transcendent reality mirrored by that nature.

The coming of biblical revelation corrects the distortion of myth, while at the same time rescuing what it validly reflects from God's natural revelation. "It has long been remarked," Father Daniélou says, "that [the first chapters of Genesis] contain elements in common with the mythical stories of the Babylonians and Chanaanites: there is the conflict of light and darkness, the antediluvian genealogies, and the story of the deluge. But it is precisely these elements which have their foundation in natural religious symbolism. They can either have a mythical or a theistic interpretation. Now the story of Genesis is a polemic against the mythical conception. It represents

[13] *Cf.* Daniélou, "The Problem of Symbolism," *Thought,* 25, September, 1950, pp. 423–440; also *cf.* Daniélou, *Advent,* Sheed & Ward, New York, 1951, pp. 50 ff.

a correction of this distortion and restores the elements of cosmic symbolism (that had been interpreted in a mythical sense by paganism) to their real value as the expression of the creative and judicial primacy of God." [14]

In the new revelation the old cosmic circle is broken, and a new symbolic dimension is disclosed: God reveals Himself in the singular, historic event as well as in the universal cosmic cycles, and the historic revelation gives to the cosmic symbolism itself an inner meaning which it did not have before; the cosmic itself is brought into line with the historic.

Henceforth the events and personages which make up sacred history become the types which reveal the divine plan as it unfolds in history—types which disclose not just the general laws of God in nature, but His particular design in history. The symbols of the Bible do not cancel out the symbols of the pre-biblical era. The myths of the pre-biblical era are rejected, but the truths they veiled are taken up into a historical and transcendental context where even the cosmic event itself is seen as a particular moment in the divine economy. Sacred history from this point of view starts with Creation itself, and concludes with the Last Judgment at the end of the world.

Unique and particular though they are, the events of sacred history nevertheless typify correspondences on several levels of history, symbolically revealing the step by step realization of the mysterious plan of God. "Christ," St. Hilary says, "throughout the course of time, by means of true and authentic pre-figurations, engenders the Church, washes it, sanctifies it, calls it, chooses it, ransoms it: in the sleep of Adam, in the deluge with Noah, in the blessing of Melchisedech, in the justification of Abraham . . . thus since the creation of the world there has been pre-figured what was to be accomplished in Christ." [15]

It is characteristic of the biblical types that they disclose many layers of symbolism: the great archetypes of cosmic symbolism, the figures of the Old Law as revelatory of the mysteries of the New Dis-

---

[14] Daniélou, "The Problem of Symbolism," *op. cit.,* p. 433.

[15] Daniélou, *Sacramentum Futuri,* Beauchesne et Fils, Paris, 1950, p. 3, quoting St. Hilary, *Tractatus Mysterium,* I, 1.

pensation, the sacramental depths of the new creation instituted by Christ. Thus the deluge figures both the waters of death and resurrection; Christ is the true Noah who triumphs over the waters of death to become the source of a new world. "In each baptism," says Methodius of Philippi, "Christ comes down again; He recapitulates His Passion and the sleep of death; and during this recapitulation . . . the Church, the second Eve, is taken from His side. In the same act, one bone and flesh that they are, the Second Adam and the Second Eve are wed, they consummate their nuptials, we are conceived and born, the Church is made Mother Church." [16]

The events of the Exodus act as a focal point rich in typology: the first born of the Jews spared the sword of the Angel of Death because they are marked with the blood of the Lamb; Christ, the first born of the new humanity, made victor over death by His own blood; the Christian spared the death of sin because in baptism he is marked with the blood of the Lamb. And not only do the seasons of Passover and Easter coincide with each other, but they coincide also with the pagan festivals which celebrate the birth of Spring. The symbolism of the Old and the New Testament is thus linked up with the symbolism of the cosmic cycles, which, in this new context, themselves take on a further depth of meaning. The network of symbolism continues: the Passage of the Red Sea symbolizes, for example, the Sacrament of Baptism; the manna in the desert symbolizes the Sacrament of the Eucharist.

Other great clusters of symbolism are found in such figures as the Garden of Eden, the Sacrifice of Isaac, the Destruction of Jericho, and so on.[17]

One final point remains to be emphasized. Whereas the sacraments of the Natural Law and of the Old Law were true symbols signifying sanctification, they did not of themselves effect that sanctification. Under the New Law, where the Sacramental order is instituted by Christ Himself, the sacraments not only signify, but they

---

[16] Louis Beirnaert, "The Mythic Dimension in Christian Sacramentalism," *Crosscurrents,* fall, 1951, II, 1, p. 68, quoting text summarized by Joseph C. Plumpe, *Mater Ecclesia.*

[17] *Cf.* Daniélou, *Sacramentum Futuri, op. cit.;* also Daniélou, *Bible et Liturgie, op. cit.*

effect what they signify (assuming that no obstacle exists in the way of wrong disposition). "The mystery of Christ," says Dom Odo Casel, "which was accomplished in Our Lord in all its historical and physical reality, is realized in us in symbol, beneath representative and figurative forms. Yet these are not mere appearances . . . they communicate to us the full reality of the new life which Christ our Mediator offers to us. This altogether special sort of participation in Christ's life, which is both presented beneath the expression of a symbol and at the same time really effected, was called by the first Christians mystic participation." [18]

The Christian believes, then, that he is literally taken up into a new kind of life, "a new world created by God, entirely different from the world of nature . . . an unknown world with a well-known inhabitant." [19] As long as the Christian chooses to remain united to Christ in this universe of grace he continues to share this sacramental life.

Material things themselves are taken up into this universe when they are used in the divine liturgy, thus spreading the effects of the Incarnation through time and the material creation, so that the universe itself becomes sacramental.

At the Mass (Dom Theodore Wesseling says) Christ is born again, suffering again, dying again, triumphing again, all in one simple action, and through this action He is breathing a new impulse of vitality again into mankind and through mankind into the whole creation. If it be asked how this can be, the answer is that the Redeeming-Act is made present again, *not* with its historical details of time and space, but *sacramentally,* mystically. A sign can recall the past as easily as it can anticipate the future. A sacramental sign can bring about the past as it can anticipate the future. The historical, temporal, graphic aspect of the Incarnation is a bygone thing; as an immanent, vital, spiritual action, integral and essential part of the Redeeming-Act it has remained, and shares in the eternal actuality, the eternal living presence of Christ, the glorified Saviour. [20]

[18] Trethowan, *op. cit.,* p. 16.

[19] E. L. Mascall, *Christ, the Christian and the Church,* Longmans, Green & Company, London, New York, etc., 1946, p. 174, quoting Dom Anscar Vonier, *A Key to the Doctrine of the Eucharist.*

[20] Wesseling, *op. cit.,* p. 26.

This, then, the continuing presence of the Incarnate Christ, is the central point of that superb synthesis of the physical and the spiritual, the natural and the supernatural, the temporal and the eternal, in which is effected the vital union of the universe with man, and in which mankind itself is made one with the God-Man in the perfect restoration of all things to God.

Bibliography

Jean Daniélou, *Advent,* Sheed & Ward, New York, 1951. (The relation of Natural Religion, Judaism, and Mohammedanism to Christianity.)

—— *Bible et Liturgie,* Cerf, Paris, 1951. (An analysis of the symbolism of the Sacraments, especially Baptism and the Eucharist; also of the symbolic reference of the major Feasts.)

—— "The Problem of Symbolism," *Thought,* September, 1950. (A condensation of Daniélou's views.)

—— *Sacramentum Futuri,* Beauchesne et Fils, Paris, 1950. (A study of the typology of the Old Testament in the Fathers of the Church.)

Mircea Eliade, *Traité d'Histoire des Religions,* Payot, Paris, 1949. (Valuable chapters on the structure of symbolism. Exhaustive bibliographies of the works published in the West on religious symbolism.)

Étienne Gilson, *Introduction à l'étude de saint Augustin,* Vrin, Paris, 1949, 2nd edition. (See Chapter 3, Pt. III, for the Symbolism of the Trinity in St. Augustine.)

—— *L'Esprit de Philosophie Médiévale,* J. Vrin, Paris, 1944, 2nd edition. (See especially Chapters V and VII for a treatment of the symbolism of creatures by the philosophers and theologians of the Middle Ages. The very full and useful chapter notes are omitted in the English translation.)

—— *La Philosophie au Moyen Age,* Payot, Paris, 1947.

R. Guardini, *Der Geist der Liturgie.*

Henri De Lubac, *Catholicism,* Longmans, New York, 1950. (For a study of the symbolism of the Sacraments see Chapter III. This work emphasizes the social aspects of the liturgy.)

—— *Typologie et allegorie,* Rech. sc. et Relig., 1947, pp. 180–226.

Jacques Maritain, *Les Degrés du Savoir,* Desclée de Brouwer, Paris, 1932.

(See especially Chapter II. The French edition contains the long and valuable appendix on the Concept, which is omitted in the English translation.)

Jacques Maritain, *Redeeming the Time,* Geoffrey Bles, London, 1943. (See the most valuable essay, "Sign and Symbol," Chapter IX, for the Thomistic theory of the sign.)

E. L. Mascall, *Christ, the Christian and the Church,* Longmans, New York, 1946. (See Chapter IX, on the symbolism of the Eucharist.)

M. Ochse, *La nouvelle querelle des Images,* Edition du Centurion, Paris, 1953.

G. B. Phelan, *St. Thomas and Analogy,* Marquette University Press, Milwaukee, 1941. (A brief philosophic treatment of the sign.)

H. Rahner, *Der Spielender Mensch,* Einsideln, 1952.

Pie-Raymond Regamey, *Art Sacré au XXe Siècle,* Paris, 1952.

Dom Illtyd Trethowan, O.S.B., *Christ in the Liturgy,* Sheed & Ward, New York, 1952.

Dom Theodore Wesseling, *Liturgy and Life,* Longmans, New York, 1938. (One of the most valuable of the brief treatments of the meaning of the Liturgy, with a particular consideration of its symbolic aspect.)

"Liturgical Arts," Liturgical Arts Society, Inc., New York, quarterly. (The topic discussed in this paper is habitually treated, from one or the other aspect in this magazine.)

"Worship," St. John's College Press, Collegeville, Minnesota, monthly. (Also, see other publications of the same press.)

See also in the *Syntopicon,* Great Books of the Western World, Chicago, 1953, the article on "Sign and Symbol."

IV

SYMBOLISM AND JEWISH FAITH

BY

ABRAHAM JOSHUA HESCHEL, PH.D.

*Associate Professor of Jewish Ethics and Mysticism,
The Jewish Theological Seminary of America*

I. *Spatial Symbols*

Art and religion

From time immemorial man has been concerned with the question how to create a symbol of the Deity, a visible object in which its presence would be enshrined, wherein it could be met and wherein its power would be felt at all times.

That religious eagerness found an ally in one of man's finest skills: the skill to design, to fashion, and to paint in material form what mind and imagination conceive. They became wedded to each other. *Art* became the helpmate of *religion,* and rich was the offspring of that intimate union. It is alone through religion and cult that the consciousness of higher laws could mature and be imposed "upon the individual artist, who would otherwise have given free rein to his imagination, *style."* "There, in the sanctuary, they took their first steps toward the sublime. They learned to eliminate the contingent from form. Types came into being; ultimately the first ideals." [1] Religion and cult inspired the artist to bring forth images of majesty, magnificent temples and awe-inspiring altars, which in turn stirred

[1] Jacob Burckhardt, *Force and Freedom,* Pantheon Books, Inc., New York, 1943, pp. 191, 318.

the heart of the worshiper to greater devotion. What would art have been without the religious sense of mystery and sovereignty, and how dreary would have been religion without the incessant venture of the artist to embody the invisible in visible forms, to bring his vision out of the darkness of the heart, and to fill the immense absence of the Deity with the light of human genius? The right hand of the artist withers when he forgets the sovereignty of God, and the heart of the religious man has often become dreary without the daring skill of the artist. Art seemed to be the only revelation in the face of the Deity's vast silence.

One is overwhelmed by the sight of the great works of art. They represent in a deep sense man's attempt to celebrate the works of God. God created heaven and earth, and man creates symbols of heaven and symbols of earth. Yet man is not satisfied with the attempt to praise the work of God; he even dares to express the essence of God. God created man, and man creates images of God.

A distinction ought to be made here between *real* and *conventional* symbols. *A real symbol* is a visible object that represents something invisible; something present representing something absent. A real symbol represents, *e.g.,* the Divine because it is assumed that the Divine resides in it or that the symbol partakes to some degree of the reality of the Divine. *A conventional symbol* represents to the mind an entity which is not shown, not because its substance is endowed with something of that entity but because it suggests that entity, by reason of relationship, association, or convention, *e.g.,* a flag.

An image is a real symbol. The god and his image are almost identified. They are cherished as the representatives of the gods; he who has the image, has the god. It is believed that the god resides in the image or that the image partakes to some degree of the power and reality of the god. A victor nation would carry off the god-image of the conquered nation, in order to deprive it of the presence and aid of its god. In the fifteenth century before the common era, a statue of the goddess Ishtar of Nineveh was carried with great pomp and ceremony from Mesopotamia to Egypt, obviously for the purpose of letting Egypt enjoy the blessings which the goddess by her presence would bestow upon the land.[2] As Durkheim remarked, the images of a totem-creature are more sacred than the totem-creature itself. The image may replace the Deity.

The rejection of the image

What was the attitude of the prophets toward that grand alliance of religion and art? What is the attitude of the Bible toward the happy union of priest and artist? Did Israel contribute toward cementing that matrimony? Did it use its talents to create worthy symbols of the One God it proclaimed by inspiring its artists to embody in stone the Creator of heaven and earth? Indeed, if a religion is to be judged by the degree to which it contributes to the human need for symbolism, the Decalogue should have contained a commandment, saying: Thou shalt make unto thee a symbol, a graven image or some manner of likeness. . . . Instead, the making and worshiping of images was considered an abomination, vehemently condemned in the Bible.[3] If symbolism is the standard, then Moses will have to be accused of having had a retarding influence on the development of man. It is not with a sense of pride that we recall the making of the Golden Calf, nor do we condemn as an act of vandalism the role of Moses in beating it into pieces and grinding it very small, "until it was as fine as dust" and casting "the dust thereof into the brook that descended out of the mount."

It is perhaps significant that the Hebrew word that came to denote symbol, *semel,* occurs in the Bible five times, but always in a derogatory sense, denoting an idolatrous object.[4]

Nothing is more alien to the spirit of Judaism than the veneration of images. According to an ancient belief, the prophet Elijah, "the

---

[2] Hugo Winckler, *The Tell-el-Amarna Letters,* Reuther & Reichard, Berlin, 1896, pp. 48 f.

J. A. Knudtzon, *Die El-Amarna-Tafeln, Vorderasiatische Bibliothek,* Leipzig, 1915, pp. 178 f. (no. 23), 1050 f.

[3] *Cf.,* for example, Deuteronomy 27:15; Leviticus 4:15.

[4] Deuteronomy 4:16; Ezekiel 8:3, 5; 2 Chronicles 33:7, 15. However, by means of a metathesis, Ibn Ezra finds the word *selem* in *sulam* (ladder); *cf.* his interpretation of Jacob's ladder in his *Commentary* on Genesis 28:11.

angel of the covenant," is present whenever the act of circumcision is performed. To concretize that belief, a vacant chair, called "Elijah's chair," is placed near the seat of the *sandek* (godfather).[5] This is the limit of representation: a vacant chair. To place a picture or statue of the prophet on it, would have been considered absurd as well as blasphemous. To Jewish faith there are no physical embodiments of the supreme mysteries. All we have are signs, reminders.

The world is not a symbol

The Second Commandment implies more than the prohibition of images; it implies the rejection of all visible symbols for God; not only of images fashioned by man but also of "any manner of likeness, of any thing that is in heaven above, or that is in the earth beneath, or that is in the water under the earth." The significance of that attitude will become apparent when contrasted with its opposite view.

It would be alien to the spirit of the Bible to assert that the world is a symbol of God. In contrast, the symbolists exhort us: "Neither say that thou hast now no Symbol of the Godlike. Is not God's Universe a Symbol of the Godlike; is not Immensity a Temple . . . ?" [6]

What is the reason for that sharp divergence? To the symbolists, "All visible things are emblems. . . . Matter exists only spiritually, and to represent some Idea and *body* it forth." [7] The universe is "a mechanism of self-expression for the infinite." The symbol is but the bodying forth of the infinite, and it is the very life of the infinite to be bodied forth.[8]

Now, the Bible does not regard the universe as a mechanism of the self-expression of God, for the world did not come into being in an act of self-expression but in an act of creation. The world is not of the essence of God, and its expression is not His. The world speaks to God, but that speech is not God speaking to Himself. It would be

---

[5] See A. T. Glassberg, *Zikron Berith la-Rishonim,* Berlin, 1892, pp. 176 ff., 231 ff.

[6] Thomas Carlyle, *Sartor Resartus,* Doubleday, Doran & Company, Inc., New York, 1937, Book III, Chapter 7, pp. 253–254.

[7] *Ibid.,* Book I, Chapter 11, p. 72.

[8] H. F. Dunbar, *Symbolism in Medieval Thought and Its Consummation in the Divine Comedy,* Yale University Press, New Haven, 1929, pp. 15 f.

alien to the spirit of the Bible to say that it is the very life of God to be bodied forth. The world is neither His continuation nor His emanation but His creation and possession.

God and space

The fundamental insight that God is not and cannot be localized in a thing [9] was emphatically expressed at the very moment in which it could have been most easily forgotten, at the inauguration of the Temple in Jerusalem. At that moment Solomon exclaims:

But will God in very truth dwell on earth? Behold, heaven and the heaven of heavens cannot contain Thee; how much less this house that I have built!

(First Kings 8:27)

God manifests Himself in *events* rather than in *things,* and these events can never be captured or localized in things.

How significant is the fact that Mount Sinai, the place on which the supreme revelation occurred, did not retain any degree of holiness! It did not become a shrine, a place of pilgrimage.

The realization that the world and God are not of the same essence is responsible for one of the great revolutions in the spiritual history of man. Things may be *instruments,* never *objects of worship. Matza,* the *shofar,* the *lulav* are not things to be looked at, to be saluted, to be paid homage to, but things to be used. Being instruments they have symbolic meaning but they are not primarily regarded as symbols in themselves. A symbol—because of its inherent symbolic quality—is an object of contemplation and adoration.

To a reverent Catholic the cross is a sacred symbol. Gazing at its shape, his mind is drawn into contemplation of the very essence of the Christian faith.

Thomas Aquinas taught that the cross was to be adored with *Latria, i.e.,* supreme worship, and argued that one might regard a cross or an image in two ways: (1) in itself, as a piece of wood or the like, and so no reverence should be given to a cross or to an image of

[9] See my, *The Sabbath, Its Meaning to Modern Man,* Farrar, Straus & Young, New York, 1951, pp. 4 ff.; "Space, Time, and Reality," *"Judaism,"* I, 3, July, 1952, pp. 268 f.

Jesus; (2) as representing something else, and in this way one might give to the Cross *relatively, i.e.,* to the cross as carrying one's mind to Jesus—the same honor given to Jesus *absolutely, i.e.,* in Himself. Adoration is also given to the Sacred Heart, as well as to images and relics of the saints.[10] In contrast, the image and shape of the scrolls, of a *shofar* or a *lulav* do not convey to us any inspiration beyond reminding us of its function and our obligation.

The spirit of Christian symbolism has shaped the character of church architecture, "a noble church structure may be 'a sermon in stone.'" According to Germanos, the Patriarch of Constantinople (715–730), the church is heaven on earth, the symbol of The Crucifixion, the Entombment, and Resurrection. From the fifth century, symbolism permeated the architecture of the Byzantine church building in all its details. "The sanctuary, the nave and aisles were the sensible world, the upper parts of the church the intelligible cosmos, the vaults the mystical heaven." [11] A similar spirit is to be found in Western Christianity, where, for example, the shape of church buildings is that of a cross, embodying the basic symbol of Christianity. The altar is often raised three or seven steps, signifying the Trinity or the seven gifts of the Holy Spirit.

In Jewish law, which prescribes countless rules for daily living, no directions are given for the shape of a synagogue building.[12]

Any form of architecture is legally admissible. The synagogue is not an abode of the Deity but a house of prayer, a gathering place for the people. Entering a synagogue, we encounter no objects designed to impart any particular idea to us. Judaism has rejected the picture as a means of representing ideas; it is opposed to pictographic symbols. The only indispensable object is a Scroll to be read, not to be gazed at.

There is no *inherent* sanctity in Jewish ritual objects. The candelabrum in the synagogue does not represent another candelabrum

[10] William Edward Addis and T. Arnold, "Latria," *Catholic Dictionary,* Catholic Publication Society Company, Kegan Paul, Trench & Company, London, 1884, p. 505.

[11] Charles R. Morey, *Medieval Art,* W. W. Norton Company, New York, 1942, pp. 104 f.

[12] Rabbi Yeheskel Landau, *Noda be-Yehudah,* Second Series, *Orah Hayim,* responsum 19.

either in Jerusalem or in heaven. It is not more than you see. It has
no symbolic content. According to Jewish law, it is prohibited to
imitate the seven-branched candelabrum as well as other features of
the Temple in Jerusalem for ritual purposes. "A man may not make
a house in the form of the Temple, or an exedra in the form of the
Temple hall, or a court corresponding to the Temple court, or a table
corresponding to the table [in the Temple] or a candlestick corresponding to the candlestick [in the Temple], but he may make one
with five or six or eight lamps, but with seven he should not make,
even of other metals [than gold] . . . or even of wood."[13] The
anointing oil must not be produced in the same composition to be
used outside the Sanctuary. "It is holy and shall be holy unto you"
(Exodus 30:32).

The purpose of ritual art objects in Judaism is not to inspire love
of God but to enhance our love of doing a *mitzvah,* to add pleasure
to obedience, delight to fulfilment. Thus the purpose is achieved not
in direct contemplation but in combining it with a ritual act; the
art objects have a religious function but no religious substance.

Jewish artists often embellished manuscripts and title pages with
pictures of Moses and Aaron. Yet such decorations were regarded as
ornaments rather than symbols.

Man the symbol of God

And yet there is something in the world that the Bible does regard
as a symbol of God. It is not a temple nor a tree, it is not a statue nor
a star. The one symbol of God is *man, every man.* God Himself
created man in His image, or, to use the biblical terms, in His *tselem*
and *demuth.* How significant is the fact that the term, *tselem,* which
is frequently used in a damnatory sense for a manmade image of
God, as well as the term, *demuth*—of which Isaiah claims (40:18)
no *demuth* can be applied to God—are employed in denoting man as
an image and likeness of God!

Human life is holy, holier even than the Scrolls of the Torah. Its
holiness is not man's achievement; it is a gift of God rather than
something attained through merit. Man must therefore be treated

[13] *Rosh Hashanah* 24a; *Avodah Zarah* 43a.

with the honor due to a likeness representing the King of kings.

Not that the Bible was unaware of man's frailty and wickedness. The Divine in man is not by virtue of what he does, but by virtue of what he is. With supreme frankness the failures and shortcomings of kings and prophets, of men such as Moses or David, are recorded. And yet, Jewish tradition insisted that not only man's soul but also his body is symbolic of God. This is why even the body of a criminal condemned to death must be treated with reverence, according to the book of Deuteronomy (21:23). He who sheds the blood of a human being, "it is accounted to him as though he diminished [or destroyed] the Divine image." [14] And in this sense, Hillel characterized the body as an "icon" of God,[15] as it were, and considered keeping clean one's own body as an act of reverence for its Creator.[16]

As not one man or one particular nation but all men and all nations are endowed with the likeness of God, there is no danger of ever worshiping man, because only that which is extraordinary and different may become an object of worship. But the Divine likeness is something all men share.

This is a conception of farreaching importance to biblical piety. What it implies can hardly be summarized. Reverence for God is shown in our reverence for man. The fear you must feel of offending or hurting a human being must be as ultimate as your fear of God. An act of violence is an act of desecration. To be arrogant toward man is to be blasphemous toward God.

> He who oppresses the poor blasphemes
> > his Maker,
> He who is gracious to the needy
> > honors Him.
>
> > > (Proverbs 14:31)

"You must not say, since I have been put to shame, let my neighbor be put to shame. . . . If you do so, know whom you put to shame, for in the likeness of God made He him." [17] Rabbi Joshua ben Levi

[14] *Mekilta* to Exodus 20:16.

[15] *tselem elohim* in Genesis 1:27 is translated in the Septuagint *kat' eikona theou.*

[16] *Leviticus Rabba* 34, 3; see also *Midrash Tehillim,* 103. Significant are the statements in *Jer. Berachoth* III, 8a, and *Moed Katan* 83a.

[17] *Genesis Rabba* 24, 8.

said: "A procession of angels pass before man wherever he goes, proclaiming: *Make way for the image (eikonion) of God.*" [18]

And what is more. Biblical piety may be expressed in the form of a supreme imperative: *Treat yourself as a symbol of God*. In the light of this imperative we can understand the meaning of that astounding commandment: "You shall be holy, for I the Lord your God am holy" (Leviticus 19:2).

It is often claimed that "Hebrew monotheism has ended by raising the Deity too far above the earth and placing Him too far above man." [19] This is a half-truth. God is indeed very much above man, but at the same time man is very much a reflection of God. The craving to keep that reflection pure, to guard God's likeness on earth, is indeed the motivating force of Jewish piety.

The *tselem* or god's image is what distinguishes man from the animal, and it is only because of it that he is entitled to exercise power in the world of nature. If he retains his likeness he has dominion over the beast; if he forfeits his likeness he descends, losing his position of eminence in nature. [20]

The idea of man's divine likeness is, according to one opinion in

[18] *Deuteronomy Rabba* 4, 4; see *Midrash Tehillim*, chapter 17. That one lives in the company of angels, "ministers of the Supreme," was something one is expected by *Jewish law* to be always conscious of. This is evidenced by the prayer *hithhabdu*, *Berachoth* 60b and *Mishne Torah, Tefillah* 7, 4. The general belief, based on Psalms 91:11, is clearly stated in *Tacanith* 11a. According to *Exodus Rabba* 32, 6, and *Tanhuma, Mishpatim*, end, angels are assigned to a person according to the good deeds he performs; *Seder Eliahu Rabba*, chapter XVIII, edition Friedmann, p. 100. Compare also the statement of the two "ministering angels" that accompany a person on Sabbath eve on his way from the synagogue to his home, *Shabbath* 119b. "Rabbi Simeon said: When a man rises at midnight and gets up and studies the Torah till daylight, and when the daylight comes he puts the phylacteries with the holy impress on his head and his arm, and covers himself with his fringed robe, and as he issues from the door of his house he passes the *mezuzah* containing the imprint of the Holy Name on the post of his door, then four holy angels join him and issue with him from the door of his house and accompany him to the synagogue and proclaim before him: Give honor to the image of the Holy King, give honor to the son of the King, to the precious countenance of the King." *Zohar*, III, p. 265a.

[19] "It was left for the Christian religion to call down its god from the heights of heaven to earth, and to represent this god by means of art." (A. D. Seta, *Religion and Art*, Charles Scribner's Sons, New York, 1914, p. 148.) Indeed, this was not the way of Judaism which insisted upon its worship being independent of art. It is life itself that must represent the God of Israel.

[20] *Genesis Rabba* 8, 12.

the Talmud, the reason for the prohibition to produce the human figure. The statement in Exodus 20:20, "You shall not make with Me (*itti*) gods of silver, or gods of gold," should be rendered as if it were written, "You shall not make My symbol (*otti; ot* means symbol), namely, man, gods of silver, or gods of gold." [21]

What is necessary is not *to have a symbol* but *to be a symbol*. In this spirit, all objects and all actions are not symbols in themselves but ways and means of enhancing the living symbolism of man.

The divine symbolism of man is not in what he *has*—such as reason or the power of speech—but in what he *is* potentially: he is able to be holy as God is holy. To imitate God, to act as He acts in mercy and love, is the way of enhancing our likeness. Man becomes what he worships. "Says the Holy One, blessed be He: He who acts like Me shall be like Me." [22] Says Rabbi Levi ben Hama: "Idolators resemble their idols (Psalms 115:8); now how much more must the servants of the Lord resemble Him." [23]

And yet that likeness may be defiled, distorted, and forfeited. It is from the context of this problem that the entire issue of Jewish symbolism must be considered. The goal of man is to recognize and preserve His likeness or at least to prevent its distortion.

But man has failed. And what is the consequence? "I have placed the likeness of My image on them and through their sins I have upset it," is the dictum of God.[24]

The likeness is all but gone. Today, nothing is more remote and less plausible than the idea: man is a symbol of God. Man forgot Whom he represents or *that* he represents.

There is one hope. The Midrash interprets the verse Deuteronomy 1:10, as if it were written: "Lo, today you are like the stars in heaven, but in the future you will resemble the Master." [25]

[21] *Abodah Zarah* 43b.
[22] *Deuteronomy Rabba* 1, 10.
[23] See *Deuteronomy Rabba* 5, 9.
[24] *Moed Kattan* 15b.
[25] *Deuteronomy Rabba* 1, 10.

II. *Conceptual Symbols*

Symbolic knowledge

Let us now turn to the problem of conceptual symbols. In the past several decades the interest in symbolism has become a decisive trend in contemporary thinking. This is no accident. As long as man believes in his ability to comprehend the world directly, as long as he is impressed by that which *is* rather than concerned to express what he *thinks,* symbolism is one of the techniques of human understanding. When man becomes the measure of good and evil, when truth is regarded as that which the mind creates, symbolism becomes the sole technique of human understanding.

Kant has demonstrated that it is utterly impossible to attain knowledge of the world, because knowledge is always in the form of categories and these, in the last analysis, are only representational constructions for the purpose of apperceiving what is given. Objects possessing attributes, causes that work, are all mythical. We can say only that objective phenomena are regarded *as if* they behaved in such and such a way, and there is absolutely no justification for assuming any dogmatic attitude and changing the "as if" into a "that." *Salomon Maimon* was probably the first to sum up Kantian philosophy by saying that only *symbolic knowledge* is possible.[26]

To the contemporary physicist the world of sense—perception— is of no relevance whatsoever. The familiar world is abandoned for abstracts, graphs, and equations. His elements are not the familiar phenomena but electrons, quanta, potentials, Hamiltonian functions, and the like. Science is purely operational, concerned merely with the manipulation of symbols.

In the light of such a theory, what is the status of religious knowledge? We must, of course, give up the hope ever to attain a valid concept of the supernatural in an objective sense, yet because for practical reasons it is useful to cherish the idea of God, let us retain

[26] See H. Vaihinger, *The Philosophy of "As if,"* Kegan Paul, Trench, Trubner & Company, London, 1935, pp. 29 f.

that idea and claim that while our knowledge of God is not objectively true, it is still *symbolically* true.

Thus, symbolism became the supreme category in understanding religious truth. It has become a truism that religion is largely an affair of symbols. Translated into simpler terms this view regards religion as *a fiction,* useful to society or to man's personal well-being. Religion is then no longer a relationship of man to God but a relationship of man to the symbol of his highest ideals: there is no God, but we must go on worshiping His symbol.

The idea of symbolism is, of course, not a modern invention. New only is the role it has now assumed. In earlier times, symbolism was regarded as a form of *religious thinking;* in modern times religion is regarded as *a form of symbolic thinking.*

Symbolism and solipsism

Is religion the sum of mind plus symbol? Is the mind-symbol relationship the only ultimate form of relationship in which man stands to God? Is symbolic understanding of God all that religion has to offer? If God is a symbol, then religion is a child's play. What is the value of searching for a goal that will forever remain unknown? Moreover, if God has no mercy and offers no light to those who grope for Him, does He deserve man's desperate efforts to reach Him?

To religion, however, the immediate certainty of faith is more important than all metaphysical reflection, and the pious man must regard religious symbolism as *a form of solipsism,* and just as he who loves a person does not love a symbol or one's own idea of the person but the person himself, so he who loves and fears God is not satisfied with worshiping a symbol or worshiping symbolically.

Symbols are substitutes

Symbols are substitutes, cherished whenever the object we are interested in is momentarily or permanently beyond our reach. Unable to find a direct approach to its object (or a direct way of expressing itself), the mind accepts a symbol in place of the original object of its interest. The premise of religious symbolism is the assumption that God lies beyond the ken of our minds and will therefore never be apprehended or expressed directly but only through the symbol. Now the second part of that premise is not logically necessitated by the first. If the knowledge of God is beyond the reach of man, what gives us certainty to assume that there is a symbol that may serve as His representative?

Symbols can be taken seriously, only if we are convinced of man's ability to create legitimate symbols, namely, of his ability to capture the invisible in the visible, the absolute in the relative. Their validity will, furthermore, depend upon our being in possession of criteria by means of which we could decide which symbols represent and which misrepresent the object we are interested in; which to accept and which to reject. Yet in order to prove the validity of symbols in general and in order to judge the adequacy of particular symbols, we must be in possession of a knowledge of the symbolized object that is independent of all symbols. To justify and to judge symbols we are in need of *non-symbolic* knowledge.

Symbols are means of communication. They communicate or convey to us what they represent. Consequently, in order to understand or to appreciate a symbol, we must be in possession of a knowledge of what the symbol stands for. Does not this prove that symbols are secondary to religious knowledge?

And is it conceivable that a religious person would, once he has realized the fictional nature of symbolism, be willing to accept a substitute for God? He will reject not only substitutes for the religious reality but also substitutes for spontaneous expression. Such substitutes distort our vision, stifle our inner life. Giving to symbolic objects what is due to God and directing the soul to express itself by proxy, symbolism degenerates into *a vicarious religion*.

The will of God is no euphemism

Of a violinist who is moving his bow over the strings of his violin we do not say, he is performing a symbolic act. Why? Because the meaning of his act is in what he is doing, regardless of what else the act may represent. In rendering a service to a friend, I am not primarily conscious of carrying out an act which should symbolize my friendship; the act *is* friendship. Symbolism is not something that characterizes all aspects of human life. Why are there no symbols in morality? Because a moral deed is endowed with intrinsic meaning; its value is in itself, not in what it stands for.

No one eats figuratively, no one sleeps symbolically; so why should the pious man be content to worship God symbolically?

Those who are in the dark in their lonely search for God; those to whom God is a problem, or a Being that is eternally absent and silent; those who ask, "How does one know Him? Where can one find Him? How does one express Him?" will be forced to accept symbols as an answer.

But Judaism is not a religion of an unknown God. It is built upon a rock of certainty that God has made known His will to His people. To us, the will of *God is neither a metaphor nor a symbol nor a euphemism* but more powerful and more real than our own existence.

III. *Symbolism and Jewish Living*

The primacy of literal meaning

Is, perhaps, the content of the Bible, the manner in which the will of God was made known to man, symbolic?

Reading carefully the words of the Bible, we realize that the essence of biblical piety is not to be found in the employment of symbols but in something quite different. When the book of Deuteronomy exclaims: "What does the Lord thy God ask of thee?" the answer given is "to fear the Lord thy God, to walk in all His ways, and to serve the Lord thy God with all thy heart and all thy soul, to keep for thy good the commandments of thy Lord and His statutes, which I command you this day" (10:12 f.).

He who loves with all his heart, with all his soul, with all his might, does not love symbolically. Nor does the term, "to serve God," refer to a symbolic attitude. The term, "service," may be used in two ways: symbolically and literally. When a person is appointed honorary president or honorary secretary of an organization, he is serving symbolically and is not required to carry out any functions. Yet there are others who actually serve an organization or a cause.

What was it that the prophets sought to achieve? To purge the mind of the notion that God desired symbols. The service of God is an extremely concrete, an extremely real, literal, and factual affair. We do not have to employ symbols to make Him understand what we mean. We worship Him not by employing figures of speech but by shaping our actual lives according to His pattern.

The symbolists claim that not the literal meaning of Scripture is the important matter but the spiritual truths hidden beneath it; while Jewish tradition insists, the biblical verse must never be divested of *peshat,* of its naked meaning; without the reality of the naked word the spirit is a ghost. Even the mystics who cherished the allegorical meaning of Scripture and regarded the hidden significance as superior to the plain, naked meaning, always insisted that the secret rests upon the plain.

The power of the Bible is in its not being absolutely dependent upon man's symbolic interpretations. The prophets do not live by the grace of preachers. Their words are significant even when taken literally. They do not speak in oracles but in terms of specific actions. Love thy neighbor as thyself has strictly literal meaning, and so has the commandment to observe the seventh day. Judaism has tried to teach that holiness is vital, that the things of the spirit are real. The Torah is not in heaven. The voice of God is unambiguous; it is the confusion of man, of the best of us, that creates the ambiguity. It tells us precisely how God wants us to act. Performing a sacred deed we are not aware of symbolizing religion; a sacred act *is* religion.

Religious observance has more than two dimensions; it is more than an act that happens between man and an idea. The unique feature of religious living is in its being *three-dimensional.* In a religious act man stands before God. He feels addressed or commanded to act. "Greater is he who acts because he is commanded by God than he who acts without being commanded by Him." [27] Symbolic meaning of an act expresses only what the act means to man in relation to an idea; it does not convey what the act means in relation to God.

Does man stand in a symbolic relation to God? To the outsider, religion may appear as a symbol, just as to those who see a man weep,

[27] *Kiddushin* 31a; *Baba Kamma* 38a, 87a.

weeping is a symbol of grief, pain, or fear. Yet, to the afflicted man weeping is not a symbol. God was not a symbol to him who exclaimed, "Though He slay me, yet will I trust in Him." [28] Do we pray symbolically? Do we implore Him for symbolic aid?

Symbols have their place in the outer court of religion. What is found in the inner sanctuary is neither speculative nor artistic pageantry, but the simplicity and immediacy of insight, faith, and dedication. There are many symbols in Judaism, but they have auxiliary importance; their status is that of *minhag*.[29] Jewish observance comprises both *mitzvoth* [commandments] and *minhaggim* [customs]. The Rabbis were careful to distinguish between law and custom.[30] Customs are symbols born of the mind of man; *mitzvoth* are expressions and interpretations of the will of God.

Mitzvoth and ceremonies

Moses was not concerned with initiating a new cult, but with creating a new people. In the center of Jewish living is not a cult but observance; the former is a realm of its own, the latter comprises all of life. Since the destruction of the Temple in Jerusalem Judaism has had a minimum of cult and a maximum of observance. The prophetic fight against the mendacity of spurious ceremonies has left its trace in our lives. There is a minimum of show, of ceremonialism in Jewish religion, even in public worship. Ceremonies are for the eye, but Judaism is an appeal to the spirit. The only ceremony still observed in the synagogue is the blessing of the priests—but then the congregation is required to close its eyes.

We rarely object to ceremonialism in the observance of state affairs or in courtroom proceedings or to the elaborate ritualism of academic celebrations at American universities. Should we not say that the private and domestic acts must likewise have something that would

[28] Job 13:15.

[29] "Said Abaye: Now that it has been said that symbols are of significance, a man should make a regular habit of eating, at the beginning of the year, pumpkin, fenugreek, leek, beet and dates (These grow in profusion and are symbolic of prosperity)" *Horayoth* 12a.

[30] *Yebamoth* 13b; *Niddah* 16a; *Taanith* 26b.

stamp them as out of the ordinary, and that *mitzvoth* are essentially ceremonies?

Ceremonialism has the pedagogical value of emphasizing the extraordinary character of an occasion. In becoming a daily habit it loses its value. A ceremony is an emphasis on a deed. Yet adding an esthetic veneer, decorum, and solemnity, it remains very much on the surface.

A *mitzvah* is performed when a deed is outdone by a sigh, when Divine reference is given to a human fact. In a *mitzvah* we give the source of an act, rather than the underlining of a word. Ceremonies are performed for the sake of onlookers; *mitzvoth* are done for the sake of God. Ceremonies must be visible, *spectacular;* a *mitzvah* is spurious when turning impressive.

Mitzvoth are sanctifications rather than ceremonies. Without faith, the festivities turn dull and artificial. The esthetic satisfaction they offer is meager compared with that obtained from listening to a symphony, *e.g.*

The myth of self-expression

Symbols are human forms of expression. Yet, is eloquence the essence of piety? Is religion a function of man's power of expression? Is it one of the many dialects of man's language, comparable to art, poetry, and philosophy? The theory that religion is a form of expression is a theory that thinks too much about what man says and ignores the fact that in the face of the ultimate problems he has nothing or very little to say.

The goal of religion is not primarily to help us to express ourselves, but to bring us closer to God. *Empathy* rather than expression is the way of piety. The function of *mitzvoth* is not to express ourselves but to express the will of God. The most important fact is that God speaks. And he who knows that God speaks cannot regard his own need for speaking and self-expression as being of supreme concern. The supreme concern is how to understand God's speech, God's expression. The *mitzvoth* are words of God which we try to understand, to articulate. The whole world was created by His word, and, figuratively speaking, all things are signs of His alphabet which we must learn to decipher.

Granted that the need for symbolization is a basic human need, the task of religion would not be to satisfy that need but rather to supply the norms for the right satisfaction of that need. Thus, the essential role of religion would be, if necessary, to prevent certain forms of symbolization. Symbolism may be characteristic of human nature, but religion is more than an aid in the development of the merely human; its goal is to raise the human to the level of the holy.

The primary function of symbols is to express *what we think;* the primary function of the *mitzvoth* is to express *what God thinks.* Religious symbolism is *a quest for God,* Jewish observance is *a response to God.* In fulfilling the *mitzvoth* our major concern is not to express our feelings but to comply, to be in agreement with the will of God.

Mitzvah and symbol

Jewish piety is an answer to God, expressed in the language of *mitzvoth* rather than in the language of *symbols.* The *mitzvah* rather than the symbol is our fundamental category. What is the difference between the two categories?

The use of symbols whether in the form of things or in the form of actions is required by custom and convention; the fulfilment of *mitzvoth* is required by the Torah. Symbols are relevant to man; *mitzvoth* are relevant to God. Symbols are folkways; *mitzvoth* are God's ways. Symbols are expressions of the human mind; what they express and their power to express depend on a mental act of man; their significance is gone when man ceases to be responsive to them. Symbols are like the moon, they have no light of their own.

Mitzvoth, on the other hand, are expressions or interpretations of the will of God; they are divine commandments. While they are meaningful to man, the source of their meaning is not in the understanding of man but in the love of God. The essence of a *mitzvah* is in its being relevant to God, *regardless* of what it may mean to man; its meaning often transcends the understanding of man. Unintelligible symbols we discard; *mitzvoth* we cherish regardless of our understanding. It is the *mitzvah* that lends more meaning to us than the meaning we ascribe to it.

A symbol is *man's reference to God;* a *mitzvah* is *God's reference to man.* As a symbol, the act of blowing the *shofar* on the New Year's Day would have no meaning to God. In carrying out a *mitzvah* we acknowledge the fact of God having addressed man and His being concerned with our fulfilment of His will.

Symbols serve a cognitive function; they try to make the unknown intelligible, to make the distant present. In contrast, the *mitzvoth* do not interpret the essence of God to us or instruct man about the mysteries.

Symbols are created for the sake of *signifying; mitzvoth* were given for the sake of *sanctifying.* This is their function: to refine, to ennoble, to sanctify man. They confer holiness upon us, whether or not we know exactly what they signify.

A symbol is a thing, a *mitzvah* is a task. A symbol *is,* a *mitzvah* is an act that *ought to be,* done. Symbols have a psychological, not an ontological status; they do not affect any reality, except the psyche of man. *Mitzvoth* affect God. Symbols evade, *mitzvoth* transcend reality. Symbols are less, *mitzvoth* are more than real.

Jewish festivals do not contain any attempt to recreate symbolically the events they commemorate. We do not enact the exodus from Egypt nor the crossing of the Red Sea. Decisive as the revelation of Sinai is, there is no ritual to recreate or to dramatize it. We neither repeat nor imitate sacred events. Whatever is done in religious observance is an original act. The Seder ritual, for example, recalls; it does not rehearse the past.

Kavanah and symbolic understanding

There was never any doubt that all ritual acts have an ultimate meaning, yet their immediate relevance to us does not lie in their symbolic meaning but in their being commandments of God. Jewish piety demands their fulfilment regardless of whether we comprehend their symbolic meaning. We may not comprehend the wisdom of God, but we are certain of understanding the will of God.

Does the absence of symbolic understanding imply that Jewish observance is nothing but a physical performance? Jewish tradition insists that no performance is complete without the participation of the heart. It asks for the *kavanah,* for inner participation, not only for external action. Yet there is a difference between symbolic understanding and what tradition means by *kavanah.*

Kavanah is awareness of the will of God rather than awareness of the reason of a *mitzvah.* Awareness of symbolic meaning is awareness of a specific idea; *kavanah* is awareness of an ineffable situation. It does not try to appropriate what is part of the divine mystery. It is *kavanah* rather than symbolic understanding that evokes in us ultimate joy at the moment of doing a *mitzvah.*

It is, for example, possible to justify the ritual washing of the hands before a meal as a reminder of a similar priestly ceremony at the Temple in Jerusalem. Yet what is characteristic of Jewish piety is not to be mindful of that reason but to forget all reasons and to make place in the mind for the awareness of God.

Indeed, the certainty of being able to do the will of God lends to the *mitzvoth* a meaning compared with which all particular explanations seem platitudes. What reason could compete with the claim, "This is the will of God"?

Moreover, who would be willing to sacrifice his dearest interests for observing the Sabbath just because it symbolizes creation or the redemption from Egypt? If the Jews were ever ready for such a sacrifice, it was not because of a symbolic idea but because of God. The ideal of Judaism is to serve for the sake of God, not for the sake of symbols.

The status of symbolic meaning

The validity of a symbol depends upon its intelligibility. An object loses its symbolic character when people forget what it stands for. Yet, in Judaism the knowledge of what the commandments symbolize was not considered essential. *Halacha* has never regarded the understanding of symbolic meaning as a requirement for the proper fulfilment of a *mitzvah.*

The striking fact is that the symbolic meaning of the *mitzvoth* was neither canonized nor recorded. Had such understanding ever been considered essential, how did it happen that the meaning of so many rituals has remained obscure? Had it been known and had its knowledge been regarded as essential, it would not have fallen into oblivion, but would have been transmitted to posterity by a people that so faithfully preserved its heritage.

Let us take an example. On the Feast of Booths we are commanded to carry four kinds of plants. The significance of that ritual is not given in the Bible. So the Rabbis offered a symbolic interpretation: The stem of the palm tree corresponds to the human spine, the leaf of the myrtle to the eye, the willow leaf to the mouth, and the *etrog* to the heart.[31] What is the status of that interpretation? It was not claimed to be the authentic original meaning of the ritual. Nor was its awareness considered essential to the fulfilment of the ritual. The symbolic interpretation is one of several offered. It has devotional meaning.

We must distinguish between that which is *only a symbol* and that which is *also a symbol*. A flag serves only one function, namely, to serve as a symbol; beyond its symbolic function it is a meaningless object. A temple, on the other hand, has a very definite meaning as a building, regardless of its symbolic function. In the same sense, religious observance, such as the ritual of the four plants, may assume symbolic meaning; it is *also* a symbol, yet its essence is in its being a *mitzvah*.

A system of symbolism implies if not established or canonized meaning, then at least some unanimity of its understanding. The teeming multiplicity of symbolic interpretations of Jewish rituals advanced in the course of the past two thousand years testifies to the fact that symbolic meaning is merely *an afterthought*. No one has succeeded in discovering a system of symbolic meaning by which all *mitzvoth* could be explained with some degree of consistency. The numerous attempts to explore the semantics of the *mitzvoth* have been futile. If Judaism is a system of symbolism, then it must be regarded as a forgotten system.

The essence of Judaism is a demand rather than a creed. It emphasizes the centrality of the act. The act of studying is more im-

[31] *Leviticus Rabba* 30.

portant than the possession of knowledge. There is more reflection about the deed than contemplation about the dogma.

Just as an image becomes an idol, a deed may become a habit. Its truthfulness is surrendered when it assumes independence and becomes self-perpetuating and more sacred than God Who commanded it.

The moment of meeting

What is the purpose and the justification of symbolism? It is to serve as a *meeting place* of the spiritual and the material, of the invisible and the visible. Judaism, too, had such a meeting place—in a qualified sense—in the Sanctuary. Yet in its history the point of gravity was shifted from space to time, and instead of a place of meeting came a *moment of meeting;* the meeting is not in a thing but in a deed.

Ritual acts are moments which man shares with God, moments in which man identifies himself with the will of God. Symbols are detached from one's being; they are apart from the soul. Yet, God asks for the heart, not for the symbol; he asks for deeds, not for ceremonies.

IV. *Symbolism and Immediacy*

Symbolism and the sense of the ineffable

Essential to human thought is not only the technique of symbolization but also *the awareness of the ineffable*.[32] In every mind there is an enormous store of not-knowing, of being puzzled, of wonder, of radical amazement. While the mind manufactures ideas, translating insights into symbols, the deeper knowledge remains: what *is* we cannot say.

Thus, what characterizes man is not only his ability to develop words and symbols, but also his being compelled to draw a distinction between the utterable and the unutterable, to be stunned by that which is and cannot be put into words. It is *the sense of the ineffable* that we have to regard as the root of man's creative activities in art,

[32] See my *Man Is Not Alone,* Jewish Publication Society, Philadelphia, 1951, pp. 3 ff.

thought, and noble living. The attempt to convey what we see and cannot say is the everlasting theme of mankind's unfinished symphony, a venture in which adequacy is never achieved. There is an eternal disparity between the ultimate and man's power of expression.

Science does not know the world as it is; it knows the world in human terms. Scientific knowledge is symbolic knowledge. Trying to hold an interview with reality face to face, without the aid of human terms or symbols, we realize that what is intelligible to our mind is but a thin surface of the profoundly undisclosed.

The awareness of the unknown is earlier than the awareness of the known. Next to our mind are not names, words, symbols, but the nameless, the inexpressible, being. It is otherness, remoteness upon which we come within all our experience.

Just as the simpleminded equates appearance with reality, so does the overwise equate the expressible with the ineffable, the symbolic with the metasymbolic.

Philosophy and religion

The awareness of the ineffable, of the metasymbolic, is that with which our search must begin. Philosophy, enticed by the promise of the known, has often surrendered the treasures of higher incomprehension to poets and mystics, although without the sense of the ineffable there are no metaphysical problems, no awareness of being as being, of value as value.

A recent publication which undertook to analyze the concept of value concludes with the following statement:

Our essay has ended with the unsayable. We cannot in a correct language formulate an answer to our question: What is value? . . . Should we not give up the whole undertaking as unnecessarily self-frustrating? I think not. I need not and I shall not conceal the fact that I have my own moments of despondency when I am tempted to throw aside the whole philosophical endeavour to find an answer to such questions as, What is value? What is fact? What is truth? What is entailment? What is designation? And I suspect that this despondency is not peculiar to me and my individual inadequacies as a philosopher; I suspect that everyone who has seriously wrestled with these issues must have at some time experienced it. . . .

It is not then to be wondered at that we end with the unsayable: This we should expect. The objective should be to postpone this inevitable result as long as possible, to push the unsayable as far back as we can, to let the object speak for itself only after we have said as much as can be said to bring out what is not obvious.

If the present essay has been successful in postponing ultimate taciturnity for a few thousand words, this is the only sort of success its author could realistically have aimed at, always providing that this postponement has not destroyed or signally lessened the final vision. . . . Nothing can be done, save to return constantly to the task of pushing the obvious further back. . . .

This whole appeal to the obvious, to the revelation of what cannot be said, as the ultimate arbiter of philosophic disputes may be disconcerting to some prosaic minds. It smacks too much of mysticism, but it is mysticism in its most plebeian and I hope unobjectionable garb. There is meant no escape to some ecstatic experience, some high, emotional plane achieved only by the few on rare occasions. The vision appealed to is that which is obvious in all experience, and which is revealed in the sense of our everyday language, a sense that is felt by everyone using that language in everyday situations.

It is hoped that this essay has met this test, that it has not only postponed by some two-hundred-odd pages the appeal to the obvious (in this sense), but, resting finally on this appeal, really has retained the obvious, that it has remained true to our feelings for everyday language in pushing back into the unsayable but seen an answer to the question, What is value? [33]

This is the difference between religion and philosophy. Religion *begins* with the sense of the ineffable; philosophy *ends* with the sense of the ineffable. Religion begins where philosophy ends.

Symbolism and immediacy

A symbol is by definition not the ultimate; it is the representative of something else. What is ultimate is not translated into symbols; the ultimate is an antonym of the symbolic.

We must distinguish between *symbolic knowledge*—which we

[33] Everett W. Hall, *What is Value? An Essay in Philosophical Analysis,* The Humanities Press, New York, Routledge & Kegan Paul, Ltd., London, 1952, pp. 247–248.

obtain through logical operations, such as analysis and syllogism—and *immediate understanding* which enables us to acquire insights which are not derived from symbols but from an intimate engagement with what is real. Insights such as the meaning of joy or the difference between beauty and ugliness or the awareness of temporality, of the transitoriness of existence, we do not acquire through the mediation of symbols but through direct acquaintance.

The soul of the religious man lives in the depth of certainty: This is what God wants me to do. Where that certainty is dead, the most powerful symbolism will be futile.

The clamor for symbols

The whole history of religion is filled with the struggle between the pursuit of idols and the worship of Him Whose name is ineffable; *between symbolic knowledge and metasymbolic understanding;* between employing symbols *as means* and accepting them *as ends.* In the past symbols have often served as substitutes for insight, for immediate perception; as an alibi for faith. The need for symbolism does not always arise when the power to pray increases. When in medieval Christianity symbolism threatened to smother the immediacy of faith, the Reformation raised its voice against it. Today there is a clamor for symbolism perceptible both in Jewish and Christian circles.

Is the present day cry for symbols a cry for God? Is the craving for ceremonies an expression of a more profound care for the will of God? These are the questions our critical sense must ask.

Symbolism—a trap

Symbolism is so alluring because it promises to rehabilitate beliefs and rituals that have become meaningless to the mind. Yet, what it accomplishes is to reduce beliefs to make-believes, observance to ceremony, prophecy to literature, theology to esthetics.

Symbols are esthetic objects: either things to be looked at that please the senses and demand nothing in return or ideas that offer enjoyment without involving us in ultimate commitments. A symbol is often like a plaything, an imitation of reality, cherished for the emotional satisfaction it affords. Symbolism, indeed, is an esthetic category.

The quest for symbols is a *trap* for those who seek the truth. Symbols may either distort what is literally true or profane what is ineffably real. They may, if employed in the inner chamber of the mind, distort our longing for God into mere esthetics.

When their meaning becomes stale, symbols die. But what is worse, the heart of faith dies of an overdose of symbolism. It is better that symbols die and faith should live.

Symbolism undermines the certainty of history, implying that even God did not succeed in conveying His will to us, and that we did not succeed in understanding His will. Man speaks in symbols; God speaks in events and commands.

Realizing all this, one begins to wonder whether symbolism is an authentic category of prophetic religion—whether it is not a device of higher apologetics, a method of rationalization?

The uniqueness of the Bible is not in its symbolism. The religions of Egypt, Rome, India were rich in symbolism; what they lacked was not the symbol but the knowledge of *"the living God."* The uniqueness of the Bible is in disclosing the will of God in plain words, in telling us of the presence of God in history rather than in symbolic signs or mythic events. The mysterious ladder which Jacob saw was a dream; the redemption of Israel from Egypt was an iron fact. The ladder was in the air, while Jacob's head was on a stone.

A new heart or new symbols

"You do not believe, said Coleridge; you only believe that you believe. It is the final scene in all kinds of worship and symbolism." [34]

Let us never forget: *If God is a symbol, He is a fiction.* But if *God is real,* then He is able to express His will unambiguously. Symbols are makeshifts, necessary to those who cannot express themselves unambiguously.

There is darkness in the world and horror in the soul. What is it

[34] Thomas Carlyle, *On Heroes, Hero-Worship, and the Heroic in History,* D. Appleton & Company, New York, 1841.

that the world needs most? Will manmade symbols redeem humanity? In the past, wars have been waged over differences in symbols rather than over differences in the love of God. Symbols, ceremonies are by their very nature particularistic. Symbols separate us, insights unite us. They unite us regardless of the different ways in which they are expressed. What we need is honesty, stillness, humility, obedience to the word of God. What we need is a *new insight,* rather than new symbols.

Symbols without faith are unnecessary baggage. Our task is to overcome the callousness of soul, to be led to a plane where no one can remain both callous and calm; where His presence may be defied but not denied, and where, at the end, faith in Him is the only way.

What we ought to strive for is to find out whether we have a common concern, whether, *e.g.,* we are interested in atonement at al¹ Then the question of what symbols express atonement is secondary. What we need is immediacy. The ultimate human need is the need for a meaning of existence. This will not be found through introducing a set of symbols.

Harsh and bitter are the problems which religion comes to solve; ignorance, evil, malice, power, agony, and despair. These problems cannot be solved through generalities, through philosophical symbols. Our problem is: Do we believe what we confess? Do we mean what we say?

We do not suffer symbolically; we suffer literally, truly, deeply; symbolic remedies are quackery. The will of God is either real or a delusion.

This is our problem: "We have eyes to see but see not; we have ears to hear but hear not." There is God, and we do not understand Him; there is His word and we ignore it. This is the problem for us. Any other issue is relevant as far as it helps us to meet that challenge.

V

RELIGIOUS SYMBOLS CROSSING
CULTURAL BOUNDARIES

BY

DANIEL J. FLEMING, PH.D.

Professor Emeritus of Missions, Union Theological Seminary

There is a silent ministry of outward things and actions that have an inner meaning. When such a function is performed, not with the aim merely of signifying an object, but rather of suggesting a connotation connected with the object, it may be called a symbol. Here I shall be dealing not with ideational symbols, but with objective, visible objects and pictures which suggest conceptions that are not actually shown, but which are apprehended in association with these symbols.

The general outline of this paper can be given in a word. We shall glance first at three symbols, and then at three religions. The three symbols are chosen because of their extensive travels across the world. The three religions are chosen because they have been consciously expansive and should therefore be able to yield data on what happens to religious symbols as they cross cultural boundaries.

I. *Three Symbols*

1. *The Swastika*

The swastika is a symbol of great antiquity and has been known to many peoples. Its simplicity, as well as its almost mystic configuration, was bound to make it attractive. Hence it is found in remnants of the bronze age and on the pottery of early American Indians.

Scandinavian inscriptions show the swastika on the battle ax of Thor. It is the monogram of Vishnu and Siva in India, and the Buddhists introduced it into China and Japan. It appears on the crown of Lama deities in Tibet, on rock carvings in Sweden, and on Celtic stones in Britain. However, the swastika seems never to have visited Africa.

The swastika is assumed by many to be exclusively a Buddhist symbol. And one does often find it engraved on Buddha's breast. It is one of the auspicious signs on Buddha's footprints. But, although found more often in Buddhism, the swastika, as we have seen, has many friends.

Rather unexpectedly the swastika is found, also, in Christianity. It was fairly common on early Christian remains in Rome in juxtaposition with the cross. It is found on many of the bronze and brass Christian crosses unearthed in North China. In modern times it could be found in the panels of a Peiping church, at the ends of the beams of a Christian chapel in Nanhsuchow, on the altar of a Hongkong chapel, and on the seals of a Baptist school in Burma, and a Methodist school in India.[1]

The original meaning of the swastika is obscure. In practice, most varied connotations are assigned to it. As an old religious symbol it typified cosmic union. Some Buddhists explain it as a sign that the heart has come to rest. Pictured on the heart of Buddha, it was believed to symbolize the whole mind of that personage. In one culture it may be merely a good omen or mark of benediction. In another it may stand for philosophy or for cosmic harmony. In India today it is used in connection with Hindu marriages, signifying a wish that the best blessings may rest upon the bride and groom. In many cases it merely stirs emotion without having conscious intellectual content. Thus the swastika has traveled to many peoples with no clear and constant meaning, but fitting into the thought forms of its environment.

[1] Daniel J. Fleming, *Christian Symbols in a World Community,* The Friendship Press, New York, 1940, figures 61, 68, 87, 91, 96.

2. *The Lotus*

The lotus is a second symbol that, in an extraordinary way, has traveled from culture to culture. It has been loved as a sacred flower in many lands and by many religions. In ancient Egypt, because the lotus grew so plentifully, it became the symbol of reproductive power of all nature and was used in religious rites. From Egypt it was carried to Assyria. The Greeks dedicated it to the nymphs. Wave after wave of foreign influence—Assyrian, Persian, Greek, Arab—carried the Egyptian lotus to India. Three of India's gods are each shown seated on a great lotus. Buddhism in India took over the lotus as one of its sacred symbols. It was introduced into Buddhist sculpture, painting, and literature. In fact, the lotus is chief among the eight symbols of Buddhism. From India, the lotus went on with Buddhism to Nepal, to Burma, and to China, where it is loved and held sacred above all other flowers—and finally to Japan. The lotus-flowered design of bowls in the synagogue in K'ai-fêng points to Buddhist influence on Chinese Judaism. As will be seen later, there are many instances of the symbolic use of the lotus by Christians in China and in India.

It is not surprising that the lotus is so widely used. In its most obvious symbolism it stands for purity and perfection because it grows up out of the mud but is not defiled. As the open flower quietly rests upon the water facing the sun it could not fail to signify meditation. In full bloom it pictures an awakened heart and spiritual enlightenment. Just as the lotus has its roots caught in the quagmire and its stem immersed in muddy water, and yet the flower rises to exquisite beauty and purity, so we are to rise above all passion and selfish striving. Neither its beautiful and fragrant flower nor its large leaves are made wet by the muddy water on which it rests; so we should live in an evil and impure world without stain.

Buddhism had adopted the lotus from Brahmanic Hinduism, and it became one of the commonest motifs in Buddhist art and literature. Because the lotus issues pure and unsullied from the waters of a lake, however impure, Hindus saw in this a symbol of superhuman or divine birth. Buddhism, borrowing from Hinduism, assigns a still more esoteric meaning to the lotus in that the many-petaled spread of the lotus is made to symbolize spatial expansion. From this it gets a cosmic significance as space whereon all existence both is supported and passes away. After Buddha began to be represented in sculpture, from about the beginning of the Christian era, his image constantly appears standing or sitting on a lotus. In symbolic language this says the Buddha is on the platform of existence and that all cosmic possibilities are at his disposal.

3. *The Cross*

The cross is a third symbol that has been at home in many cultures. By no means has it always been uniquely and distinctively Christian. Long before the Christian era it had a prominent place among the many sacred and mystic figures connected with widely scattered mythologies and religions of antiquity. Pre-Christian crosses were thus used in Assyria, Persia, and India, and among some of the Scandinavian peoples of the north, generally with a symbolic religious significance.

One of the meanings of the cross was consecration. The Tau form was common in ancient Egypt as a symbol of life. This form is also sometimes called the cross of the Old Testament, raised by Moses in the wilderness. Early Christian apologists, when taunted as "cross-worshipers," pointed out that their persecutors themselves adored cruciform objects.

However, the cross has come to be regarded as distinctively Christian. When one considers the central fact of Christianity, it would seem inevitable that the cross should become the characteristic symbol of the faith. One need not illustrate how universal is its use by Christians. Besides the objective representation of the cross, there is the ritual of making the sign of the cross—original in Christianity. This sign has manifold meanings, such as blessing, protection from danger or temptation, expulsion of evil spirits, an expression of the Faith, confession before man, or a mark of Christ's ownership. In fact, one way of demonstrating the ecumenical nature of the Christian faith would be to follow the cross as it has entered almost every land.

We see, thus, that symbols travel and persist. The swastika, the lotus, and the cross are just three illustrations showing that symbols capable of carrying deep meanings are not the private language of any individual, century, or religion. In fact, the late Ananda K. Coomaraswamy of the Fine Arts Museum of Boston, well known authority on Indian art, wrote that "there are no symbols private to any religion. If, as an historian of art, I were asked to point to a specifically Christian or specifically Buddhist symbol, for example, I should be hard put to it to find an answer."

From this first part of our study, let me submit the following principle for your consideration: that it is easier to put new meaning into an old symbol than to introduce a new symbol.

II. *Three Religions*

In the second part of this paper, we shall consider symbolism in the three so-called "missionary" religions—Islam, Buddhism, and Christianity. It would be supposed that one would in them, if anywhere, discover conscious and intentional shift in religious symbolism as an instrument in their efforts for expansion.

1. *Islam*

Let us, then, first consider symbolism in Islam. Here we have a worldwide religion. There is no continent in which Muslims cannot be found. One would expect, therefore, that its expansion would provide rich material for this paper.

But, possibly to our surprise, we find that Islam has no distinct and original symbolism.[2] From the first, Islam has forbidden any religious plastic or pictorial art. Fear of images and idols led to

[2] *Cf.* Thomas Walker Arnold, *Painting in Islam*, Clarendon Press, Oxford, 1928, p. 116.

severe condemnation of the sculptor or painter in the traditions of the Prophet.[3] Hence, throughout the Islamic world (excepting Iran whose people are artistic non-conformists) painting and sculpture have had practically no place in religious art. Islam does have its rich tradition of architecture, arabesque decoration, geometric design, and use of the beautiful forms of Arabic writing. But symbols in any exact sense do not exist in mosques. Symbolic art, then, has not been a handmaid to orthodox Islam as it has crossed the many cultural boundaries in its great expansion. This is in striking contrast to practice in Buddhism and Christianity.

Moreover, this new religion had no sacraments. Orthodox Islam had no priesthood properly so called. Its expansion so far as it has been peaceful, came largely from the influence of lay merchants, for there were no missionary societies or specially trained propagandists among Sunni Muslims until the end of the nineteenth century. Hence any architectural or cultural adjustments made through the centuries were the result, not of planned, but of unconscious, action.

Many of the features of Islam into which symbolic meaning could be read are really functional. For example, in many areas, the minaret is the visible outward sign of a mosque. The minaret, by itself, like the Qutb Minar in Delhi, might be interpreted as a finger pointing heavenward in testimony of the unity of God in a pagan land. But, as a matter of fact, the minaret is utilitarian, not symbolic, erected to fulfil a need, a vantage point from which the call to prayer may be made. A Chinese minaret may be for observation, or the mosque itself may have neither dome nor minaret, differing only slightly from an ordinary Chinese temple. In Java, the summons to prayer may be from no more than a balcony of palm branches.

The crescent could be a wonderful symbol in Islam. Occasionally, it is suggested that it signified the Prophet's great miracle of splitting the moon, or that it represents the new moon which heralds the sacred month of Ramadan. The crescent conceivably could stand for the dawning of the light of Islam. However, against such in-

[3] *Mishkat ul-Masabih*, translated by A. N. Matthews, Hindoostanee Press, Calcutta, 1809, II, pp. 368–370.

terpretations, it may be noted that the origin of the crescent in Islam is certainly secular, and late in history. When the Turks took Constantinople in the fifteenth century they put on their banners the Byzantine crescent. It thus became the ensign of the Ottoman Empire. Christian Europe was most closely in touch with this area of Islam, so it is not strange that for four hundred years Westerners have tended to think of the religion of Islam as symbolized by the crescent in contrast to the cross. We have such Western titles as "The Cross and the Crescent," "The Crescent and the Rose," "The Crescent in Northwest China," "The Crescent in the Land of the Rising Sun," etc. But there are areas other than the Near East which would resent the association of the crescent with Islam as a religion. Hence it is a mistake, though a common one, to think of the crescent as a universal symbol of Islam.

The color green is often associated with Islam. Mohammad greatly preferred green. The garments and the couches in Islam's paradise are green. War flags were often green; and the national flags of Egypt, Persia, and other Muslim lands have green as a predominant color. But while green may stand for life and vigor, and hence might symbolize Islam's hope for victory, the writer has found no evidence that this meaning lies back of its widespread use by Muslims.

The elaborate ablutions, so much a part of Muslim worship, might be used to suggest the necessity of careful attention to inner cleanliness before standing in prayer before Allah. In the tank connected with a mosque the orthodox Muslim washes his hands three times, gargles water three times, then washes his nostrils and his face, his right arm, his left arm, the inside of his ear and then the outside, and finally the right and the left foot. Sometimes prayers are said at certain points in the washing. When drawing the fingers over the face, a worshiper may say, "O Allah, whiten my face on the day when thou doest whiten and blacken faces." On washing the feet he may say, "O Allah, establish my feet in the straight path on the day when the feet slip."

But here again the objective is mainly functional to free the worshiper from impurity rather than symbolic. There is very little internalizing of the rite even by such a recognized leader as Al Ghazzali who tried to spiritualize rites as much as he could. The traditions hold that ablutions have the utilitarian or even magical effect of removing evil of all kinds.[4] For most, however, the ceremony is just a formality commanded by Allah which must be faithfully performed in detail as directed if the prayers which follow are to be acceptable. One mistake in order or act may spoil the whole result.

The various postures of the formal Islamic prayer (*salāt*) have symbolic possibilities. These prayers constitute one of the five foundations or "pillars" of the religion, and are required of each Muslim five times a day. The ordered gestures and genuflections, with only minor differences among the various sects and legal schools of Islam, characterize the religious practice of followers of the Prophet in all countries. It is quite possible to give an interpretation to each of the various postures. An occasional mystic may say that the raising of the hands implies that whatever was in them has fallen away, indicating that one stands empty handed before Allah as a mendicant; that, as the hands are the seat of power, by raising the hands the Muslim worshiper confesses that the power is God's, not his own; that raising the hands to the chest signifies that God is in front of him; that raising the hands to the ears signifies that God is above him; that placing the forehead in the dust symbolizes the literal meaning of Islam as "submission."[5] In conclusion the hands are raised to the shoulders, and then are drawn over the face and down over the breast as if to convey the blessing of the final prayer to every part of the body.

But it is decidedly questionable whether these successive postures in prayer should be treated as symbols. In the literature on Islam, although prayer positions are often carefully described, it is significant that one seldom finds any symbolic meaning assigned to them. One gets the impression that only isolated interpreters or individual worshipers apply symbolic meanings, and that we are inclined to read more into some of these things than anything of which Muslims are aware. Similarly, fasting, another of Islam's five "pillars," may be

---

[4] *Ibid.*, I, pp. 91 ff., p. 119.

[5] *Encyclopaedia of Religion and Ethics,* edited by James Hastings, Charles Scribner's Sons, New York, 1913, 12, p. 146.

given an interior, spiritual meaning. But like *salāt* it is primarily observed in obedience to Allah's command.[6]

While Islam, as has been noted, has no absolutely distinctive symbol, there are other recognized practices which could have meaning. Hajjis (pilgrims to Mecca) go through a washing ceremony before they reach the sacred place. Each dons a simple white garb of two pieces of cloth. All Hajjis are expected to throw stones at certain fixed places. To us, this fifth pillar of Islam (pilgrimage) can be a symbol of the ecumenical nature of Islam. Similarly, to us, the congregational prayers on Friday, where lines of worshipers stand side by side irrespective of class or race, may be taken as symbolizing the really remarkable way in which Islam transcends such barriers.

In traveling from Arabia to Spain, east to China, and south to Africa and the isles of the Pacific, the objective postures in prayers and ablutions remain practically constant. Thus, wherever a non-Muslim sees an isolated worshiper facing toward Mecca, faithfully performing his prayers wherever one of the five stated hours may find him, this identifies a Muslim. This punctiliously followed rite is actually a most effective practise for propagating Islam. In Africa especially, Islam owes its steady advance largely to the impression made on less developed peoples by the regimented prayers and worship of the faithful. However, these are signs, not symbols of Islam.

One arrives at the opinion, therefore, that while there are many acts which to us might be symbolic, these acts are to the Muslim functional, utilitarian, or merely part of his obedience to Allah's commands without other necessary meaning. There is a difference between putting meaning into rites *ex post facto,* and having rites officially intended to be symbolic. Islam certainly has no objective symbol corresponding to the cross. We have, here, a zealous missionary religion which makes a minimum use of symbolism.

2. *Buddhism*

Turning from Islam to Buddhism, we pass to an opposite extreme. Where Islam used a minimum of objective symbolism, Buddhism uses

[6] *Mishkat ul-Masabih, op. cit.,* I, p. 462.

a maximum. There is a wealth of images of Buddhas and Bodhisatt-vas, each with his characteristic and meaningful hand gesture, and with their varied accompanying symbols, such as the wheel of law, footprint of Buddha, conch shell, umbrella, lotus, swastika, jar, fish, etc.

Images of Buddha did not come into use until six hundred years after Buddha lived, because, at first, no one dared represent the Il-lumined One. He had consistently deprecated any attempt to give him special honor or reverence and made no claim to divine power. But it was not long after the first image was carved in India soon after the first century A. D., that figures of the Buddha could be found wherever Buddhism had found its way. The figure of the Founder did not always remain central, but, in general, it would be found in some form in all Buddhist art and imagery.

As one observes from land to land this omnipresent, endlessly repeated symbol, one is struck with the profound impression made by Buddha on the souls of successive peoples. However, the use of the Buddha image must not be taken for idolatry as we ordinarily under-stand this. Except for the very ignorant the images are visible re-minders of invisible spiritual powers. For the enlightened worshipers and spiritual Buddhists, they stand for the Buddha-nature which is in all things. These images speak a language of their own.

At their best, you feel the dignified serenity of the features, and that the half-closed eyes look down with pity on the sorrow of the world. There is a complex impression of immense sympathy with all who suffer, combined with harmony and peace of soul. Contemplation is emanating from the calm face. In one image you may catch, in spite of otherwise impassive features, a half-smile of supreme wisdom before universal vanity. Another figure may show peace in the eyes but triumph in the mouth. From another one gains the impression of the weariness of life or sees a being who looks out beyond the world, beyond the ego, into the unfathomable inner and cosmic vacuity. In fact, the best images in Japan rank among the most spiritual creations of religious art. Unquestionably the great peace reflected by some of the finer images in the various Buddhist lands has had its silent influence on many a worshiper who kneels in meditation before these impressive symbols. Possibly some understand Buddhism less through its documents than by gazing at the calm inward-looking face of the seated Buddha.

As Buddhism has been characterized throughout by missionary zeal, it is not surprising that objective symbols have been used in its attempts to penetrate one culture after another. The great emperor, Asoka, as a part of his successful effort to introduce Buddhism into Ceylon, sent to that land a living branch from the sacred Bodhi Tree under which Buddha had attained enlightenment. Similarly, a branch of the Bodhi Tree and various relics accompanied the victory of Hinayana Buddhism in Siam. Venturesome Chinese pilgrims to India, braving the dangers of the overland route over half of Asia, seem to have been almost as eager to take back statues and paintings of the Buddha as to obtain precious Sanskrit texts for translation.

This interest in objective symbols as instruments of propaganda is further shown in that the Chinese monk who brought Buddhism to Korea carried 372 sacred images and books with him. In the sixth century a Korean king, eager to share his devotion to Buddhism with Japan, sent to the Emperor of Japan a copper image of Buddha plated with gold, some flags, an umbrella, along with a royal letter as a starting point in Buddhist propaganda. About two centuries later a Japanese emperor ordained that every household in the land should have a shrine in which there would be a Buddha image. Not only were parts of Buddhist scriptures distributed, but an imperial rescript demanded that every province should erect a sixteen foot image of Buddha.

As an aggressive religion Buddhism was represented symbolically by its early artists in a way to proclaim its superiority to other religions. For example, in both Burma and Ceylon various Vedic and post-Vedic gods were assigned subordinate roles in Buddhist temples. In Cambodia, also, one finds Hindu deities in Buddhist temples, but occupying lesser positions than the Buddha. A sixth century monument so portrays relationships between Buddha and the emblems of Confucianism and Taoism that it is clear that Buddha ranks above the two indigenous religions.

Statues of Buddha have taken three forms. The seated Buddha is much the most usual, representing the Enlightened One in the act of meditation under the Bodhi Tree. Sometimes this seated form is found many times in the same place of worship. There is one temple with ten thousand Buddhas, suggesting how the perfected spirit fills the whole universe. Less frequently one finds the standing position, representing Buddha in the act of preaching. A third position, least often found, represents Buddha's attainment of the blissful calm of Nirvana, and shows the figure recumbent with a face retaining its thoughtful and placid aspect.

The actual sculptural style of a Buddha image may change from culture to culture. For example, the waists of Burmese and Siamese Buddhas may be narrower than those in China; or those in Cambodia may have African lips and broad noses. But, in general, local artists did not presume to change the dignified serenity of Buddha's features which carried the impression of calm, untroubled repose.

In the many journeyings of Buddhism there has been variety, also, in the number and arrangement of figures. In Hinayana Buddhism, Sakyamuni usually sits alone. This southern form of Buddhism is practically a religion without a god, so the image symbolizes the Dharma more than the Founder who is considered by Hinayana as now in the world of the ideal rather than the actual, and hence not one to whom prayer is addressed. In contrast, Mahayana or northern Buddhism recognizes more than one Buddha, in general five in China, and four in Japan. These can be found grouped so as to give prominence to one or the other. Most frequently it is Amida Buddha who displaces Sakyamuni. In China and Japan, Mahayana surrounded these main Buddhas with numerous Bodhisattvas— those Buddhas designate who in this preliminary stage dedicate themselves in unselfish devotion to their fellow creatures, and hence to whom homage can be paid and from whom assistance may be received. One Bodhisattva personifies mercy, another wisdom, still another courage. However, all are more than ethical abstractions. They symbolize gracious spiritual presences. Because local divinities are often elevated to the rank of future Buddhas, obviously there could be no uniformity in the number, character, and arrangement of these many figures as one passes from country to country. While the peaceful impression from Sakyamuni's figure is conserved, local artists found an opportunity for variety and lavish adornment in the Bodhisattvas that surrounded the main figure. In this way Mahayana for the common man became practically polytheistic, thus encouraging a veneration at the opposite extreme from the teachings of a Founder who repudiated any claim to divine prerogatives.

The symbolism of hand positions is found in practically all images of Buddhas and Bodhisattvas. These simple but impressive gestures indicate some act or function of the particular being represented, and Orientals find it easy to catch these subtle suggestions. Out of scores of these positions, several examples may be given.[7] Thus Sakyamuni's entrance into profound meditation is symbolized by placing the right hand on the left, bending both index fingers, and laying each thumb on its corresponding finger.

An important hand symbol represents "the turning of the wheel of the Law," *i.e.,* the preaching of the Dharma. It is believed that this position was assumed by Sakyamuni when he preached for the first time soon after he became the Enlightened One. It symbolizes the crushing effect of Buddha's preaching upon all delusions and superstitions. The manifold spokes of the Wheel correspond to the many rules of conduct laid down by the Buddha; and they suggest, also, the rays of light issuing from the Enlightened One. It is made by bending both hands, pressing them to the chest, turning the left palm inward and the right palm outward, with ring finger of each hand bent to touch the tip of the corresponding thumb.

One of the most popular hand symbols represents Amida welcoming the dead into Nirvana. Both hands are pressed against the chest, palms turned outward with the tip of the thumb joined to the tip of the index finger, thus making a circle in each hand.

One of the most mystic hand symbols signifies that Buddha's spiritual power and virtues reach everywhere in the Buddha world, just as do the air or sky. It is made by placing the palms together against the chest, causing the tips of the forefingers to touch their

---

[7] Aisaburo Akiyama, *Buddhist Hand-Symbols,* Yoshikawa Book Store, Yokohama, 1939.

corresponding thumbs and interlacing the tips of the remaining three fingers.

Of special interest is evidence of syncretism when a religion in its expansion comes in contact with other religions. Buddhism in its pilgrimage has been particularly marked by this phenomenon. Although Buddhism, unlike other religions of southern and eastern Asia, was aggressive, it seems to have had no destructive animus against other faiths. In fact, it manifested such an aptitude for syncretism that its insights were often accepted as additions to the local faiths. Buddhism has been quick to respond to the varying needs of the different lands to which it has been carried and to the different periods during which it has served its followers. However, these adjustments must not always be considered as conscious and reasoned.

In Ceylon, Buddhism took over scores of Hindu *devas* (gods) as attendants of Sakyamuni. In Burma, Buddhism allowed the *nats* or native animistic gods, to have the place of subordinate spirits. As Buddhism traveled northward and eastward through Kashmir, Nepal, and Tibet, it had to carry with it, both in doctrine and in symbolism, a certain amount of demon worship. In China, acting with diplomacy and tolerance, Buddhists put Confucius and the god of literature into the fourth class of tutelary deities. There was even a Buddhist temple to Confucius. Another Bodhisattva was presented as the incarnation of Lao-tse, the founder of Taoism, and one painter showed Lao-tse not only transformed into a Buddha, but seated on a lotus, the favorite Buddhist symbol.

This syncretistic adjustment to local deities is found also in Siam. Here, Buddha had to share the people's worship with tree spirits and local genii just as it did with the *nats* of Burma. Similarly, in Japan as in other lands it entered, Buddhism showed a willingness to see truth under various forms and to accept some of the symbols of other religions. The Shintoist mirror, symbolizing purity and reflection, is found near the altar in the temples of several Japanese sects of Buddhism, and in a Buddha temple court there may be several Shinto shrines. Notwithstanding the fact that at first there was a century of struggle between Buddhism and Shinto, there was finally a compromise by which the Shinto deities were recognized as guardians and worshipers, but by no means as Buddhas.

Summarizing, we see that Buddhism makes a maximum use of symbolism. The Buddha image has made a profound impression on successive peoples. Objective symbols were consciously used as instruments in missionary propaganda. The superiority of Buddhism to local religions was asserted through symbols. In the extensive pilgrimage of Buddhism through the Orient, there has not only been cultural variety in the number, posture, arrangement, and adornment of Buddha and Bodhisattva images, but there has been syncretism in objective symbolism. However, in general, the dignified serenity of the Buddha features has been preserved.

3. *Christianity*

In the third place we turn to Christianity. Here we find that some of its advocates shrink from any adaptation in its Western symbolism as their religion enters a new culture. Thus there are many Christian missionaries who believe that conversion to Christianity should be marked by a complete break with the previous religion. There are nationals, also, who believe that a breach with the past is the only wise procedure. Countries differ in this respect. Japanese Christians have no desire through the suggestions of art to be reminded of the religion they have left. Perhaps they feel instinctively that new wine should be kept in new bottles. Moreover, they may feel that a Christianity sharply distinguished from everything that suggests Shinto or Buddhism is the best safeguard for a young church set in vigorous non-Christian surroundings. To adopt or to adapt from older faiths might seem like an attempt to curry favor. In Korea, there is almost no assimilation of local symbolism by the Christian church.

However, one of the most common objections to Christianity in Asia has been that it is a foreign, a Western religion. Hence strong encouragement has been given to the expression of Christian thought in indigenous art and symbols. This use of a people's own thought forms is held to be a help toward, as well as a result of, the naturalization of Christianity in another culture.

The simplest way of doing this is to incorporate into one's iconography some symbol identifying the church or institution with its local or national environment. For example, the choir chairs in an Anglican church in Hongkong are carved with waves of water. A carved panel at the entrance to a Nanhsuchow church has a conventionalized representation of the pathway up a nearby mountain as symbolic of "the Way, the Truth, and the Life." The crest of the Diocese of Hokkaido, Japan, portrays a swimming fish, typifying the principal industry of this province. The sun's rays behind a mountain on the seal of the Diocese of Kyoto signify that it is in the Kingdom of the Rising Sun. A conventionalized representation of the "golden stool," which is the symbol of the soul of the Ashanti, is embodied in the tower of a Christian college on the Gold Coast. A crocodile, very common in the Nile, stands for the power of evil to be conquered through the cross of Christ in an Anglican diocesan crest in Uganda. Because the oil-palm is the chief source of wealth in a Nigerian diocese it appears on the crest of that area.

Other examples of this effort to symbolize identification with the national environment can be given. The most conspicuous item in the seal of Judson College, Burma, was the peacock, the national emblem of Burma. The motto of Anatolia College in Greece is from the words of Isaiah, "The morning cometh." Every morning the sun's rays burst out from behind the profile of a large mountain near the college, and this view is clearly represented on the seal of the college as symbolic of the faith and hope embodied in the motto. It is not surprising, in like manner, that the University at Beirut uses the cedar of Lebanon to localize its position, or that an Egyptian diocese uses the Nile, the Sphinx, and a pyramid, to symbolize that Christianity has been naturalized in Egypt. Twin windows of pierced stone are in an Irish Presbyterian church in India. At the top of one is the shamrock, atop the other is the lotus, the two emblematic that Ireland and India are united in the worship of Christ. The Church of the Cross Roads, in Hawaii, in order to symbolize the cultural blending actually in process in the congregation, incorporated in its new building wood from the Philippines and Samoa, as well as the local monkey-pod. Rich red columns impart a Chinese element to the building and other motifs intentionally suggest Polynesia and Japan.[8]

A still more definite step toward consciously naturalizing Christianity in a new culture, or evidencing that Christianity has actually entered into the art life of a people is the incorporation in a church or its insignia of symbolic decoration peculiar to the given culture, thus imparting a local flavor. Behind this trend is the desire that the suitable and valuable elements in the given culture should be consecrated to the service and worship of the Christ.

For example, from the capital of every Dravidian pillar in the cathedral designed by the great Indian Christian, Bishop Azariah, is the conventionalized representation of a banana bud, issuing out of the open flower of the datura (deadly nightshade). Everyone in India knows that the banana tree perpetually propagates itself from the same root, so this represents for the congregation a divine savior who brought life out of death and ever lives to communicate that life to his followers. All the capitals of a church in Tirupatur represent a bunch of bananalike fruit hanging from a tree with their flowers at the end, thus symbolizing deep Christian joy, for it is a South India custom to tie up plantains with flowers as a sign of joy on the occasions of festivals and marriages. In China, the carp is seen on the roof ridges of some churches with the Chinese signification of courage, of perseverance, and of struggle against the current. As red in China stands for joy and happiness, a red cross, or red candles, red pillars, or an entrance gate painted red are often used to symbolize that we should take God into all our joys. In a Nanking prayer hall the familiar *yin-yang* symbol with its distinctive dual division is changed to a triple division in order to represent the Christian Trinity. Branches of bamboo appear on the seal of a Shanghai college, because bamboo grows very rapidly and so, to a Chinese, would be symbolic of growth.[9]

As for Japan, the language of flowers is a realm of symbolism

[8] Fleming, *op. cit.*, figures 42, 66, 94, 167, 168, 181, 182, 194, 196, 207, 208, 217.
[9] *Ibid.*, pp. 75, 76; figures 20, 23, 112, 136.

that is peculiarly dear to that beauty loving people. Many Christian schools, colleges, and churches have incorporated flower symbolism in their seals or crests all the more freely because it is little associated with religion. The cherry blossom symbolizes not only Japan itself, but also those ideals of character which the Japanese most respect. The blossoms falling just when they are at their best, suggest the shedding of one's blood ungrudgingly for a noble cause. Just as the cherry blossom does not cling tenaciously to its branch, so we should not cling to life, if called to give it for a higher loyalty. The plum is the first blossom to appear in Japan, braving the cold and the snows of winter. Hence, this frail flower with its delicate pink buds has long been the theme for moralists and poets, betokening virtue triumphant or valor breaking through benumbing obstacles. Again, the pine, which grows to a very old age, stands for longevity. The flowers of Japan and Hawaii are painted in each of the squares of the coffered ceiling of a Honolulu church. The date palm and the pomegranate, two of the most natural symbols of fruitfulness, appear in an old Cairo church.

Special attention should be given to the widespread Christian use of the lotus. With such a wealth of metaphysical and popular symbolism connected with the lotus, and in view of its widespread use in Hinduism and Buddhism, it is not strange that Christians in Asia have quite often been attracted by its symbolism, assigning their own local meaning to its use. Such adoption is found all the way from the church of Al Mu Allakah in Egypt to Dr. Karl Ludwig Reichelt's Christian monastery near Hongkong.

In a large church in Ahmednagar, India, the lotus constitutes the sole decorative motif. There is a lotus flower window behind the pulpit. Around the gallery, in carved wood, runs the same design. Lotus flowers on chancel, chairs, and communion table join with all the rest to voice welcome by this church to a design that embodies India's sense of beauty. Each of the fifty columns of Ceylon's Trinity College has a lotus capital. Two rows of lotus buds appear upon the seal of a Christian college in Burma, representing the spiritual aspirations of the East.[10]

[10] *Ibid.*, figures 9, 66.

It is not only in church architecture that the lotus appears. It is found in Christian poetry, also. For example, the great Marathi poet, Narayan Vaman Tilak, using the imagery of his own land, makes his tribute to Christ in words that carry emotion to an Indian. Addressing Christ, he says:

> A loving garland I entwine
> and offer at thy lotus feet.

Moreover, we are not surprised to find the lotus appearing in Christian paintings. Alfred D. Thomas, an Indian painter, in portraying the Adoration of the Shepherds, uses this symbol in its more esoteric, or Hindu-Buddhist meaning. Each of the shepherds is shown as presenting a lotus to the Holy Child, because this is a traditional offering by a Hindu to his god, implying a rendering up of one's existence to its Source, a resignation of one's own nature and ground of separate existence.[11]

One of the ways in which the lotus is introduced into Christian symbolism is to represent the cross above, or issuing from, the open lotus flower. In many a church of indigenous architecture in India and in China the cross is sculptured or carved above a lotus on pillars, on doorways, on chapel furniture, on altar, or on lecterns. The design may appear, also, on diocesan seal or on seminary shield. Popularly, this is taken to signify that Christianity is the "fulfilment" of Buddhism or Hinduism, as the case may be. However, each local usage may have its own meaning. In a Christian Ashram at Tirupatur this design betokens the heart of a believer (lotus) accepting what is meant by the cross of Christ. In a theological seminary at Tumkur the cross in the circle of the white lotus (where the circle stands for infinity and the lotus for purity) suggested that the infinite and holy love of God is fulfilled through the historic fact of the cross of Jesus Christ.[12]

A still further step is the adoption in Christian ceremonial of symbolic indigenous customs. For example, in India, flowers have been used in worship from time immemorial. Some have urged their

[11] *Ibid.*, figure 40.
[12] *Ibid.*, figure 25.

use in Christian worship as symbolizing the beauty, creative power, and love of God. In several churches, flower petals are strewn, India fashion, over the congregation as they leave. To the Indian it seems so fitting to offer flowers in worship to God that some have encouraged churches to have small gardens, so that fresh flowers may be placed upon the altar.

Ceremonial bathing before worship is common in India, and facilities for this are generally provided outside mosques and temples. Hence, a few churches have provided pools near their entrances with the definite idea of symbolizing the purification that is needed as one comes into God's presence. In many country churches in India there is the custom of removing sandals before entering as a symbol of reverence.

What most rejoices anyone interested in evidences of the vitality of a religion in a new culture is to find quite new symbols developed out of the religious experience of the people concerned. Thus in South India burdens are commonly carried on the head. In order to rest the bearers, stone shelves have been erected here and there along the dusty highways. Some Christian wayfarer must have exclaimed: "Why, that is what Christ does! He is our burden bearer." As a result of this new insight, this common roadside stone mantel has become a symbol for the One Who said, "Come unto me, all ye that labor and are heavy laden, and I will give you rest." [13]

India, also, has developed a new symbol for a missionary church. All, doubtless, know how the banyan tree sends out branches on all sides, how each branch drops down roots and then goes still further out until, as in a fine specimen in the Public Gardens of Calcutta, it may cover an acre. This, some Christian said, is what the church should do, "starting from Jerusalem" and spreading out in evangelistic zeal as it founds daughter churches on every side.[14]

In certain parts of Africa it is customary for the leader to go ahead on the jungle path and take the dew upon himself. Hence, Christ as "dew-man" becomes a symbol in that area. A bursting pomegranate carved on the communion table for one congregation re-

[13] *Ibid.,* pp. 6, 7; figure 48.
[14] *Ibid.,* figure 55.

minds them of the resurrection of the Lord, Who was able to burst
the tomb on Easter Day. In Japan, the crescent moon has been used
in the spirit of Luke 2:52 as a symbol of growth in body, mind,
spirit, and social usefulness.

A negative influence on Christian symbolism appears in certain
idolatrous areas. For backward people the physically tangible symbol may take the place of the thing signified. In that case the symbol becomes a fetish or an idol. For example, an illiterate low caste
man, on entering a church in India for the first time and seeing an
eagle with outspread wings at the lectern, bowed with clasped hands
before it as a god. When a new cross was introduced in the chapel
of a Christian school a little Indian girl garlanded it and left a
clay lamp burning near it, as one honors a Hindu god. Therefore,
converts coming from an idolatrous background are often definitely opposed to the use of objective symbolism. A similar negative
adjustment is reported from Nigeria, but for a different reason.
There, due to surrounding and predominant Muslim influence,
with mosques free from symbols, the Christian community has no
meaningful art forms. In such cases, a check is put on symbolic representations where it is judged that the people are not yet ready to
invest outward things with inner meanings as aids to meditation or
worship.

A positive adjustment to Islam was practiced by the great English missionary, the late Canon Gairdner, in Egypt. We are familiar
with the impressive way in which in a mosque the leader and the
whole congregation at Friday prayers turn in successive rows as
one man toward Mecca. Canon Gairdner felt that converts from
Islam might miss this impressive practice. Therefore he always
left the reading desk to stand in front of the first row of Christian
worshipers, facing the same way as they, for the common affirmation of their faith. For Gairdner, this conscious adaptation was symbolic of the turning of one's whole being to God.

As did Buddhism, Christianity as an aggressive religion has attempted to show its superiority to other religions through symbolism.
That Christianity is able to meet the needs and fulfil the spiritual
aspiration of the various peoples to which it goes is repeatedly sym-

bolized. The Leonard Theological College in India on its shield shows at the bottom a lotus, standing for the beautiful spiritual heritage of India and her aspiration after the Divine. Above is a Muslim type of arch, suggestive of Islam and the glories of the Mogul Empire. At the center is the cross, implanted in the lotus as the very heart of India and within the arch as the open door of opportunity in India today.[15]

With a similar objective, a church in Iran has placed on the reredos above the altar a cross shown as filling the space under the double depressed Persian arch, betokening the permeation of Persia by Christianity. One Chinese Christian painter has used the visit of the Magi to the Holy Child to convey the idea of the superiority of Christianity. The three Magi are depicted respectively, as a formal and correct Confucianist, a Buddhist monk with shaven crown, and Lao-tse with the bottle of the water of mercy in his hand. Thus, the artist means one to see Confucianism, Buddhism, and Taoism bringing their gifts to the new religion of Christianity. In like manner the American University at Cairo on its seal portrays a large star with the sphinx at its center, symbolizing Egypt bathed in the light of Christianity.[16]

A conscious effort to symbolize a liberal, irenic, friendly attitude to other cultures and religions found expression in the planning of the Oriental Hall at the American University in Cairo. "First and foremost, it is a symbol," says the dedication pamphlet. American gifts express themselves in lines of Oriental beauty and art, symbolic of international, interracial, intercultural sympathy. On its walls are inscribed great names that reveal how Greek and Hebrew, Muslim and European minds and hearts have labored to place the richest values of the Orient at the disposal of the world. A similar liberal attitude led the Church of the Cross Roads, Honolulu, to symbolize the variety of religious heritage among its members by large carvings on either side of the lectern and pulpit. These carvings represent Hinduism, Buddhism, Zoroastrianism, and the Old Testament.[17]

[15] *Ibid.,* figure 63.
[16] *Ibid.,* figures 199, 209.
[17] *Ibid.,* figures 14–18, 203.

Thus we see that in Christianity's modern expansion from land to land there has been marked flexibility in its use of sign-symbolism. There has been a conscious effort to naturalize Christianity in the new culture through such symbols, and there is a wide welcome to any evidence that Christianity has actually entered into the art life of younger churches. Symbols are adopted that identify an institution with the local or national environment. Use is made of the cultural symbolism of colors and flowers. Symbolic customs are Christianized and new symbols are created. The symbolism actually used is affected both positively and negatively by the surrounding religious climate, and symbols are used to suggest how Christianity meets the spiritual needs and aspirations of the peoples to which it goes. The cross is universal, but there has been much imaginative creation in efforts to evoke less central conceptions.

4. Conclusion

Certain inferences may be drawn from this study:

1. We should not allow ourselves to be incapable, still less unwilling, to recognize meaning or beauty in unfamiliar forms. It may easily be that a given bit of symbolism will seem capricious or even distasteful. Yet, if we are convinced that it expresses the intelligible and reasonable tastes, interests, and aspirations of those who originally produced it, that distaste may change to appreciation based on understanding.

2. We must be flexible in attaching different meanings to any given symbol. In the color symbolism of the Renaissance, white stood for purity, joy, and life; but in China, white invariably has been the color of mourning. In the religious iconography of the West the dragon represents temptation and the evil one; but to Chinese the dragon is the spirit of change and, therefore, of life itself.

3. Similarly, we must be ready to use different symbols for the same meaning as we pass from culture to culture. Sins that are made "white as snow" in northern Europe or America may have to become "white as a coconut" in Ceylon. If the sheep is abhorred by a certain African tribe which places cattle highest in relative value,

one may need to speak of the cow at the right hand of God; or, instead of "lamb of God" for the Eskimo, substitute "the little seal of God."

4. Symbols have to contend with different physical climates as they cross cultural boundaries. Western Christianity built the suggestions from Europe's various seasons into the Church Year. But we find Francis Xavier appealing to Ignatius Loyola, the Father Master of the Jesuit Order, to change the time of Lent and Easter; for while Spring in Europe speaks of the Resurrection, that period is one of incredible heat in India—"so hot," said Xavier, "that fish begin to rot as soon as they die."

5. World symbolism must take account, also, of different psychological climates. That such differences have existed through the centuries is obvious—the mystic emphasis of the medieval mind in contrast to the modern stress on science. But anyone expecting to express truth symbolically on a world stage will need to remember that all the psychological differences of the centuries are present in today's cross-section of humanity.

6. If we are to catch the significance of symbols used in cultures other than our own we must pass beyond curious observation to intelligent apprehension of inner meaning. Laying aside our personal preferences, we must find what the artist in some distant land is attempting to say in terms of his environment and tradition. As Goethe said of pictures, "who would understand the painter must go to the painter's country."

7. Lastly, we must not only realize that our world community is made up of varied tribes, peoples, and tongues, but be aware of certain corollaries that flow naturally from that fact. Among such corollaries we must, as world citizens, recognize that each race has its characteristic thoughts about God; that each tongue has its favorite metaphors; and that each people has its meaningful representations. We must, therefore, pass beyond the provincial to that enlargement of self wherein we are ready to understand and to appreciate what is worthy in the artistry of all lands and all religions.

Bibliography

Islam

Thomas Walker Arnold, *Painting in Islam,* Clarendon Press, Oxford, 1928.

Marshall Broomhall, *Islam in China,* Morgan & Scott, London, 1910.

L. Bevan Jones, *The People of the Mosque,* Student Christian Movement Press, London, 1932.

Duncan Black MacDonald, *Aspects of Islam,* The Macmillan Company, New York, 1911.

Mishkat ul-Masabih, A. N. Matthews, translator, Hindoostanee Press, Calcutta, 1809, 2 vols.

A. S. Tritton, *Islam: Beliefs and Practices,* Hutchinson House, London, 1951.

Samuel M. Zwemer, "Green the Sacred Color of Islam," *The Moslem World,* XXXIV, April, 1944, p. 150.

Buddhism

Aisaburo Akiyama, *Buddhist Hand-symbol,* Yoshikawa Book Store, Yokohama, 1939.

Masaharu Anesaki, *Buddhist Art in Relation to Buddhist Ideals,* Houghton Mifflin Company, New York, 1915.

Ananda K. Coomaraswamy, "Origin of the Buddha Image," *Art Bulletin,* Providence College Art Association of America, June, 1927, IX, pp. 287–328.

Alfred Charles Auguste Foucher, *Beginnings of Buddhist Art,* F. M. Thomas, translator, Geuthner, Paris, 1917.

Alice Getty, *The Gods of Northern Buddhism,* Clarendon Press, Oxford, 1914.

William Henry Goodyear, *The Grammar of the Lotus,* Sampson Low, Marston & Company, London, 1891.

René Grousset, *In the Footsteps of the Buddha,* G. Routledge & Sons, London, 1932.

Karl Ludwig Reichelt, *Truth and Tradition in Chinese Buddhism,* The Commercial Press, Shanghai, 1927.

Christianity

Daniel J. Fleming, *Christian Symbols in a World Community,* The
Friendship Press, New York, 1940.

William Ernest Hocking, *Living Religions and a World Faith,* The Macmillan Company, New York, 1940, p. 291 (religion must be universal
and particular), pp. 31–43.

E. R. Morgan, editor, "The Christian Approach to non-Christian Customs," *Essays Catholic and Missionary,* Society for the Propagation of
Christian Knowledge, London, 1928, pp. 115–151, 332.

Henry Paget Thompson, *Worship in Other Lands,* Society for the Propagation of the Gospel, London, 1933.

General

Catholic Encyclopaedia, Robert Appleton Company, New York, 1907.

Dictionary of Islam, W. H. Allen Company, London, 1935.

Encyclopaedia Britannica, Encyclopaedia Britannica, Inc., Chicago, 1943.

Encyclopaedia of Religion and Ethics, James Hastings, editor, Charles
Scribner's Sons, New York, 1913.

VI

THEOLOGY AND SYMBOLISM

BY

PAUL J. TILLICH, DR. PHIL.

Professor of Philosophical Theology, Union Theological Seminary

The subject of my address is "Theology and Symbolism." The first thing I have to do is to say a few words about what theology means. Theology, as the word indicates, is "logos of theos," and as logos it deals with concepts. Theology is a creation of thought and, as the history of theology has shown, a creation of most penetrating thought. And theology is a whole, a totality, and ideally is a system of concepts concerning divine matters.

But when we develop a system of concepts, then we must have material out of which to develop it. Every thought, if it is not empty, must grasp being, something which is *given* to thought as the material which it conceptualizes. A thought which does not grasp being is empty, and even if it deals with itself, as it does in logic, it deals with something which has being, in this case the being of thought. Thought, of course, is a very limited kind of being, and it is one of the bad things about our present philosophical situation that of all the innumerable aspects of being, just this one, namely, thought itself, has become the main concern. Nevertheless, even in the case of logic, something which is given, something which has being, precedes thinking.

But where is God given to us? Where can we find the being which must be the material for theological thought? God, in contrast to everything else, is not given. He is not something which we can find in the context of reality. He does not appear as an object beside other objects. He is not a being beside other beings, within the totality of our world. This makes it impossible to give a conceptual explanation of God. It is His very nature, that which makes Him God, to transcend such possibility. But if He does not appear within the context of experience, if He cannot be explained in terms of concepts, how can He become manifest for theology; how can He become the object of that conceptual discourse which is theology and which theology must always remain?

In other words, if God is the object of theology, how is theology possible? The answer is that the direct object of theology is not God; the direct object of theology is His manifestation to us, and the expression of this manifestation is the religious symbol. This is the basic relation between theology and symbolism. The object of theology is found in the symbols of religious experience. They are not God, but they point to God. God may be said to be the object of theology but only indirectly. The *direct* object of theology is found only in religious symbols.

In these symbols there is expressed that which is the content of every religion, the basis of every religious experience and the foundation of every theology, the divine-human encounter. Theology, then, is the conceptual interpretation, explanation, and criticism of the symbols in which a special encounter between God and man has found expression. This is the basic statement about the relationship between theology and symbolism.

What is the nature of religious symbols? As symbols they participate in the general character of all symbols. I could speak at length about the general character of symbols, but I want to give here only a very few of their main characteristics.

The first is that they point beyond themselves. Every symbol points to something beyond itself; this is its first characteristic. But the second characteristic must be added immediately, namely, that which distinguishes symbol from sign. Signs also point beyond themselves. The red light at the street corner points beyond its own redness to the summons to the driver to stop his car. But there is no intrinsic relationship between this sign and the stopping of the car. It is a way of indicating something to the individual driver.

Symbols have a different quality. Although the word, "symbol," does not make this immediately clear, the symbol actually participates in the power of that which it symbolizes. The symbol is not a mere convention as is the sign. It grows organically. The symbol opens up a level of meaning which otherwise is closed. It opens up a stratum of reality, of meaning and being which otherwise we could not reach; and in doing so, it participates in that which it opens. And it does not only open up a stratum of reality, it also opens up the corresponding stratum of the mind. Symbols open up, so to speak, in two directions—in the direction of reality and in the direction of the mind.

They make accessible to our minds levels of experience from which we otherwise would be shut off; we would not be aware of them. This is the great function of symbols, to point beyond themselves in the power of that to which they point, to open up levels of reality which otherwise are closed, and to open up levels of the human mind of which we otherwise are not aware.

This is true of all symbols, and this is the reason nobody can invent them. They always are results of a creative encounter with reality. They are born out of such an encounter; they die if this encounter ceases. They are not invented and they cannot be abolished.

I may use as an example the symbolic power of art, for instance, of visual art. The symbolic power of visual art is not that special symbols are painted (as is true of bad art) but that if you paint a picture, whatever the content of it may be, a landscape or a portrait, or a story, it expresses a level of reality to which only the artistic creation has an approach. We never would see it if art did not reveal it to us. In this sense even a very naturalistic landscape—let us say, by a Dutch painter in the seventeenth century—is a picture in which everything is symbolic in the sense that it points to a reality and a meaning, to a level of reality which the painter in his creative encounter reveals to us. Now we can see it; now we can be *in* it. That is the realm of artistic symbols. There are, of course, other types of symbols to which I cannot refer here.

The religious symbol has special character in that it points to the ultimate level of being, to ultimate reality, to being itself, to meaning itself. That which is the ground of being is the object to which the religious symbol points. It points to that which is of ultimate concern for us, to that which is infinitely meaningful and unconditionally valid. Religious experience is the experience of that which concerns us ultimately. The content of this experience is expressed in religious symbols. How can this be done? The ultimate transcends all levels of reality; it is the ground of reality itself. It transcends all levels of meaning; it is the ground of meaning itself. But in order to express it, we must use the material of our daily encounter. We cannot do it otherwise. Therefore, religious symbols take their material from all realms of life, from all experiences—natural, personal, historical. All realms of being have contributed to religious symbolism. In themselves they all are of preliminary import. They have a limited meaning, they have a conditioned validity; but they are used in order to point beyond themselves to that which has unconditional, unlimited, and infinite meaning.

This is how we should understand a religious symbol. It is material taken out of the world of finite things, to point beyond itself to the ground of being and meaning, to being itself and meaning itself. As a symbol it participates in the power of the ultimate to which it points; or, to use a word which we commonly use when we speak of the power of ultimate being, it participates in the "holy." "Holy" and "sacred" point to the presence of the ultimate power of being and of meaning in an individual thing or situation. The religious symbol participates in the holiness of that to which it points, that is, to the holy itself. Religious symbols are not holy in and of themselves, but they are holy by their participation in that which is holy in itself, the ground of all holiness. This participation gives them their meaning, but at the same time sets limits to their meaning. A holy book, a holy building, a holy rite, a holy person—they are not themselves *the* holy; they are not the ultimate; they never should be a matter of ultimate concern. I repeat, they are more than signs. They not only point beyond themselves to something else; they also participate in the power of that to which they point. This participation, which, on the one hand, is the reason for the greatness and holiness of the symbol, and, on the other hand, accounts for its smallness and limitation, must be understood in reference to every religious symbol. Religious symbols open up the mystery of the holy and they open up the mind for the mystery of the holy to which it can respond.

Theology can neither produce nor destroy religious symbols. They are that which is *given* to theology; it is not God that is given, but the symbols of the encounter between God and man. As such, they are the objects of theology.

What theology can do with these symbols is to conceptualize them, to explain them, and to criticize them—these three things. But theology cannot produce them and cannot destroy them. Nevertheless, religious symbols are born and die. They are the expression of an encounter with ultimate reality, and they disappear if this kind of encounter disappears. The gods of polytheism did not disappear through philosophical criticism; rather they could be successfully criticized philosophically only *after* the encounter out of which they were born already had ceased to be.

Therefore, the theologian in order to be a real theologian must stand within this encounter. In my *Systematic Theology* I have called this the "theological circle." The theologian must participate in that encounter out of which grow the symbols with which he deals. Otherwise he would be an observer from outside but not a theologian. Even in the situation of extreme doubt he lives in the realm, the atmosphere, of the symbols of his special religious encounter. If this encounter changes, some of these symbols also will change—some of them might even die. It is not theoretical criticism which kills religious symbols, but rather a change in the actual encounter.

Theology deals with religious symbols by conceptualization, explanation, and criticism. Conceptualization discloses the relation of the symbols to each other and to the whole to which they belong. For instance, the theologian describes the relation between the symbols of the divine omnipotence and of human sin, of divine love and divine justice, of the Creator and the creature, of faith and works, of God and the Christ. In all these instances theology deals with symbols of that divine-human encounter which we find expressed in Bible, Church, and Christian tradition.

The second function of theology in relation to symbols is explanation. To explain does not mean to invent arguments for the validity of the symbols. That would be a self-contradictory enterprise, and it never could succeed because that which must be expressed in symbols cannot be expressed in concepts, conveyed through argument. It has its own standing rooted in the actual encounter between God and man. "Explanation" in theology means something else. It means an attempt to make understandable the relation of the symbols used to that to which they point. For instance, we use the word, "Bible." Christians and Jews use it, and holy scriptures exist in most religions. The biblical writings as such are literature, religious literature, written by different people who stood in a particular culture, used a particular language, lived under particular social conditions. What is it that makes religious literature a Bible? How does this material become "the Word of God"? What is the relationship between the Bible as religious literature and the Bible as the Word of God? That is what theology has to ask. Human existence as described in poetry, in literature, in philosophy, and in depth psychology shows finitude and estrangement and leads to the question, "What does this mean in the light of the symbol of creation?" What does it mean that we are creatures? What does it mean for the relationship of God and man, of the infinite and the finite? Or, we may consider the symbol of the Kingdom of God. "Kingdom" is taken from the political realm. Theology asks, "How is the political reality, how is the historical development, related to this symbol?" What does it say about the meaning of history in religious terms, in terms of ultimate concern? Again, we have the symbol, "Church." From the one side, Church is an assembly of people, an object of sociological analysis. In another perspective we call this assembly a "Church." Theology must ask what makes an assembly of religious people a Church, *i.e.,* an "assembly of God." Or, consider the message of Jesus, whom we call the Christ, using the Jewish symbol, "Messiah." How does it happen that an individual man is called the Christ? What is the relationship of Jesus and the Christ?

That is what I would call the theological explanation of the given symbols. It explains the relation of the religious meaning of the symbolic material to its original and simple meaning.

The third function of theology in relation to religious symbols is criticism. Again, this criticism does not seek to dissolve the symbol as historically or scientifically or psychologically untrue. That would mean criticizing symbols on a non-symbolic level, and no symbol can be criticized on a non-symbolic level. If a symbol is criticized, it must be criticized within the bounds of symbolic meaning. We must criticize it from the inside, comparing elements of it with the whole of the symbolic system to which they belong. It is one of the reasons for the disintegration of religion in recent centuries that the symbols have been taken literally. Then they provoke criticism on a non-symbolic basis, and disintegrate because on this basis they are meaningless.

That is one of the greatest problems of theology today, Christian as well as Jewish. Many people take religious symbols literally and criticize them after they have been taken literally. Symbols, I have said, are born and die. Only if the religious encounter out of which they grow changes may they change or disappear.

Theological criticism has to do three things. First, it has to prevent the reduction of the symbols to the level of non-symbolic thinking. The moment this happens, their meaning and their power are lost. Secondly, theology has to show that some symbols are more nearly adequate than others to the encounter which expresses itself in symbols. And, thirdly, some symbols must be shown to be inadequate in the light of the totality of the symbolic meaning which they represent; they contradict the fundamental symbolic structure. This is the way in which theological criticism of symbols is possible; but it is never possible on the non-symbolic level.

Sometimes it happens that the theologian is a prophet and that as a prophet he changes the encounter between God and man. But this happens through him as a prophet and not as a theologian. As a theologian he is as dependent on the material given to him in the symbols as the historian is dependent on the historical facts and the scientist on the natural facts.

This leads me to a consideration of the different levels of religious symbolism. I distinguish three levels. The first is the transcendent level. On the transcendent level lie those symbols which point to the holy itself. This is, first of all, God seen as Highest Being, symbolizing that which concerns us ultimately, the ground of our being and meaning.

The theological function on this level is to resist the idolatrous identification of the ground of our being with the God of ordinary theism Who is a being existing in addition to other beings. The God of traditional theism is a symbol for the God beyond the God of theism. The God beyond the God of theism is the ground of being and meaning. The true God is not a being existing beside others but He is the symbolic expression of our encounter with the ultimate itself, with the ground of being. The God Who is really God is the abyss of the symbolic material which we apply to Him. On the other hand, we can speak of Him only if we apply this symbolic material to Him.

This leads us to God's attributes. Classical theology knew that if we affirm anything about God we say something which we must doubt in the next moment. Everything we assert about God has the double character of yes and no. Why is this so? Classical theology taught that in God all attributes are one, and therefore, there is no possibility of distinguishing them as literally valid; they point to something in our immediate experience; they are true symbols. The same is true of God's actions—creating, judging, helping, determining, fulfilling, and their emotive causes—love, wrath, justice, mercy, patience.

Religious symbols have the reality of the religious encounter from which they come. They use realities which are rooted in the ground of being to express truth about the ground of being. They are true, but true as symbols and not in a non-symbolic sense.

The second level of religious symbols is the sacramental level, namely, the appearance of the holy in time and space, in everyday realities. Realities in nature and history are the bearers of the holy on this level. Events, things, persons can have symbolic power. The danger in sacramental holiness is that the holy is identified with that which is the bearer of the holy. Where this happens religion relapses into magic. I believe that the vigorous opposition of the Reformers to the transubstantiation theory was the belief that it was a regression into the magical identification of the Divine with the bearer of the Divine. When we speak of Jesus we have the same problem. He is the bearer of what in symbolic terms is called the Christ. The same is true of the Church. The Church is a sacramental reality. It is sociological, historical as is every group, and at the same time, it is the "Body of Christ." In all these cases, the confusion of the holy itself with the bearer of the holy is the beginning of the distortion of religion.

There is a third level, the liturgical level, where all kinds of signs are elevated to symbolic power, *e.g.,* special objects, special gestures, special garb; the vast realm of sign-symbols as I call them, including water, light, odors, colors, sounds. As signs they are replaceable; as symbols they are consecrated by tradition, but with less power than genuine symbols. They are a mixture of symbols and signs. It is the fate of religion that again and again the levels are confused; that the sacramental level is confused with the ultimate level, that the level of sign-symbols is confused with the sacramental level. We must distinguish them as clearly as possible.

I will use my last few paragraphs to write as a Protestant *against* myself as a Protestant.

Protestantism has lost the whole realm of sign-symbols, and it has lost most of the sacramental symbolism. It has retained only one thing, namely, the transcendent symbolism, but this has been used in an intellectualistic and moralistic way. It is, however, a good symptom that in recent decades Protestantism has become more aware of what the depth psychologist Jung has said about it—that it is a "continuous iconoclasm," meaning a continuous breaking and destroying of symbols. Today Protestantism is trying to regain much of the lost symbolism. But how can this be achieved? Symbols cannot be invented; they grow. And beyond this, we have today in Protestant theology the now famous discussion about the "de-mythologization" of the New Testament. That is a simple consequence of the fact that we must understand the New Testament's symbols *as symbols.* Configurations of symbols are myths and we must understand them as such. That is what Bultmann means with his attempt to demythologize the New Testament.

We need demythologization against the confusion of literalism with symbolism, and we need at the same time symbolization as full and rich as possible. How can this be realized? That is the great problem of Protestantism. It must develop an attitude in which it is again able to accept symbols. Protestantism has gone through four hundred years of rational criticism and has learned that symbols are symbols, that they cannot be taken literally and that if they are taken literally they evoke a justified unfavorable reaction from the secular world. Against literal symbolism I have the same critical attitude as the rationalist, but only in order to protect religion. For it is the first step in the deterioration of religion when it identifies symbols with the world of finite interrelations which furnishes the material of the symbols—which are the material and not that which is signified. That which is signified lies beyond the symbolic material. This is the first and last thing we must say about religious symbolism.

VII

A PSYCHOLOGIST'S VIEW OF RELIGIOUS SYMBOLS

BY

GOODWIN WATSON, PH.D

Professor of Education, Teachers College, Columbia University

For some five hundred centuries *homo sapiens* has been experiencing and expressing life in symbols. For less than one century psychology has been searching for its own symbols with which to represent and to systematize our understanding of man's ubiquitous symbolizing process. Influenced by a mechanistic and atomistic physics, early psychological theories were concerned with putting the pieces together. Associationists, in nineteenth century Europe, noted that ideas are bound to others which have come close to them in time or space. (If they had gone further with their interesting concept of association due to *similarity,* the ensuing questions might have advanced the awareness of symbols.) Structuralists like Titchener tried to start at the beginning with pure sensations and to discover how these became combined into percepts, images, and concepts. Units of behavior were viewed by Pavlov and Thorndike as connections between a specific stimulus and a defined response. Learning was seen as forming and reinforcing bonds to tie a new, or conditioned, response to a predetermined stimulus. The fact that man is even more prone to manipulate metaphors than he is to push and pull objects was largely ignored, because, under the impact of evolutionary theories, it was deemed more fundamental to study behaviors which are not distinctively human, but are shared with other animal species. Even rat-psychologists have recently, however, had to concern themselves with what Tolman calls a "sign-Gestalt."

Several movements in psychology during the past two generations have opened the way to deeper insight into symbolic processes. The most radical change in conceptions was introduced by psychoanalysis. Freud revealed that the unconscious, which finds expression in dreams, neurotic symptoms, fantasies, fairy tales, legend, myth, ritual, and many other forms of art, uses a language of metaphor and symbols. Symbolism, like pantomime, is so basic to human make-up that it may transcend barriers of language and culture. Erich Fromm in his book, *The Forgotten Language,* writes:

The myths of the Babylonians, Indians, Egyptians, Hebrews, Greeks are written in the same language as those of the Ashantis or the Trukese. The dreams of someone living today in New York or in Paris are the same as the dreams reported from people living some thousand years ago in Athens or in Jerusalem. The dreams of ancient and modern man are written in the same language as the myths whose authors lived in the dawn of history. . . . It is the one universal language the human race has ever developed, the same for all cultures and throughout history.[1]

To Gestalt psychology we owe another tremendous advance in our appreciation of the significance of symbolic patterns. Wertheimer, Koffka, Koehler, and their associates were not studying dreams arising from within the psyche—they were reopening the question of our powers of conscious observation of the real world around us. Their ingenious experiments demonstrated that perception comes to us not in bits and pieces to be stuck together by some after-act of mind, but immediately coherent, patterned, and structured. The baby looking up into his mother's face sees no discrete hair, eyes, nose, mouth, and chin, but the beloved face experienced as a whole against some sort of dim background. Brunswik has suggested the analogy of a lens. The image thrown on the screen of our consciousness does properly represent the outside world. It appears in its entirety with all parts in approximate proportion. It is representative and symbolic. Sights and sounds do not come to us knocked down into elements which we must mentally assemble, they come all put together in workable and meaningful units of experience. The Gestalt

[1] Erich Fromm, *The Forgotten Language,* Rinehart & Company, New York, 1951, p. 4.

psychologists have helped us realize the ease with which similar patterns can be identified despite very different stimuli. A melody is recognized, although transposed. A live duck, a clay model of a duck, and an outline drawing of a duck present three quite different sets of sensory data but a child soon can match them. The writer recalls a memorable evening with Wertheimer when he stepped to a piano and with a few chords portrayed each of several different persons so vividly that no one present had any difficulty in knowing which personality was to be equated with which music. The essential pattern or Gestalt was communicated without words or other conventions. Minds are metaphoric by nature.

A third insight into symbolism has come with the progress of social psychology and the study of social norms. We have become aware of the fact that our beliefs and attitudes are acquired in social settings. They are seldom as distinctively individual and private as they seem. Any notion that each person can devise his own religious creed on the basis of his own unique experience and reason will have to be somewhat amended. The symbols he uses when he does his private thinking have been given their meaning in socially shared experiences. The word, "prayer," for example, carries to even the most independent thinker meanings acquired when the word was used by his parents, friends, religious teachers, and all the writers or speakers who may have influenced him. Their tone of approval or disapproval inevitably becomes part of his feeling when he thinks of "prayer." If he happens to be an adolescent (of whatever chronological age!) engaged in the unavoidable struggle for independence from his parents, that social context influences the way in which his innermost mind reacts to any symbols acquired during his period of dependence. His need to belong to his peer group and neighborhood and religious community cannot be laid aside while he cogitates on ideas which are products of his participation in such groups. It is well known that most people carry about as their own firm convictions the attitudes concerning religious, moral, and other controversial issues which they acquired in their homes. It may not be so well recognized that when they change, they do so again as part of a new social context. Our own still unpublished study of individuals whose prejudice against those of different race or religion has undergone great changes—for better or for worse—showed that in every case the new attitude took form in a new social context. Social psychology is confirming in its special area of science the doctrine that we are all members one of another. It is challenging the fancy of self-made minds. It affirms with John Donne that "No man is an Iland intire of itselfe."

Before attempting to develop further the implications of social psychology, Gestalt psychology, and psychoanalysis for our understanding of religious symbolism, it may be well to define what we are here to mean by "symbols." Carnap, Langer, and other philosophers of language have introduced an important distinction between *"discursive"* and *"presentational"* forms. In reasoning, we arrange word-symbols in a logical sequence appropriate to "discursive thought." We make propositions the truth of which might conceivably be experimentally tested. Our discursive symbols are set in certain relationships to one another by the rules of logical syntax. Mathematics is made up of discursive symbols. The sciences have little use for any but discursive symbols, the meaning of which can be operationally defined. In the religious traditions discursive symbols make up the substance of creeds, commandments, and apologetics. The psychology of discursive symbols as they appear in discussions of religion is not notably different from the psychology of language, semantics, and logic in any other context.

The really rich field for psychological study is the other type of symbol—the expressive or presentational. Most people "picture" things in their minds. They may talk about the image they see in their mind's eye and the feelings it inspires, but words will never exhaust nor adequately convey it. The parts are united in a Gestalt; the key idea is not linkage but lens-image. The fact that feelings cannot be communicated by testable logical propositions does not argue against their real existence. It is the words which fall short, not the experience. To share the meaning of profound experiences we must turn to metaphor. The lover speaks of a treasure, an enchantment, eternal bliss, a song in the heart, or a morning star. These are not denotative propositions—they are efforts to translate realities of experience into some representations which will come closer to the mark than scientific measures ever could.

The presentational symbols of religion center naturally about the mysteries of life and death, seedtime and harvest. In ceremony and ritual the human community shares the meaning of procreation, birth, puberty, vocation, maturity, and bereavement. The most vital activities of the group—foodgathering, hunting, planting, reaping, care of the sick, administration of justice and conduct of war— are closely integrated with religious celebrations and institutions. The relation of man to his brothers, his enemies, to sun, water, earth, and to the cycles of stars and seasons finds expression in religious symbols. Persistent moral problems such as resistance to temptation, courage in face of danger, and sacrifice for others provide the framework for tales of gods and supermen. Deep inner needs for integrity amid distracting pressures and for spiritual renewal when existence grows tedious may be served by symbols as different as silence and the Hallelujah Chorus.

Some of the confusion among both believers and skeptics arises from failure to distinguish between discursive and presentational religious symbols. The sophomoric mind asks scornfully: "Do you expect me to believe that a snake talked Eve into eating that apple— that the Ark of the Covenant contained such magic that one who touched it to steady it, fell dead—that Jonah journeyed inside a whale?" Treated as propositions of fact such reports raise difficulties. One who has studied the basic language of mankind, however, reads the same statements quite differently. "What would it mean," one might ask the sophomore, "if you dreamt that a strange serpent which you felt was very old and wise told you that you need not be afraid to open a forbidden door and that if you did you would become master of earth's mysteries?" It might help him understand the tale of Uzzah and the Ark if he would ask ethnologists: "What kind of stories do Indian tribes tell to convey to others their feeling of awe before the mana of their Great Spirit?" Jonah will acquire a universal meaning for him if he asks himself: "What recurrent human experience finds expression in a poem with these images: going down into the belly of a ship, sinking into sleep, falling beneath the billows of the sea, being swallowed by a great fish, finding oneself cast down to the bottoms of the mountains, and feeling the bars of the earth close over one forever? What would it mean to come out of such experiences, to stand free and erect again, with the sun overhead and the breeze in one's hair?"

Symbolic interpretations are sometimes resisted by the devout as well as by the agnostic, because the language of myth is felt to be less trustworthy than the language of science. If discourse is not rational, must it not be irresponsibly irrational? If the rules of logic and evidence are not to hold, what check can there be? Is a painting as revealing as a photograph? What validity can reside in such nonsense as Burns's:

> Oh, my love's like a red red rose,
> That's newly sprung in June;
> Oh, my love's like the melodie
> That's sweetly played in tune.

Can there be as much truth in theatres as in theorems? What does a sonata prove?

"We are not talking nonsense," answers Susanne K. Langer, "when we say that a certain musical progression is significant, or that a given phrase lacks meaning, or a player's rendering fails to convey the import of a passage." [2] Expressive symbolism does not follow the laws of logical proof but it may meet requirements of validity in its own way. Art may be genuine or spurious. The parables of Jesus are not less true but true in a different sense than are the chronicles of a historian.

Psychological study of the genesis of presentational symbols leads to a few suggestions for improving religious education. Fromm has distinguished three ways in which symbols arise, classifying the products as accidental, conventional, and universal.

Consider first the accidental—a connection arising by mere contiguity in individual experience. Morton Prince's famous clinical case found herself depressed by the sound of church bells; the con-

[2] Susanne K. Langer, *Philosophy in a New Key,* Harvard University Press, Cambridge, Massachusetts, 1942, p. 101.

nection had been formed by chimes outside the room where this young woman nursed her father in his fatal illness. By the process psychologists call "conditioning" the bell became a signal which reinstated in her the despair of those hours of suffering. The memory itself was repressed. She did not know why bells symbolized deep melancholy to her.

Religious symbols vary in their effect upon minds that have been formed by different childhood experiences. The most striking example is the idea of Father, used to symbolize God's relationship to man. Happy the child for whom that symbol is filled with a sense of warmth, security, intimacy, generous provision, complete understanding, and perfect reliability! But we human parents are so fallible. The symbol, "father," might well imply to a child in some suburban families a tired and irritable figure appearing at rare in·tervals to rest up from busying himself in a far away office with matters of no concern to that child. Do we want to tell the children often severely punished by a harsh disciplinarian father that God is like that? And what about children in families deserted by the father?

Other religious symbols likewise acquire special colors and connotations by accidents in the careers of individuals. Bread and wine used in a sacrament have the most holy implications, but are not thereby freed from other meanings for particular children who are chronically hungry, or who are rebelling by rejecting food urged on them by parents. One of the problems of religious education is to free individuals from distorted associations with the common symbols. Some of our most powerful associations may be unconscious, steering us along courses of feeling which rationally we reject. It might be helpful to try a kind of group therapy approach in religious education. Within a congenial group of adults or teenagers, present briefly a religious symbol (perhaps a term, a phrase, an art form, or an act of ritual). Then ask each member to close his eyes, relax, and let arise whatever images or feelings are associated for him with that symbol. Try to discover the common core of response and to help each individual correct for his deviations.

Fromm's second category of symbols is the conventional. These are shared by all members of a culture, but differ from one society to another. Within Nazi circles the swastika had a meaning fundamentally different from its significance as a good luck charm among the Indians of our Southwest. In one society black is the color of mourning, in another the appropriate dress is white. Dances which are central in the religious ritual of some cults would be shocking to others. To the Roman Catholic, prayers in Latin, and to the Jew, prayers in Hebrew, impress the worshiper as devout, reverent, and inspiring, even if no word of the language is understood. The symbolism, let us remember, is not discursive but presentational. The authenticity of the experience is not dependent on logical explication of the course of thought but is a product of images and feelings associated with the ritual since early childhood. This experience is shared by the family and congregation. It has become for them a conventional symbol. Each individual has some understanding of the meaning of the ritual for other members who share in the convention, although to an unaccustomed outsider, the ceremony may seem ridiculous.

Our growing knowledge of social norms and the way in which individuals internalize them suggests that education in appreciation of religious symbols is best when it is collective. Ceremonies in which all members of a family, a neighborhood, a congregation, or a community participate together are the most influential. In one Friends' Meeting which I occasionally attend, all the children of the Sunday School, including the tiny tots of nursery school age, come in for the last ten minutes of the service to sit on their little chairs alongside all the adults in the main Meeting, sharing those few moments of collective silence.

Collective symbols unite persons in social groups. The heart of the vital issue between public schools and parochial schools seems to be more a matter of social context than of religious content. The point is that in the church's own school, children get their sense of belonging and at-home-ness-in-my-group focused upon religious symbols under consistently religious auspices, with their fellow religionists. Identical religious subject matter read in a book by an individual child in a public library would lack those social ties and be less effective. The supporters of public education want all children of the neighborhood, regardless of their religious affiliation or lack of any, to join in school activities which will unite them as citizens of a democratic community, loyal to civic symbols. The difference lies not so much in *what* is studied as in *with whom* the strong ties of collective symbolism are established. The outcomes differ not so much in individual character as in group coherence.

Fromm's third category—the universal symbols—raises the most farreaching questions. Gestalt psychology has demonstrated that the human mind is constructed to give preference to certain forms. A complete circle or square fits our psychic preconceptions better than does one which is unclosed. We do not need to be taught to laugh or to cry; we understand immediately those behaviors in others. Anthropologists and ethnologists report that "upward" seems always associated with the better and "downward" with the worse. The forces of light (a symbol President Eisenhower used effectively in his Inaugural address) seem always favorable to man; the powers of darkness are threatening. The association of springtime with love and procreation is as inevitable as the implication of old age and death in the withered leaves of winter. Fire is consistently an exciting dynamic symbol, while deep waters serve both to bring forth life and to receive the dead. How much further our nature predisposes us toward specific symbols is not certain. Efforts to contrive appropriate rational symbols and to inculcate them, as, for example, immediately after the French Revolution, have not been very successful. C. G. Jung has devoted many years of study to the universal symbols which reappear in the dreams, the myths, the art forms, and the fantasies of both sane and insane minds in widely different cultures. He tells us that these arise from levels within us deeper than our conscious self and deeper than the personal unconscious which contains, as Freud has shown, memories repressed during the course of our early years. The figure of the hero who kills giants or dragons, the child wonder, the holy saint, the seductive temptress, the pure virgin, the vile witch, the trickster, the wise teacher, or the savior may be given a different name and history as it reappears in each dreamer or in the folk tales of each culture but there must be something in the human psyche which predisposes to such patterns. Psychology has not yet begun the serious exploration of these fascinating problems. Having now become aware that human consciousness is a never ending flow of symbols and that the energies of the unconscious come to us in symbolic form, perhaps psychologists will soon be prepared to approach the mighty mysteries which concern all religions. If so, you need have no fear that under the microscopes of science the realities of the spiritual universe will be dissipated. We have every reason to believe that as our concept of the physical universe has been enriched because of what scientists can tell us of worlds within the atom and worlds beyond our galaxy, so the more intensive study of the inner world of man will bring increased appreciation, wonder, and awe.

> The wise man also may hear and increase in learning
> And the man of understanding acquire skill
> To understand a proverb and a figure—
> The words of the wise and their dark sayings.
>
> (Proverbs 1:5–6)

Bibliography

Egon Brunswik, *The Conceptual Framework of Psychology,* University of Chicago Press, Chicago, 1952. (A rather technical analysis of the way psychologists have looked at mental life and of possible improvements in the "models" used in constructing psychological theory.)

Erich Fromm, *The Forgotten Language,* Rinehart, New York, 1951. (An introduction to the symbolic activities of mental life, especially dreams, myths, and fairy tales. Probably the best single volume to follow up the ideas in this paper.)

Edna Heidbreder, *Seven Psychologies,* Century Company, New York, 1933. (Useful as a readable overview of the several "schools" of psychology discussed in the introduction of this paper.)

Susanne K. Langer, *Philosophy in a New Key,* Harvard University Press, Cambridge, 1942. (The best arguments for the distinction between "discursive" and "presentational" forms of thought. Excellent approach to the meaning of art forms.)

John F. Markey, *The Symbolic Process and Its Integration in Children,* Harcourt, Brace & Company, New York, 1928. (One of the early psychological studies of how children acquire words and meanings.)

I. Progoff, *Jung's Psychology and Its Social Meaning,* Julian Press, New York, 1953. (The best presentation in English of the basic ideas of C. G. Jung, a psychologist who has concerned himself profoundly with the study of symbolism and with man's religious needs.)

VIII

SYMBOLISM IN CONTEMPORARY CHURCH ARCHITECTURE

BY

ARLAND A. DIRLAM, M.A.

Architect

Perhaps the most loosely employed word in the entire vocabulary of architecture is the term, "symbolism." This is understandable, as symbols may exist in a multitude of forms and may be created from an inexhaustible choice of building materials. Color, light, mass, and detail independently function, or collectively combine to express a message. A specific description of symbolism borders on the impossible.

To the layman, the word is even more confusing because of its lack of limitation. The guide on a conducted tour of a cathedral will point out some peculiar graining in an obscure marble slab and proudly insist that one can distinguish in this graining a visible profile of the Master, and this is a symbol; or the group of sculpture located at the west portal, according to page 3 of the cathedral book-let, symbolizes faith, hope, charity, and as many other virtues as the writer of the brochure can bring to mind. It is, therefore, necessary, before attempting any discussion of contemporary symbolism to establish certain standards that may be used as a basis for proper evaluation.

In the past, the major function of symbolism was to educate. Walls and windows of our medieval churches became the poor man's Bible. Here from the paintings and the glass, the sculpture and the tracery, the goodness and the mysteries of God, he could learn the history of secular events and the role of the church in the community. The dramatic portrayal and the tangibility of the symbolic message often proved far more effective than the spoken word. Constant repetition and yet varying significance, depending upon the emotions and moods of the individual worshiper, caused the symbol to become an indispensable part of ecclesiastical architecture. Symbolic forcefulness caused the church to be the generous patron of the arts. Vulnerability of the symbolic message lay in the growing development of imagery and the tendency of the worshiper to place his emphasis upon the symbol and to neglect the message.

The use of and need for symbolism as an educational medium still exist today. But in this more literate era its educational value is much reduced. Its continued use cannot be justified by assigning to it the mere role of an illustrated alphabet, but only when for twentieth century man it fulfils that part of the order of worship to which we refer as the Service of Meditation. Symbols must suggest and inspire. They must serve the masters for whom they have been designed.

W. T. Stace in his recent book, *Time and Eternity,* says that religious symbolism stands for an experience. The symbol does not mean, but evokes an experience. It evokes in us feelings, moods, and emotions, much as the varying sounds of music evoke them in us. Continuing, Dr. Stace says that all religious language is symbolic and that symbolism is a relation to which there must be two terms. One term is a sensuous image or picture, which is the metaphor or symbol. The other term is the thing which the symbol or image stands for and represents. He finds that the condition for the valid use of symbolic language is that both terms should be in some sense present to the mind. Both terms must be in some way known.[1]

If we accept this statement, and its validity is difficult to challenge, then our review of architectural symbolism must distinguish between those elements that are purely ornamental and whose symbolic significance has been hastily discovered in time for publication in the dedication booklet, and those significant details or forms

[1] W. T. Stace, *Time and Eternity,* Princeton University Press, Princeton, 1952, pp. 91–115.

which from the original conception of the design were deliberately created to evoke, instil, and inspire.

Before we permit ourselves to limit our thinking to single elements or disconnected details as the sole media for symbolic expression, let us first review the primary purpose of church architecture. Basically, it is a functional composition whose pattern of plan and development, of façade and internal sections, have been deliberately formed to serve a specific end. The order of worship, the liturgical requirements, and the denominational characteristics are the elementary concern of the church architect. Upon these, he gauges his conception and from these he charts his course. Not until he has designed the tree and arranged its branches does he concern himself about the shape of the leaf or the color of the blossom. Yet it is in this elementary stage of conception that the truly valid story of symbolism begins. The tree itself becomes the symbol: the branches, the leaves, the blossoms are but accents incorporated to dramatize the story and to tell in fuller content the magic mysteries of the whole.

The physical emphasis placed upon the sanctuary or *bimah,* the determination of flow lines from the narthex to the nave, the recessing of entrance portals or projection of side chapels, the orientation to catch the rising or setting sun, the recognition of climatic conditions, the awareness of neighboring environment, become points in plan which, when projected vertically, determine the elevations and sections, the physical elements that compose symbolism. It is the skill in setting forth these salient projection points that establishes that quality which architects call scale, but which laymen recognize as an element that suggests intimacy or grandeur. It is these same salient points that set the stage for the ultimate development of those intangible and almost atmospheric qualities which spell mystery, awe, welcome, and light. It is these very primary points that determine whether the structure will physically become a house of worship or merely a secular building adorned with ecclesiastical designs. Grace of proportion and coordinated emphasis of space are architecture's springboard to the field of symbolism, and become the noun and verb of the sentences that are to be told.

In the tempo of our age, and in keeping with the manner in which we live, comes the constant clamoring for the new and the ready discarding of the old. This discontent with the *status quo* marks our period of civilization and produces a healthy situation that spells progress. Like science, medicine, and art, architecture has made mighty strides during recent decades. It has broken itself free from the nineteenth century contentment with archeological copying. It has discovered freedom of expression, ability to pioneer, and daring to explore the realms of tomorrow. Advanced knowledge in methods of construction, new discoveries of building materials and new and greater uses of the old have greatly expanded the architectural vocabulary of the designer. New forms, new masses are arising from newly arranged salient points, and ecclesiastical architecture has embarked upon a new quest for physical expression that may prove to be the greatest advance since the rise of medieval Gothic. At no time in the past century has the opportunity to create been so fresh and so challenging. At no time has the lay public, mentally conditioned through the advertising of commercial and domestic products, been so ready to accept a departure from the past. With abounding enthusiasm architects have set forth to display the wonders of their new found tools.

Tempering this enthusiasm, however, is the cold awareness that history has proved lasting architecture evolutionary, not revolutionary, and that the new of today does not contain only that which is good, nor is the past composed only of decadent and archaic forms. Our perspective is yet too close to determine which parts of these efforts are merely stylistic or faddish and which by their studied integrity indicate a trend. At best, we must recognize that all that is current modern is but transitional.

To avoid the stigma of the term, "modernistic," which was generally applied to the early endeavors in this new field—unfortunately for the most part stylistic and faddish—the word, "contemporary," has been employed. Eventually, this word came to be used only for those forms of architecture which dissociate themselves from a basic traditional form. Such connotation is misleading. It suggests that our total building efforts today are limited to an expression in a single style.

In many parts of the country, and particularly in the field of church architecture, newly erected, traditionally inspired structures still outnumber those of modern design. Although conservative in their approach, and usually retaining a more normally accepted form, their departure from their architectural antecedents rightly proclaims them as modern. Their recognition of and adaptation to current problems, plus their continued adoption by building committees, classifies them as contemporary. Thus, when we think of contemporary symbolism, we must include in this category all that has been done in this and the preceding decade.

Furthermore, as we endeavor to evaluate and compare the symbols of varying styles, we must keep uppermost in our minds that it is usually the skill and ability of the designer that establish the success of the creation, rather than the medium in which he works.

The skill of the designer, however, has many controlling limitations, frequently beyond the point of his own choosing. We can agree that the perfectly designed church would be one that would recall the glories of the past, express the problems of the present, and project our thinking into the promises of the future. The difficulty, and perhaps impossibility, of achieving this utopian goal is that churches are not, and should not be, mere architectural monuments. To warrant their erection, they must be specifically designed to serve the needs of a particular community. Churches are erected to God, by His people and for their use. Academic creations, no matter how perfect, must bow to the views of the congregations who are to worship in them and who cause them to come into being. The architect's function is to lead, but not to dictate. The symbolism he causes to be formed must be significant and evoking, to the people who are to be served.

Of what value is the finest suit, even if made of the best cloth and meticulously tailored, if it neither fits nor feels comfortable upon the wearer? Modern, as well as traditional architecture, no matter how perfect in its concept or design, can become but a mere museum piece, if it fails to inspire or is not enjoyed by the people who use it. Consequently, as we search for symbolism, we must appreciate the background of the parish and the locale and environment in which the structure has been set.

One's first awareness of symbolism is derived from the total building. Its unity of mass, its suggestion of strength, its ability to proclaim its purpose and to extend a message of invitation to the passerby, are as symbolic and as evoking as any particular carving or painting that one may perceive upon closer scrutiny.

The properties that cause a structure to identify itself as a place of worship are not confined to those cozy little churches that adorn Christmas cards nor are they limited to those modern ecclesiastical designs so frequently used as a background in commercial advertising. Instead, they find a common ground between these two extremes, and each in its own language spells out the same or similar words to capture the imagination of the layman.

Nor is size or budget the controlling factor. Many a little mission or parish church has expressed its message with more dramatic and intimate appeal than does the lofty grandeur of certain cathedrals.

In the vicinity of New York there are several examples of the work of men in the modern field which illustrate the accomplishments to which I refer. In a church in Manhasset, one readily catches a vital freshness, an interesting interpretation of form, a clever handling of the vertical lift, a pleasing treatment of non-traditional fenestration. Its setting among other structures of non-traditional form, reflects an awareness in keeping with the time, and establishes for its outward religious message an architectural story as current as any secular building that has been designed to serve some particular phase of community life. It seems to say that here is a structure in which people recognize religion as an integral part of modern life, a group who have availed themselves of the increased knowledge of modern construction and who, by the form of building that they have chosen to erect, have striven to relate their religious life to their weekday activities. The same can be said of other modern churches. St. Peter Clavier Mission, designed by Albert Hoffman in Montclair, New Jersey, although built before the recent war is still an outstanding example of modern expression in art and architecture. On the West Coast the works of Pietro Belluschi, and in the Midwest the creations of Saarinen speak the same language. Architects Thorshov and Cerny, in their Church of St. Frances Cabrini, in Minneapolis, with its simple stone cross set against a plain brick front, express religious aspiration in its lines. St. Clements Church in Alexandria, Virginia, whose entrance portals are integrated with the cross, and are flanked by Old Testament figures, departs from the usual form, yet tells a religious story. The Blessed Sacrament Church in Stowe, Vermont, also modern, is symbolically effective.

The geographical distribution of these illustrations demonstrates the nationwide acceptance of this form. Its acceptance in fact is worldwide; even today some of the best thinking in modern church architecture originates in Scandinavia and Switzerland. The continued development in this modern field dramatically declares to the observer that religion has met the challenge of the twentieth century and has adorned itself with proper garb.

But who will say that the recently constructed little white wooden church in the Colonial town of Easthampton, Connecticut, and the Mary Martha Chapel in Sudbury, Massachusetts, do not, in their setting, equal their modern contemporaries in appeal, and express as dramatic a symbol story? Chaste in design, beautiful in their simplicity, inspired by but not copying the Colonial form of their ancestors, these pleasing structures whose slender spires reach skyward, embody the richness of tradition. They suggest a continuing stability. Adorned with green lawns and accented by colorful foliage, their quiet form spells peace and rest.

Such Colonially inspired structures and other recently built but traditionally patterned churches are the contemporary expression of what many communities feel, and must be recognized as reflecting the mood of a large proportion of our church-going people.

Assuming equal ability of the architects, working in the modern and traditionally inspired fields, their resulting efforts produce a symbolic story. Although employing contrasting architectural vocabularies, each proclaims its message as forcibly as the other. How-

ever, though equal in appeal, comparable in story, and on an inspira-
tional par with each other, neither the modern formed nor the traditionally inspired structure could be transposed to the environment or
locale of the other without suffering a decided loss in architectural
importance and a diminished value in ecclesiastical function. The
modern form would appear strange and non-conforming in the Colonial atmosphere and the Colonial structure would be so incongruous
in a surrounding of modern buildings that instead of inspiring, it
would tend to stamp a note of archaism upon the very purpose it was
designed to serve.

Therefore, as we project the salient points of function to their vertical and horizontal locations, which permit us to create a composition
or style, let us ever be mindful that all styles have symbolic stories to
tell, but the environment of the reader and the atmosphere in which
he reads the message will increase or lessen in direct ratio with the
architectural sentences we employ for a given situation. Again the
challenge to the designer is not merely to produce interesting architecture of his own interpretation and understanding, but rather to
provide forms and patterns that can be read by those whom he serves.

The second great field of symbolism is the atmosphere of the interior, that intangible quality that evokes in the worshiper an awareness of God: that certain something that distinguishes a church from
a public auditorium and suggests to the layman the desire for meditation. Although certain combinations of architectural elements have
proved helpful in the past in creating this suggestion, probably the
greatest achievement is the control of the quantity and quality of
light and shadow.

Aldo Guigola, in a recent article about lighting, referred to the
moment when shadow invaded the Gothic cathedral, flames of the
lamps and torches concentrated the light in the lower part of the
nave, leaving above an unexplored darkness, while the rays fled along
pillars and ribs with no rest into the black vastness, the interior seem-
ing thus to melt into that endless space where is God. He concludes
with the statement that light is today a positive force capable of bid-
ding us by scientific means to be active, productive, or relaxed. Some

day, we will understand the shadow, and from that day on, we will know how to make light more beautiful.

Modern architecture uninhibited by established forms and capable of absorbing in its fluid pattern the recent advances made in the field of illumination, holds more promise for capturing these essential qualities than does the usual traditionally patterned church. The mystical quality of trickling sunlight through a clerestory, the vitality of color of the western rose, the transparent intimacy of the small clear panes of Colonial may some day be surpassed by the freedom of fenestration or absence of it that keynotes modern, and with the assistance of artificial light new dramatic stories may be told. Although the transitional period may tend to the theatrical, the future for modern in this sphere is unlimited.

However, despite the dramatic appeal of the tower, silhouetted against the sky at twilight, or the emotional lift of a masterfully executed interior, some persist in thinking that the art of symbolism is confined to a third aspect, namely, that field of detail or ornament which has been applied upon or incorporated into the mass design as a decorative part. This reason is proved by a reading of traditional pattern. Alphabets and literally sentences and paragraphs of symbolic stories have been handed down to us in specific details through the ages. To these accepted and significant forms we have applied our nationalistic touches and adjustments. Dozens of books have been written about their meaning and origin.

Because of this background, the designer who bases his study on the traditional form has a readymade inventory from which to draw. Having established his mass composition, his treatment of detail has frequently been merely one of modifying a truly traditional form to a point where it achieves harmony and consistency with the surrounding design. This may consist of flattening the relief, establishing a bolder treatment of pattern, the elimination of fussiness, and occasionally the introduction of new forms, adjacent to or combined with, the traditional. The success of the resulting effect is dependent upon the ability of the designer. In most cases, however, this process of evolutionary design has resulted in a conservatism which, while sound and logical, frequently has failed to kindle that spark of vitality which signified advancement. The architect, while fulfilling his obligation of providing elements of significance and understanding for the congregation, has faltered in his task of leadership by failing to create elements sufficiently current and sufficiently stirring to evoke an expression that might bring the congregations present day understanding of God to a closer, more personal relationship.

To add this feeling of new to the old, without resulting in a hodge-podge of architectural formation is one of the most difficult tasks of designing. Few men have been able to accomplish it successfully. But that it is possible is exemplified by the works of the late Bertram Goodhue.

Goodhue's Gothic was not the Gothic of the medieval ages, but a fresh and modern conception of mass and detail which equals any ecclesiastical work that has been erected during this past half century. Yet Goodhue's success in this effort was without a sudden radical departure from the accepted form. He created his architecture as a living thing. While working in a proven form he preserved those elements that had served well, and discarded those points which had been purely transitional and of no current meaning. He added to his creations contemporary concepts that reflected the century in which we live. Other designers emulated the work of Goodhue, and although they succeeded to a lesser degree, the patterns that evolved from their drawing boards also spoke the feeling of the twentieth century. Translating their efforts to our mechanical period, it was as if they had said, in their designs, that we are living in an automotive age, the need of the buggy whip and duster has gone, four wheels on which to ride are still necessary, certain body changes are desirable, and while the day of the space helmet may yet come, it has not yet proved itself sufficiently to warrant its incorporation into permanent architectural form.

The worshipers in the churches of Goodhue and his followers were not forced to adjust themselves to new and strange forms in order to catch the current and living quality of the work. Instead, the very positive awareness of the blending of the new and the old evoked a vitality and continuity of religious growth like those of the great churches of the past which spoke in comparable terms of the period in which they were built.

This point is stressed not to deprecate the great pioneering that has been and is being done in the ecclesiastical architectural field by our modern architects, but rather to show that the evolution of traditional form still holds forth to men of ability an opportunity to speak in the mid-twentieth century tongue. The great treasures of the past are far too great and too important to be quickly cast aside.

No, we should not belittle the contribution of the architect who works in the modern field; rather, it is upon his efforts that we should, with attention and hope, bestow our plaudits. I refer now, not to the man who merely seeks to be different, and whose prime qualification is to attract attention and thus acquire personal publicity, but rather to that rapidly growing group of modern architects who studiously and sincerely seek to contribute to the church field a freshness and rejuvenation similar to that which led the early builders of Gothic churches to depart from the earlier traditional forms. Their leadership, their spearheading the advance gave to the world the great cathedrals and the greatest expression of symbolism. These modern men have within their reach the opportunity to set the stage today for equal and perhaps even greater accomplishments.

Their efforts in the art of detail symbolism have just begun to show. The simplicity of their expressions has been dramatically revealing. Their new concept of space and accent has been impressive. Nevertheless, uninhibited by accepted form, yet producing designs to be viewed by traditionally environed readers, they have created symbolism which, in many of its aspects, has come to be the most disputed segment of modern church work. One is reluctant to accept some deliberately distorted corpus, which by its form perplexes rather than inspires, merely because such distortion is supposedly necessary to prove its modern qualities. One finds it difficult to see why crudity in sculpture or extreme angularity are needed to proclaim their expression as the new art.

The complete avoidance of accepted form or the total distortion for purely stylistic effect creates a disturbing lack of understanding on the part of the worshiper and eliminates the very purpose for which the symbol has been created.

In one Roman Catholic church recently visited, the Stations of the Cross were so extreme in their modern execution that their only identification was the numerals placed at their bases. Certainly such a radical expression was limited in its appeal to those few who were highly educated in the appreciation of modern art, and left upon the average layman who piously sought assistance only the impression of a meaningless and confusing mass.

Photographic realism, of course, destroys the vital import of the symbol and tends toward the development of imagery. In fairness, when criticizing the lack of realism in modern symbolism, let us acknowledge that frequently it is the demand for photographic likeness that despoils the traditional form. An illustration is the memorial to Aunt Emma. The loving nephews and nieces in recognition of the legacy they shared, directed the leaded glass man to incorporate in his design an exact likeness of their departed aunt, and for his guidance provided him with a photograph of their deceased relative. With careful diligence, he followed line for line and tint for tint. When the great work was completed, it pictured Aunt Emma proudly displaying one eye of brown and the other of azure blue. The donors, however, were highly pleased because Aunt Emma had had a glass eye.

But aside from glass eyes, traditional symbolism in the past has had its share of lipsticked statuary and rouged angels. Even today, stock catalogs list great bargains (with special discounts for quantity purchase) of unlimited numbers of items which are supposed to serve as symbolic elements that will instil or evoke the proper reactions at stated appointments in the course of the liturgical service. As we discover the extreme opposite of realism in modern symbolism, let it be recalled that certain forced distortions and deliberate changes of balance have always been employed in all art for dramatic emphasis, and are as well justified today as in centuries past. It is only the overzealousness on the part of some designers to exaggerate their point that gives rise to this criticism of the modern.

In the handling of the Cross and similar symbols of more geometric form, the modern architect has encountered less controversy regarding the manner in which he has presented his message. In fact, it has been the Cross treatment that has supplied the total symbolic story for many a modern designer and has done so with greater force and vividness that we encounter in many traditional patterns.

The tall, slender cross of St. Frances Cabrini Church has a lifting quality. It removes itself from all association as an instrument of torture. It seems to reach beyond the limits of earthly patterns and proclaims a risen Lord of Salvation. Its marked relief, almost as if free-standing and yet part of the structure, has a mystical rather than a fearsome quality, and conveys the suggestion of a medium of transition to the world beyond. Saarinen's crosses of Calvary of various sizes, tell the story of the penitent and impenitent sinners, creating an indelible impression, not often achieved by traditional forms. Monograms and dramatically placed and spaced lettering have a more forceful role in modern design than was true of much of the medieval or even contemporary Gothic script.

Murals have played a major role in modern symbolism. Here the artists have ranged from simple childlike primitives to complex overlapping formats. They have employed every medium from the simple execution of tempera on cinder block to rich, brilliant, colorful mosaics. Like the statuary, modern church murals have been highly controversial. Only the passing of time will prove their ability to establish themselves as a permanent contribution to the art, or their doom as a passing fad employed to enliven what might have otherwise been a dull, barren design.

One of the more interesting of the mural-dominated churches was recently pictured in *Life* magazine. It is the creation of Father Couturier in his development of the church in the village of Assy in the French Alps. Instead of standard portrayals of saints, the Assy church windows and walls are a blaze of abstract designs by fifteen of France's leading modern artists. The decorations have aroused considerable opposition not only because they are abstract, but because most of the artists are non-believers.

This latter point provokes a highly important question in any review of modern symbolism. Can an artist or craftsman who himself does not participate in the awareness of the experience, evoke in others the emotional lifting quality of the message to be told? Father Couturier declares the church must place priority on the creative genius of the artists, not on their beliefs. However, there are many who disagree with this premise and insist that the message must be intimately known by the writer if it is to be intelligently understood by the reader.

Color is the fourth and final medium for symbolic expression. For the past several years, aided by the advertising efforts of paint and fabric manufacturers, the lay public has become color conscious. The therapeutic values of certain color combinations are known and can be proved by the designers of hospitals and sanitariums. Color is playing an ever increasing part in our homes and in our factories. Its power in our everyday life to create moods, to stir emotions, to warn of danger, to provide peace and tranquillity, is known to all. The traffic light with its red to stop, green to go, and yellow to walk, has expanded into many combinations capable of creating positive behavior reactions. So integrated has color become with our daily endeavors that it is natural to find its use in church design expanding. No longer is the use of color limited to liturgical, seasonal expression or vestments. And no longer are we dependent upon the hues of the leaded glass window to dispatch the cold somberness of gloomy interiors.

Finally, the day of institutional buff has gone from our traditionally inspired structures and the traditionally minded and the modern bent architects have united to grasp the potentialities of the color field. Dark brown stained wood trusses and ceilings have given way to deep tones of blue, maroon, or green. The standard cream tints of Colonial interiors have yielded to the more expanded palette of Williamsburg, still authentic and traditionally correct, but more in keeping with our time in the matter of color. And in modern, sensing the ability to add richness and warmth to cinder block and concrete, architects have indulged in endless painting combinations. Color accent of tapestries, overtones of draperies, directional pointers of colored runners or carpets, are but a few of the features which indicate a new awareness of the power of color and give promise of a more extended use of it in future work.

As we endeavor to sum up the various media of symbolic expression—mass, light and shadow, detail, and color—it is obvious that each of these different forms has its own particular attributes, enabling it to tell its significant story in a manner distinct from all others. Yet, upon closer study, the story of a single medium seems but a mere sentence or paragraph of a total message, when the capabilities of all media are combined into a common effort. The same is true of traditional as compared with modern symbolism. For certain groups of people and in a certain fixed environment, each has the capacity to express something destructive in symbolic form, and to evoke experiences not called forth by the others. Perhaps with the passing of time a more coordinated blending of the two will produce a form of symbolism even more dramatic, more positive, and more vital than any we have yet known. Responsibility for insuring this outcome rests heavily upon us who are interested in the future of the church. It falls most heavily on those who are entrusted to design the churches desired by particular groups of people, and on those who are selected to direct the development of the design.

Modern architecture is a potent tool. Its concern to pioneer, its wish to explore, can, if not controlled, result in perversion. Materialism in its crudest form may supplant our hope for spiritual expression. But this danger has been present whenever man has dared to step out of the past and move toward the sunlight of tomorrow. The steps that symbolism has thus far taken toward that elusive tomorrow, have, even though sometimes strange in form, been sound and logical. If we labor with devotion, seeking the guidance of Him to Whom we would build, we shall as in ages past create monuments and symbols worthy of His name.

Bibliography

The following list of books affords excellent reference material for specific symbols or mode of symbolic expression in modern work. Although not attempting to define or describe any particular symbols, Stace in his book, *Time and Eternity*, sets forth the need of and justification for symbolism in ecclesiastical art and shows that symbolism need not be limited to any prescribed form or diagram, but rather may assume any pattern or expression that will evoke within the viewer the awareness of an experience.

Eleanor Bitterman, *Art in Modern Architecture*, Reinhold Publishing Corporation, New York, 1952.

Elizabeth E. Goldsmith, *Life Symbols*, The Knickerbocker Press, New York, 1928.

A. Cassi Ramelli, *Edifici Per Il Culto*, Antonia Vallardi, Milan, Italy, 1950.

Rudolf Schwartz, *Vom Bau Der Kirche*, Verlag Lambert Schneider, Heidelberg, Germany, 1947.

W. T. Stace, *Time and Eternity*, Princeton University Press, Princeton, 1952.

"Architecture Réligieuse," L'Architecture Française, 1952.

"The Assy Church," *Life*, June 19, 1950.

IX

RELIGIOUS USE OF THE DANCE

BY

TED SHAWN, M.P.E.

*Managing Director, Jacob's Pillow Dance Festival and
The University of the Dance*

I am not a professional writer, and I have done a great deal more communication and expression through movement than I have through words—so do not expect an erudite discourse. I am going to begin this in a very personal manner in order to give you a little background which some of you may not know. I am going to be a bit autobiographical.

From early childhood, as far back as I can remember, I had a fixed idea that I was going to be a minister. As a matter of fact, an aunt of mine tells an embarrassing story, which aunts usually do, that when I was first able to speak and they asked, "What do you want to be when you grow up?" I said, "I want to be a preacher on Wednesday nights and Sundays, and an actor the rest of the week."

I went through to my junior year in college studying to be a Methodist minister, with no other idea consciously in my mind. Then I had diphtheria, and was quarantined for three months, alone in a hospital room. I had nothing to do but think (which is the most dangerous thing you can do). And I realized I had never done any thinking. I had never said anything but yes to what my pastor told me. I had said yes to what I read out of books. I had said yes to what my teachers, as well as my parents, told me, but I had done no original thinking.

So I made the very brave gesture of cleaning my entire inner house, and said, "I will not put any furniture back into this house unless I myself have made it; I will believe as truth only that which I have demonstrated and made work." Of course, that is too big a job for anybody literally to do, but it did start me out of the hospital with a completely clean mental slate, although, physically, I was paralyzed from the hips down.

When I was able to walk again I took up the dance as therapy; that is, it was a way in which I could regain my physical strength, and at the same time it seemed to me the ideal form of exercise in which to gain an expressive and intelligent use of my body as contrasted with any kind of sport or ordinary gymnastic activity.

But I had, after I went into the dance professionally, a split consciousness. I felt that I had left the church for the theatre, that I had left religion for the dance.

And then, in 1910, I saw for the first time Ruth St. Denis. She danced among other things that night a dance called "Incense," which was a pure expression of worship; and I had that experience which is sometimes referred to as conversion. I had the greatest religious experience of my life, and I was healed of that inner conflict because I realized that dance and religion could be the same thing, and that the dance could be the finest medium of religious expression. And so I carried over my feeling for the ministry into this career of the dance, and had naturally the urge to do research in order to confirm this experience (which had been an emotional experience), to confirm it with facts.

First I picked up a Concordance and looked to see what the Bible had to say about it. Some seventeen times the words, "dance" and "dancing," are mentioned in the Bible, and never once with disfavor. As a matter of fact, we have a clear, curt, concise command in the Psalms: "Praise ye the Lord in the dance."

Many years later I preached from a Methodist pulpit in New York City and used that sentence from the Psalms as my text. There were some whitehaired elders sitting in the front row, and I said to them, "Have you praised the Lord in the dance today? If not, you have committed a sin of omission." And they shouted, "Amen, Brother!"

I began experimenting with my own expression of religion in the dance, and took a vocal setting of the Twenty-third Psalm which had been composed for a singer. It was very simple and pantomimic and was the beginning of many things that developed later. By 1917 I had composed an entire Protestant church service in dance form, with an opening prayer, dancing the Doxology, the Gloria, an anthem, Fauré's "The Palms." I did a sermon in the form of symbolic dance with a dramatic theme, to the text, "Ye shall know the truth and the truth shall make ye free." I danced a hymn and a benediction.

I have kept up this interest—it is more than interest—in the religious dance all through my career. There has never been a program in my forty solid years of one-night stands that has not included some dances on religious themes. For instance, in my recent (December, 1952) tour of forty-nine cities, my program contained the "Dance of a Whirling Dervish," a Negro Spiritual, "Nobody Knows the Trouble I've Seen," and a Methodist revival hymn, "Give Me the Old Time Religion."

I will refer briefly to some of my other dances. One was based on the bronze images of "Siva as Nataraja," which Ananda K. Coomaraswamy has described as the clearest image of the activity of God of which any religion can boast. As a matter of fact, we find that all through the ages, when writers have tried to describe the activity of God or the activity of angels, they have had to fall back on choreographic forms.

I remember how thrilled I was when I first read Nietzsche's *Thus Spake Zarathustra* and learned that he could believe only in a God Who would know how to dance. It was such a corroboration of my own feeling that I then began to define God in terms of a divine dancer. Could we imagine Him as being anything but infinite grace, infinite rhythm, infinite expression of beauty, of lightness? All of the attributes we strive for in the dance may be thought of as descriptive of God.

I found also in my research that the dancing of primitive people is almost entirely a religious expression. A study of the history of all the great religions of the world shows that they have used the dance as their finest medium of religious expression, and that includes even the Christian Church in its early centuries when it was vital and young and undegenerate.

During my own career I have done not only Negro Spirituals, which I have mentioned, but also have used a great many of the Bach Chorals. "Jesu, Joy of Man's Desiring" I did with my company of men dancers as a processional dance, and I have danced solo, "I Call Upon Thee, My God."

The "Whirling Dervish," already mentioned, is an ecstatic, fanatical, individual expression of man's use of a magic formula by which he believes he can attain absolute union with God and return to his unconscious body which has been spinning all the time. He comes back refreshed, revitalized, and regenerated by the experience.

I have gone back into ancient civilizations such as that of Crete and the pre-Minoan, which is earlier than the golden ages of Egypt and Greece. I have gone into the primitive dances of the American Indians. One that I have probably done more than any other dance in my career is called "Invocation to the Thunder Bird," which is a dance prayer for rain. Also, I have taken the life and character of St. Francis of Assisi and have made of that a dance, where in ecstasy and an almost trancelike condition he received the divine stigmata.

There are three major divisions or types of religious dance. The first is formed out of the individual's own experience, separate from his relationship with other men. Primitive man found very early that in the monotony of repeated rhythmic movements he induced a supernatural, an ecstatic, state. He believed that that was the finest method of putting himself in harmony with cosmic forces, and that by becoming one with these cosmic forces he could then shape them toward beneficent ends either for himself or for his tribe.

The "Whirling Dervish" is an example of this individual, ecstatic type of dance. Although it is sometimes done in company with many other people, it is not a group dance as such, because each individual is inducing his own individual ecstasy. All over the world these dance forms are found.

I have described at some length in my book, *Gods Who Dance,* something I happened by mere accident to see about two-thirty or three o'clock in the morning during my stay in India. I went near

Calcutta to a temple which was almost completely deserted, and there on a platform, in front of an image of a goddess, was a single figure, dancing. I do not know to this 'day whether it was a man or a woman. There were about four musicians present, and I do not know how long this had been going on. I stayed, fascinated, an hour or two, and when I left it was still in progress. This individual had reached some tremendous spiritual crisis in his or her life, and had made a pilgrimage of perhaps hundreds of miles to arrive at this particular shrine and there dance out an ecstasy of communion with his or her god.

I have seen all over the world, different types of this individual ecstasy, this ecstatic dance. Here in America, of course, we are descended largely from North European, very inexpressive stock. We are afraid of emotion and we shrink from expressing it. We are also a little bit suspicious of emotion. But there are sects in this country like the Holy Rollers, the Jumpers, who *move* their religion, and I must say I have tremendous respect for that, because, if religion is anything at all, it is emotion, and if God comes into you it is something so terrific that you are shaken by it. I despise the kind of religion which allows people to sit relaxed against the back of the seat and listen to somebody preach at them, or to sing some dismal hymn like, "Oh, Happy Day," about as happily as if it were wash day.

Even in our own language we say, "I was deeply moved by that experience," and it means exactly what it says. If you really get religion, your body cannot stay still. You are shaken. You are in the midst of the most terrific force in the universe. How can you be placid? How can you be merely intellectual about it? I have seen Negro revival meetings. I have seen the voodoo dances in Haiti, and to me this really is a genuine and much to be admired and respected form of religion, where people are moved, and *physically* moved, by what they sincerely feel.

The second major type of religious dance is a dance drama used symbolically, used as a treasure chest to hold and preserve and pass on the beliefs of a church or a people. We find these in ancient civilizations like those of Egypt and Greece, and they were called "The Mysteries." It is strange, isn't it, the transition in the meanings of words through the centuries? Today, a mystery is a twenty-five cent paperbacked book, a "Who Dunit?" But the original meaning of "mystery" was a great, sacred, secret doctrine which was put into symbolic dance drama and performed by the elder priests for the student priests, and in that way perpetuated. It was remembered emotion, rather than immediate experience, as in the ecstatic individual dance; it was remembered emotionally, and recreated and patterned in purposeful ways in the form of the rhythmic, expressive, and symbolic movement of the dance. Some of it was pantomimic, and realistically so, and in that form it represented the purest form of religious dance drama.

But as time went on much of the realism, the actual pantomimic acting out, of understandable drama gave way to more abstract, more stylized, and more symbolic forms. Dr. Johnson tells me there is much argument over what is the proper definition of the word, "symbol"; so I will stay out of that controversy. However, I will just pridefully say that movement symbols are more universal, they are closer to man's heart and life, and they are, therefore, more potent than any symbol that is projected into the graphic or plastic arts.

This form of the dance has arrived at what we call ritual, where it now is so patterned and so stylized and so abstract that only the people who are "in the know," those who are already initiated, can understand the meaning of the ritual movement. During my travels I have seen the dances of the most "primitive" people living on earth today, the Australian aborigines. I had the great privilege of having a five-day corroboree planned and performed in my honor. Among other things, I saw an example of their pure ritual. I saw a dance that was performed to celebrate the coming of age of a girl of the tribe, her passing from childhood into adult status. A serpentine line of women came out of the bush across the corroboree grounds. The leading woman, who had the appearance of a priestess, carried a burning brand in her arms. The girl who was to be initiated was the second in line, and all the women of the tribe followed in a serpentine line (which is used among all primitive people because evil spirits can travel only in a direct line).

The girl was eventually led up to her own physical mother, who was sitting at the foot of a tree with her legs outspread and in a very stolid pose, with no facial expression, no movement. She was like a statue. The girl was brought up to·her and she turned and knelt with her back to her mother and assumed the foetal position. Then the mother very gently took her and lifted her to a standing position and presented her to the world as a grown woman. It was a very simple, very touching, and very sincere ceremony, and the symbolism of rebirth was readily understood.

I have seen processional dances on the birthday of the Buddha in Kandy, Ceylon, at the great Temple of the Tooth. These processional dancers came from villages all over the island, followed by people bearing gifts and sometimes very decorative banners—long streamers held over the gifts—always preceded by the temple dancers and drummers. Here was pure dance; that is to say, the movement had no symbolic or dramatic or pantomimic significance. It was sheer rhythm that led these different groups of pilgrims to the temple where they made their offerings.

I have also seen in Ceylon the use of dance as healing, by the so-called devil dancers. I think that name must have been applied to them by missionaries, because the dance is a pure and very fine form of religious dance in which the participants, in masks, dance around the patient. If you have malaria you send word, and the dancers come with malaria masks. The family puts out food, flowers, grain, sometimes money, on platters. The dancers perform their dance of healing, and if they accept the gifts they are believed to take the disease out of the body. If they refuse the gifts, a death sentence has been pronounced. Incidentally, many physicians, trained in Western medical schools, have told me that the percentage of recoveries is high.

I have seen the Tibetan Lamas, up in the Bhutia Monastery on the border of Tibet, perform dances which have a documented history of twenty-seven hundred years. These dances have been done with the same movements and in the same design of costumes during all these centuries, which means that they predate Buddhism and are an expression of the early animistic beliefs of ancestors of the Buddhists.

There are many uses of the dance as a way of teaching. The ancient Chaldeans are supposed to have taught astronomy and astrology to the youth of the nation by means of vast astronomical ballets.

We may assume that the form of service at the beginning of Christianity was patterned somewhat on the rituals of existing religions. Nothing is born full bloom and completely different from what it was, or has grown out of, and because dance was used in perhaps three-fourths to four-fifths of the rituals of all religions preceding Christianity, it is reasonable to assume, on that basis alone, that dancing played a great part in early Christian worship.

I have often read arguments contending that the word, "choir," meant a group of dancers or a place to dance, and that the word, "prelate," meant a *premier danseur,* or one who bore himself before and was the leader of the dance. It has also been argued that the early Christians, when obliged by reason of persecution to meet secretly in the catacombs, found satisfaction in the silence of the dance.

We know that in the early centuries of the Christian era there were rituals that were both danced and sung, and there are still extant the words of a hymn used in one such ritual. It is called "The Hymn of Jesus," and in it the solo dancer danced the character of Jesus, and the twelve ensemble dancers danced the twelve Apostles. In this hymn are the words, "I came unto you in order that you all might come into the general dance." Such antiphonally sung dance rituals survived in the Christian Church for several centuries.

I hope I will not tread on any toes in what I am about to say, but all I can do is to speak from my heart, honestly. I think that Paulism did violence to original Christianity. Paulism is quite a different thing from Christianity. Certainly with Paul something came into Christian thought that cannot be in any way sustained by any reported words of Jesus: the denial of the body, deprecation of sex as something that was too foul to mention, such phrases as "flesh and the devil," the idea of mortifying the flesh in this life in order to reach some unknown paradise, the whole attitude that the body was somehow or another inherently evil, sinful, obscene, indecent. That conception swept over the Christian Church, with the result that the dance, the one art which employs the whole person, because it was so identified with the body was gradually pushed out under a false asceticism. Other arts, such as sculpture, could create religious figures, statues, and decorations on buildings. Painters could paint saints, architects could design churches, and musicians could compose and sing church music; but you cannot dance without using the body.

Dancing survived, however, particularly in certain cathedrals in Spain, down to my own lifetime. I had the privilege of seeing a religious ballet performed in front of the high altar in the Cathedral of Seville when I was there about 1923, and it was a very stately, very simple, and very sincere form of religious expression. Whether it is still going on since the civil war, I have never been able to learn.

The Mass of the Catholic Church today has been described by a very renowned Catholic in the terms of a religious ballet. In the book, *Papers of a Pariah,* by Monsignor Robert Hugh Benson, there is a chapter entitled "Dancing As a Religious Exercise," in which he shows in great detail how all these movements are rhythmic, patterned, purposeful, and expressive, and are, therefore, dance.

We have undergone many changes. At the beginning of my lifetime we had inherited a Victorianism, a Puritanism, and there was still—it seems hard to remember—a feeling that somehow or other the body was evil. And certainly when I was a theological student and intending to be a Methodist minister, it was written in the rules of the Church that card playing, theatre-going and dancing were forbidden as sins. That has changed, fortunately.

I think that my doing a complete church service in dance form in 1917 in San Francisco, under the auspices of the First Interdenominational Church, helped in reversing this attitude. In this service Dr. Henry Frank lectured on religion and dance for the preceding half hour, and then I did the entire church service without a word spoken or sung, accompanied by the string section of the San Francisco Symphony Orchestra. I was frankly terrified. The newspapers were there in full force, and it was a wonderful oppor-

tunity for them to do critical acrobatics and make ridiculing comments on it, but I got by very nicely. They accepted it for what it
was intended to be, a sincere and reverent excursion, both backward
and forward—backward into the universal use of dance in religion,
and forward into the hope that we would restore it.

Shortly after that, here in New York, Dr. Norman Guthrie began experiments at St. Mark's In-The Bouwerie, for which he
suffered the withdrawal of Episcopal visits. But he persisted in
dance rituals as a part of his church service up to his death, or re-
tirement. I witnessed those ritual dances. They were performed
almost entirely by girls of adolescent age, very simply costumed in
great long robes. The only fault I found with this was that it was a
little pretty, a little anemic. But considering what a daring thing it
was for him to do, I suppose it was wise for him to be cautious;
otherwise, he could not have done it at all.

Any robust expression of religion must use men equally with
women, and it has to have, if I may use the vulgar word, more guts
to it than pretty girls making pretty poses. Dance is too big a thing
to be limited to any segment of humanity.

When I first had the great experience of seeing Ruth St. Denis
dance—and a great religious experience I had that night in the
theatre—I did not know, of course, that later I would meet Ruth
St. Denis and that we would be married and would found a dance
school. But for years and years we discussed this problem of the
relationship of the dance and religion.

She had danced not only an expression of Hindu religion, but
she had given expression to the principle of God in the form of a
goddess. She had danced as Kwannon of Japan, Kuan Yin of China,
Isis of Egypt, and Ishtar of Babylon. But she said to me, "I wonder,
if I had to do it over again, if I would clothe religion in these alien
art forms, because the American public said, 'Oh, yes, the Hindus,
they may dance their religion, but after all, they are heathens, and
that has nothing to do with us!' " Being so ignorant of the history
of their own religion, they did not realize that Christianity had also
used the dance. In the exclusion of dance from religion, I think a

great loss occurred. Dance is a powerful medium, and I think that we have the right to use it as we use all of the other arts.

I know that the word, "dance," still has clinging around it many cheap and tawdry associations, but there was a time, even in our country, when instrumental music also had such associations, and the idea of anyone playing a violin in church was unthinkable because the violin was an unholy instrument. As we outgrew those false associations with music, so we should outgrow the false associations with dance.

Later, Ruth St. Denis came to the point of tackling the expression of the Christian religion in dance form, and right here in New York at the Riverside Church she did a great pageant dance drama called "The Masque of Mary," in which the entire Christmas story was told. Two clergymen read the text alternately from two pulpits, and Miss St. Denis and a large company reenacted the several sections, from the Annunciation through the flight into Egypt, to the Adoration of the Infant by the Magi. This was done in front of the high altar of the Riverside Church on a Sunday night. At Eastertime, she did another great religious dance drama based on the theme of the Resurrection. This was later repeated in many New York City churches, in Philadelphia, Pittsburgh, and all across the country.

Five or six years ago Ruth St. Denis founded what she calls the "Church of the Divine Dance" in Hollywood. As there is such a great variety of churches in southern California, she saw no reason why she should not have her own Church of the Divine Dance! There she has a group of people who are interested, sincerely interested, in the use of dance as a medium for religious expression, and they have done many very fine and interesting experiments in this field.

Margaret Palmer Fisk, the wife of a minister in Hanover, New Hampshire, has been experimenting for a good many years with dance in her husband's church. Out of this has grown a book, *The Art of the Rhythmic Choir,* which is very informative as to the possibilities of the use of dance as ritual in present day churches.

I have seen some of Mrs. Fisk's work, and there are still the same pretty, adolescent girls, very discreetly robed, and doing very pretty poses. I think we have got to go a long way farther than that. The whole trouble is, we need training. There should be dance training in theological seminaries. In the first place, from the standpoint of good health alone there is no form of exercise that is so complete a physical education as the dance. It makes for a healthy man—"sound mind in sound body." That is basic. Secondly, it is the form of movement training that enables a man to use his body expressively, and certainly a preacher in a pulpit should not only be able to express meaning through inflection of voice, but should be able to be expressive in his gestures. And if he is so trained, and is intelligent in the use of the body as a means of expression, he will be able to pass that training on to the young people in his church.

The main drawback is the architecture of most churches. Dance is an art form which works in four dimensions. It works in the three dimensions of space and simultaneously in the fourth dimension of time. It needs space I danced my dance of St. Francis on a Methodist rostrum in Milwaukee and the choreography, which was planned for a floor area of twenty feet by thirty feet, got squeezed into a sort of spaghetti shape on a very narrow platform. How that problem will be solved, I do not know; but there are churches in which there is sufficient room.

Ideally, the whole congregation should move. That makes a more difficult architectural problem because there is not room for movement between the rows of chairs or up and down aisles. There should be open spaces in church in which the congregation could move and use all of themselves to express what they feel and what they believe in, and not just remain still and use the soundmaking instruments of the tongue, the teeth, the vocal chords, and the palate.

It is just as legitimate to use dance as a part of a church service as it is to use speech, song, or instrumental music. There is nothing in any scripture in the world which says that our vocal chords are any more sacred than any other part of our body. On the contrary, our body, our *whole* body, is the temple of the living God, and it should *all* be used simultaneously, as a unit, for praise and for worship. We have to outlive the childish, narrow, outmoded notion that there is anything inherently wrong about the body. A more wholesome, a truer conception of the body will allow us to use our *entire* bodies for expression of worship.

Bibliography

Eugene Louis Backman, *Den religiösa dansen inom kritsen kyrka och folk medieine,* P. A. Norstedt & söners, Stockholm, 1945.

Robert Hugh Benson, *Papers of a Pariah,* Longmans, Green & Company, New York, 1913.

Edward Carpenter, *Pagan and Christian Creeds,* Harcourt, Brace & Company, New York, 1921.

Havelock Ellis, *Dance of Life,* Book League of America, New York, 1929.

Margaret Palmer Fisk, *Art of the Rhythmic Choir,* Harper & Brothers, New York, 1950.

Sir James G. Fraser, *The Golden Bough,* The Macmillan Company, New York, 1926.

La Meri (Russell Meriwether Hughes), *Dance as an Art Form,* A. S. Barnes & Company, New York, 1933.

William Oscar Emil Oesterley, *The Sacred Dance,* The Macmillan Company, New York, 1923.

Curt Sachs, *World History of the Dance,* translated by Bessie Schoenberg, W. W. Norton & Company, New York, 1937.

Ted Shawn, *The American Ballet,* Henry Holt & Company, New York, 1926.

—— *Dance We Must,* The Eagle Printing & Binding Company, Pittsfield, 1940.

—— *Gods Who Dance,* E. P. Dutton, New York, 1929.

X

RELIGIOUS SYMBOLISM IN
CONTEMPORARY LITERATURE

BY

NATHAN A. SCOTT, JR., PH.D.

Associate Professor of the Humanities, Howard University

If the world is, in the words of Baudelaire, a vast system of contradictions, the preoccupation of the artist is to discover order where chaos exists. What is order in the world must of necessity be spiritual.
—Wallace Fowlie, *Clowns and Angels,* Sheed & Ward, New York, 1943.

In order to get a point of leverage upon the issues and problems that I suppose I am expected to discuss in the present symposium, I have found it necessary to approach my task in a manner somewhat oblique and circuitous. For the subject as formulated—"Religious Symbolism in Contemporary Literature"—suggests, I think, that there is some special unitive body of iconological material in the literature of contemporary poetry and the novel that may be set apart by the term, "religious symbolism." And, in fact, I suppose there is, in the work of writers who have taken up a positive and unequivocal relation to some tradition of religious orthodoxy—writers, for example, like T. S. Eliot and Graham Greene in England, and Robert Lowell and W. H. Auden in America. But such writers, of course, constitute only a small minority within the larger republic of contemporary letters, for the modern writer has not often been able to accept the creedal commitments that these men have undertaken. And thus to draw so narrow a circle of definition about our subject, as by implication the announced title of my paper does, is, in effect, to exclude from our consideration many modern writers of the highest interest whose work, though not presenting a symbolic language of the conventionally religious sort, is yet clearly focused upon basic dimensions of the spiritual problem and is also illustrative of significant new patterns of symbolism. So perhaps the more fruitful method of approach to our problem is to think of religion, as Professor Paul J. Tillich urges us to do, as being related primarily not to orthodoxies of creed and dogma but to man's ultimate concerns "with the meaning of life and with all the forces that threaten or support that meaning." [1] And if this be our point of view, in turning to the writers of today who are presenting the most important testimony about the human condition, we may then regard the significant patterns of symbolism implicit in their work as religious in whatever degree to which they suggest the ultimate concerns of contemporary man. In other words, what is here subsumed under "religious symbolism" should not properly be regarded as a special property of the work of those writers who have taken their stand within a formal tradition of orthodoxy. And thus my first impulse was to desire that the qualifier "religious" be stricken from my subject, so that it might simply read: "Symbolism in Contemporary Literature."

But then, on further reflection, I came to feel that the word, "symbolism," did not perhaps point with sufficient suggestiveness to those aspects of contemporary literature with which I should be expected to deal. For the word is likely to connote that special linguistic technique of the poetic mind whereby images and tropes are arranged about a feeling or an action or a state of being in such a way as to create a sensuous figuration capable of performing an analogical function. But symbols are really only minor elements of the richness that literary art displays. And what, I suspect, I was really asked to discuss is the more ulterior and radical technique of the imagination, whereby the poetic mind gives consent to a ruling myth that introduces order and coherence into the whole of that experience from which particular symbols spring and from which, in fact, they take their meaning. Myth is, in other words, I am

[1] James Luther Adams, "Tillich's Concept of the Protestant Era," Editor's Appendix, Paul Tillich, *The Protestant Era*, University of Chicago Press, Chicago, 1948, p. 273.

suggesting, the larger, the more inclusive, term that hovers over the area of meaning in modern literature with which I have been asked to deal. And so I have preferred to think of my subject, then, as being "Myth and Symbol in Contemporary Literature."

Now, having arrived at a somewhat sharper focus upon our problem, what we must first of all recognize is the indispensability of myth and symbol to those procedures of the imagination from which great literature springs. In discussing these questions in his little book *The Enchafèd Flood,* Mr. W. H. Auden has remarked:

A constant aesthetic problem for the writer is how to reconcile his desire to include everything, not to leave anything important out, with his desire for an aesthetic whole, that there shall be no irrelevances and loose ends.[2]

That is to say, the artist wants always to convey a vision of the rich plenitude of experience, and yet, if he is not himself to succumb to it, he must have some counterpoise in faith and reason that supports his imagination and that does not leave him too much exposed to the deracinative force of that plenitude. He must have, in other words, at his disposal, as Mr. Eliot said many years ago in his famous review of James Joyce's *Ulysses,* some means "of controlling, or ordering, of giving a shape and a significance to the immense panorama of . . . anarchy which is contemporary history."[3] There must be operative within his deepest instinctual life a set of *archai,* of first principles, which furnish him a technique of metaphysical and ethical valuation, for without this he cannot bring order and intelligibility to experience: in the traditional Aristotelian language, he cannot produce an imitation: that is to say, he cannot impose form upon the formless stuff of life itself.

And just here we come upon the reason for the extreme difficulty that has been involved in the creation of art in our time. For modern culture, though it has had many other gifts to bestow upon the artist, has not been able to provide him with the essential thing—"a positive

[2] W. H. Auden, *The Enchafèd Flood,* Random House, New York, 1950, p. 66.

[3] T. S. Eliot, "Ulysses, Order, and Myth," *Forms of Modern Fiction,* William Van O'Connor, editor, University of Minnesota Press, Minneapolis, 1948, p. 123.

affirmation, the intensity of a great conception," [4] an illuminated point, a still center around which the tumultuous and fragmentary world of contemporary life might be ordered and given meaning. Our poets and novelists have not received from their culture, as Sophocles and Dante and Shakespeare did from theirs, any central myth or body of symbol which, when applied to the modern world, was capable of radical organizing power. The multiplicity of myth or belief—or of what is sometimes called ideology—has often been noted in modern discussion, but by no one with more remarkable concision and vividness than by the American poet Karl Shapiro, who, in his *Essay on Rime,* at one point observes:

> So various
> And multifoliate are our breeds of faith
> That we could furnish a herbarium
> With the American specimens alone.
> A choice anthology of a few of these
> Made its appearance just before the war;
> It is an album of philosophies
> Called *I Believe.* The essays it contains
> Have nothing in common but proximity. [5]

And thus it is that Mr. Shapiro provides us with some measure of the degree to which the modern writer has been unable to presuppose agreement between himself and his audience about the ultimate issues of human existence—the kind of agreement, that is, that might furnish his imagination with the premises of its functioning. The modern artist has needed a large and pervasive myth, a frame of traditional values, out of whose logic he might speak with poise and certitude to his contemporaries. But he has had to live and work in a cultural situation in which his position has been very much as that of Dante would have been, if he had had himself to elaborate the whole massive structure of Christian myth and symbol before beginning to compose the *Commedia.* This has been the enormous burden and expense not only of literature but of all the other arts in our time—as is indicated, for example, by the restlessness with which

---

[4] Alfred Kazin, *On Native Grounds,* Reynal & Hitchcock, New York, 1942, p. 451.
[5] Karl Shapiro, *Essay on Rime,* Reynal & Hitchcock, New York, 1945, p. 63.

Stravinsky in music and Picasso in painting have raced from first one idiom to another: they, too, along with, let us say, Joyce in the novel and Eliot in poetry, have been in search of a myth, of an appropriate mode of vision and of a usable vehicle of communication. Their misfortune has been that of having to live in an age without organic order, presided over by a philosophical and religious pluralism of the most extreme sort. We realize, of course, when we read today Eliot's *The Waste Land* or Joyce's *Finnegans Wake,* when we look at Picasso's *Guernica* mural, or listen to the last quartets of Schoenberg, that this very situation of extreme cultural disorder is capable of stimulating work of great power, and yet we feel, at the same time, that it spells a certain decadence. And when I say this I do not want to be interpreted as implying the pejorative and dismissive judgments with which J. Donald Adams of *The New York Times* bludgeons us every Sunday: I mean only to suggest that the tendencies which these monuments of modern art represent seem "to exhaust the possibilities of further development and to tend towards the point of absolute incoherence." [6]

Now, in remarking upon the modern artist's search for myth, I have already anticipated the second observation that we must make, which is that, having found his culture to be unstable in its beliefs, he has had to try to supply himself with a usable myth, with a focus of vision whereby the astigmatism to which his age inclines him might be corrected. And immediately, of course, many spectacular examples come to mind. There is the example of William Butler Yeats, who, in the process of creating what is perhaps the most notable body of poetry in this century, amalgamated in the most eccentric fashion the traditions of pagan Ireland and of theosophic Rosicrucianism. There is the even more familiar example in modern poetry of T. S. Eliot, whose great poem of 1922, *The Waste Land,* was erected out of a scaffolding whose sources range all the way from Sir James Frazer to Dante and from the Elizabethans to the French Symbolists. And in the novel we have the dazzling pyrotechnics of Joyce and the highly sophisticated, though by no means wholly successful,

---

[6] J. M. Cameron, "Poetry and Metaphysics," *Dublin Review,* 220, autumn, 1947, p. 57.

effort of Thomas Mann in the *Joseph* stories to rehabilitate biblical myth. Still much closer to home, we have the examples of Hart Crane in poetry and Thomas Wolfe in the novel, for whom the theme which seemed to promise a subject of mythic proportions was that of America itself.[7] And in the work of younger poets and novelists of our own day like Dylan Thomas and Randall Jarrell, Delmore Schwartz and George Barker, William Sansom and Paul Bowles, the search for myth is continued and goes on without interruption.

It has, however, during all this time been slowly dawning upon us that the kind of myth for which the modern writer has striven is not something that can be created by an act of will. Vital myth and symbol are not produced by fiat. They are, rather, the expressions of a deep sense of organic unity that, gathering over a long period of time, binds a people together with ties of sympathy and of fellow feeling, and they become the means whereby that people is united, as Philip Wheelwright has said, "with the unplumbed Mystery from which mankind is sprung and without reference to which the radical significance of things goes to pot." [8] And when the mythical consciousness has been lost—as it has very largely been lost to us through the corroding acids of modernity, the acids of behaviorism and instrumentalism and semantic positivism and all the other secular and naturalistic heresies of the modern world—when the mythical consciousness has been lost, the poet is without that common background of transcendental reference by which the imaginative faculties of his readers and of himself are oriented and so brought into profounder rapport than would otherwise have been possible. In such a situation the writer must be content either with turning inward upon himself and reporting on his own malaise or simply with making the barest of indicative statements about his environing world. In the one case we have the literature of pure sensibility—the novel, say, in the hands of André Gide or Virginia Woolf—and in

[7] *Vide* William Van O'Connor's discussion of Crane in this connection in his *Sense and Sensibility in Modern Poetry,* University of Chicago Press, Chicago, 1948, Chapter II.

[8] Philip Wheelwright, "Poetry, Myth, and Reality," *The Language of Poetry,* Allen Tate, editor, Princeton University Press, Princeton, 1942, p. 32.

the other case we have the literature of naturalistic metajournalism, the novels of Farrell and Dos Passos or of the young postwar Americans, Norman Mailer and James Jones.

Neither is, of course, today quite satisfactory. The purveyors of pure sensibility do not satisfy us because our generation, having inherited in the past thirty years not the world of John Dewey but that of Nietzsche, "the artist's estrangement is no longer a phenomenon unique but rather something shared." [9] And so we expect our writers, when they write out of their own discomforts, to do so in such a way as to suggest a recognition on their part of their implication in a collective tragedy. We look to them for some hint of how the self-encystment of the ego may be broken and we may gain release from the awful prison of our private fantasies into a public world of fellowship and community. We want them to give us some sense of man as Man, and thereby to give us a presentiment of abiding values beyond the despair of our age. But we do not get this in the novels of Proust and Virginia Woolf, of Italo Svevo and André Gide, and so there comes a time when we feel that we must refuse their enchantments.

The literary naturalists, on the other hand, do not satisfy us because, in their subversive way, they cooperate with all the impulses of a secular culture to disenthrone the imagination, whether in its esthetic or in its religious phases, in the interest of "the scientific observation of fact." The names of men like Dreiser and Dos Passos, Farrell and the early Steinbeck, or, among younger writers, Norman Mailer and James Jones, put us in mind of that current in our literature which has wanted to give us the illusion of history by eradicating the distinction between life and art and by giving us so large a slice of the crude, raw stuff of life as to make us forget when we read their novels that we are reading a novel. And thus by banishing themselves from their books and muffling their own voices, in the manner of the competent photographer or reporter, they have, as Lionel Trilling has said, only "reinforced the faceless hostility of the world and have tended to teach us that we ourselves are not creative

---

[9] Nathan A. Scott, Jr., *Rehearsals of Discomposure: Alienation and Reconciliation in Modern Literature,* King's Crown Press, Columbia University, New York, 1952, p. 7.

agents and that we have no voice, no tone, no style, no significant existence." [10] But surely, as Trilling goes on to say in his book, *The Liberal Imagination,* "what we need is the opposite of this, the opportunity to identify ourselves with a mind that willingly admits that it is a mind and does not pretend that it is History or Events or the World but only a mind thinking and planning—possibly planning our escape." [11]

What is perhaps at the root of our dissatisfaction with both the literature of pure sensibility and the literature of naturalism is their failure to give us what the naturalists have unsuccessfully tried to furnish—namely, a clarified and deepened vision of history. The distinguished French man of letters, Jean-Paul Sartre, tells us that we are living through what he calls an "extreme situation," by which, presumably, he means to bring us up short against the great and sobering fact of our time—which is that tidal forces "powerful enough to . . . nullify the bequest of centuries" [12] are today sweeping across the earth and thundering upon the door of our children's future: he means to tell us that our crisis is radical and that we have been brought to bay at the extremity of the human situation. And in such a world, where the fire is put out and the sun is lost, what little light remains must be used for the quest of the one thing needful, and imaginative literature must, therefore, be a way of reading the human condition and a counterpoise to chaos, for that is what our time requires. This is not, of course, to say that our writers must be "public health officers, criers of economic and political cures," as Diana Trilling has said we have sometimes mistakenly insisted that they be.[13] In their office as "renovators of the spirit," their one task is to be "spokesmen for the self and the self's mysterious possibilities" [14] and, in the present time, to seize upon the crises and dis-

[10] Lionel Trilling, *The Liberal Imagination,* The Viking Press, New York, 1950, p. 270.

[11] *Ibid.*

[12] Stanley Romaine Hopper, *The Crisis of Faith,* Abingdon-Cokesbury Press, Nashville, 1944, p. 15.

[13] Diana Trilling, "Editor's Introduction," *The Portable D. H. Lawrence,* The Viking Press, New York, 1947, p. 13.

[14] *Ibid.*

tempers of modern history as means for the conveyance to us of a deeper knowledge of ourselves and of what is sometimes called our "boundary situation." And in spite of all the unfortunate excrescences that attach to Sartre's theory of "engaged literature," it is, I think, the chief merit of that doctrine to make this assertion. In speaking of his own literary generation in France, he remarks upon the "historicity" that has flowed in upon the pages of the books they have written and says:

we are Jansenists because the age has made us such, and insofar as it has made us touch our limits I shall say that we are all metaphysical writers. I think that many among us would deny this designation or would not accept it without reservations, but this is the result of a misunderstanding. For metaphysics is not a sterile discussion about abstract notions which have nothing to do with experience. It is a living effort to embrace from within the human condition in its totality.

Forced by circumstances to discover the pressure of history, as Torricelli discovered atmospheric pressure, and tossed by the cruelty of the time into that forlornness from where one can see our condition as man to the very limit, to the absurd, to the night of unknowingness, we have a task for which we may not be strong enough . . . It is to create a literature which unites and reconciles the metaphysical absolute and the relativity of the historical fact, and which I shall call, for want of a better name, the literature of great circumstances.[15]

But this—namely, a literature of great circumstances—is precisely what we have not obtained from either the creators of the literature of pure sensibility or from the modern naturalists: in the one case because the writer has not been able to cross-question himself out of his solipsism into an awareness of the public world of which both he and his readers are living members; in the other case because a fiction committed to the mere enumeration of social and political detail, though it may reproduce the disorder of the contemporary world, is incapable of giving its drama the dimension of tragic grandeur. This is perhaps, of course, to say that neither current within our recent literature has possessed an adequate myth or body of sym-

[15] Jean-Paul Sartre, *What is Literature?*, Philosophical Library, New York, 1949. p. 222.

bol whereby, in Mr. Eliot's words, "a shape and a significance" might be given "to the immense panorama of . . . anarchy which is contemporary history."

But if imaginative literature is to engage itself profoundly with the historical drama of our time, it must somehow lay hold of new myths and symbols that are appropriate correlatives of that drama, and the writers who move us most deeply today are, I believe, those in whom we feel the mythmaking imagination to be most powerfully at work. And in this connection I am impelled to recall the testimony of many young men who saw active service during the past war and who have told me of the excitement with which they rediscovered, somewhere in the Pacific or in Europe, Herman Melville's *Moby Dick*. The voyage of that old monomaniac Captain Ahab and his fellow pilgrims gave these young soldiers, they have told me, a kind of release: that is, the journey of Ahab's strange crew in their small bark over the uncharted waters of the deep gave the soldiers a sense of what their situation then really was and of what man's condition in the world has always been: as they considered the infernal land upon which they fought and the storm tossed seas over which the Pequod rolled, they found, as Melville had predicted, a strange analogy to something in themselves. And the late F. O. Matthiessen similarly recalled in his journal, *From the Heart of Europe,* the many young American soldiers who told him after the war of the release that they were given by Henry James while they were in the army. "They had felt a great need," said Matthiessen, "during the unrelenting outwardness of those years, for his kind of inwardness, for his kind of order as a bulwark against disorder." [16]

Here, then, is evidence of how intense a preoccupation among sensitive young people of our day is the search for new symbols and myths, and thus it is not at all surprising that this is what we value most highly in the literature of the recent past and in the literature of our own period. So it is perhaps one of the most important cultural inquiries that can be made at the moment to ask what are some of the more pervasive myths or patterns of symbolic statement about the

[16] F. O. Matthiessen, *From the Heart of Europe,* Oxford University Press, New York, 1948, pp. 45–46.

human condition discernible in contemporary literature. And there are four that I should like briefly to discuss. There are, of course, others, and these that I shall treat might be differently named, but I shall call them the Myth of the Isolato, the Myth of Hell, the Myth of Voyage, and the Myth of Sanctity.[17] The form of our excursion will, in other words, resemble that of Dante's *Commedia:* we shall begin in "the dark wood," and we shall end with bliss of which, to be sure, there is not a great deal in contemporary literature; and such as there is does not perhaps resemble very greatly the bliss of the *Paradiso.* But, nevertheless, if justice is to be done to the modern writer, we must attend not only to his anatomy of melancholy but also, finally, to his anatomy of blessedness.

Our most abiding impression, however, of the report that the literature of our period submits on contemporary man's spiritual estate is that his condition is described in terms of isolation and estrangement. In the earlier part of Melville's *Moby Dick* there occur two chapters which are devoted to a description of the men who composed Captain Ahab's crew, and toward the close of the second of these two chapters Melville says: "They were nearly all Islanders in the Pequod, *Isolatoes* too, I call such, not acknowledging the common continent of men, but each *Isolato* living on a separate continent of his own." And it has been with this sentence in mind that I have called the first of the symbolic patterns in modern literature to which we now turn the Myth of the Isolato. William Faulkner tells us of Joe Christmas, the mulatto protagonist of *Light in August,* that "there was something definitely rootless about him, as though no town nor city was his, no street, no walls, no square of earth his home. And . . . he carried his knowledge with him always as though it were a banner, with a quality ruthless, lonely and almost proud." The same might also be said of Conrad's Heyst in *Victory,* of Joyce's Bloom in *Ulysses,* of Graham Greene's Pinkie in *Brighton Rock,* and of Robert Penn Warren's Jeremiah Beaumont in *World Enough and*

[17] Mr. Wallace Fowlie, in discussing Rimbaud, has spoken of "the Myth of Hell" and "the Myth of Voyage" in the beautifully executed little book which he has devoted to that poet (*Rimbaud,* New Directions, New York, 1946), and it is from him that I borrow a part of my phraseology.

Time. For the image of man that recurs most frequently in these and many of the other memorable books of our time is the image of man as *Isolato,* of the individual as "living on a separate continent of his own." That this emphasis upon alienation and lostness should be a hallmark of our literature is easily explained by reference to reasons which it is beyond our purview here to explore. The fundamental explanation is doubtless that the shape of the modern writer's imagination has been but an analogue of the historical situation in which he has found himself. He has lived in a world struck through by profound social and political dislocation, and he has also, more often than not, lived in urban communities the primary quality of whose life has been impersonality and uprootedness from the soil, from the family, and from all those other basic organic unities of life from which the spirit of man derives its deepest nourishment.[18] Indeed, it is significant that the City—which is one of the most recurrent symbols in modern fiction—is, in Joyce's *Ulysses,* in Dos Passos's *Manhattan Transfer,* in Albert Camus's *The Plague,* an image of despair, as it is in Isaiah and Jeremiah.[19] So it should not, therefore, be at all surprising that the sense of deracination, of spiritual insecurity, and the preoccupation with the theme of moral isolation are pervasive throughout the work of the more serious writers of our day. Their characters are, as a rule, homeless derelicts in search of self-definition and the Mystery of Being.

It is perhaps in the novels of Franz Kafka (who, it has often been said, bears much the same relation to our age that Dante, Shakespeare, and Goethe bore to theirs) that we get the most archetypal presentation of the contemporary hero. His is the religious consciousness of our age—by which I mean what Wallace Fowlie means when he makes a similar claim for the French painter Rouault: I mean that Kafka's is "a mind which contains the terrors and nightmares of the age which most of us can't face."[20] What is perhaps first to be re-

[18] *Vide* Amos N. Wilder, *The Spiritual Aspects of the New Poetry,* Harper & Brothers, New York, 1940, Chapter VIII, "A World Without Roots."

[19] The English critic, J. Isaacs, in his book *An Assessment of Twentieth-Century Literature,* Secker & Warburg, London, 1951, has written suggestively of the symbolic uses to which the image of "the City" has been put in modern literature.

[20] Wallace Fowlie, *Jacob's Night: The Religious Renascence in France,* Sheed & Ward, New York, 1947, p. 42.

marked upon is the atmosphere of isolation that pervades his books, enveloping and conditioning the destiny of his hero who holds no definite position in the world and whose name consists of only one letter. At the center of his novels there is always the single individual, the lonely and uprooted "isolato," for whom there is no fixed abode and who, in becoming a kind of clown, grows "more conscious of his center, of his distance from God, of the mechanical awkwardness of his gestures, of the dizzying somersaults his spirit performs before the revolving universe and the eternal peace of God." [21] In *The Castle,* for example, K. arrives one night in the Village, to which he believes himself to have been called to practice the profession of Land Surveyor. But he discovers after his arrival that there is no prepared place for him and that, as the life of the Village is controlled by the Castle which is situated on a hill above the little hamlet, in order to remain there he must secure a special dispensation from the Castle officials. The novel becomes, then, the story of his progress toward this end which will be his salvation. But the "progress" is precisely the thing that remains always in question and that is the chief problem. K.'s goal is clear: it is acceptance. And we do not doubt the reality of a road that leads to this goal. But how to discover this road and, in the absence of any clearly defined signs, how to remain on it, once it is discovered—these are the chief problems. K. has no good guide, such as Dante had in Virgil, and so he must discover everything for himself. All the accumulated lore of the folk and even his own intuitions appear to be unreliable. He is the prototype of the modern man who, as Mr. Auden has well said, no longer being supported by a living and vital tradition, must "do deliberately for himself what in previous ages had been done for him by family, custom, Church, and State—namely, the choice of the principles and presuppositions in terms of which he can make sense of his experience." [22] Of course, K. never really gets anywhere: he never succeeds in getting from the Castle an unequivocal declaration of his right to remain in the Village. But, paradoxically, this is his triumph, his assurance that he is on the right road, for were he to

---

[21] The phrase is used by Fowlie in a characterization of the modern artist in his book on Rimbaud (*op. cit.,* p. 111).

[22] Quoted in J. Isaacs, *op. cit.,* p. 112.

become convinced of having achieved some simple *modus vivendi* between himself and the Castle, we should know that he had failed. He must, that is, as St. Augustine advised, delight to find God in failing to find Him, because (as Auden said not very long ago on the occasion of a laymen's Sunday service in a New York Episcopal church), though "our dominant experience [today] is of God's absence, of His distance . . . for our time, the distance of God may be something He wishes us to learn."

"The distance of God"—this might, indeed, be regarded as a major lesson of many of the most memorable books of our time, of Céline's *Journey to the End of Night,* of Djuna Barnes's *Nightwood,* of Nathanael West's *Miss Lonelyhearts,* of Robert Penn Warren's *World Enough and Time,* and of André Malraux's *The Walnut Trees of Altenburg.* Joseph Conrad tells us in *Nostromo* that "Solitude from mere outward condition of existence becomes very swiftly a state of soul in which the affectations of irony and skepticism have no place. It takes possession of the mind, and drives forth the thought into the exile of utter unbelief." And it is this dialectical unfolding which is exhibited in a great deal of modern literature. So it is no wonder, then, that we have been made familiar with Hell— which is but the moment in which man, in the arrest of his melancholy, makes the discovery that he is something less than what he should be. Of the *personae* in his early novels, in whom he would have us see ourselves, Graham Greene has said more than once, "Hell lay about them in their infancy," and Kate Farrant remarks at one point in Greene's *England Made Me:*

"We're all thieves . . . Stealing a livelihood here and there and everywhere, giving nothing back . . . No brotherhood in our boat. Only who can cut the biggest dash and who can swim."

"It is the moment of the whirlpool," says the poet Archibald Fleming, "moment/Of the abyss where all things stream" [23]—the moment in which we are surprised to learn "That Death so great a legion had undone." [24] And so Sartre puts the three characters in his play

[23] Archibald Fleming, "The Destroyers," *The New Republic,* July 13, 1938, p. 273.
[24] Dante, *The Divine Comedy,* Laurence Binyon, translator, and Paolo Milano, editor, The Viking Press, New York, 1948, "Inferno," III, 57.

No Exit in Hell, which is portrayed as a Second-Empire furnished living room. Their sentence condemns them to eternal wakefulness in a room lit by a glaring light which will never go out, and their condition is infernal, we are given to understand, because each is utterly out of harmony with the others. Their situation is summed up at the end of the play by Garcin, the male member of the trio, who declares: "Hell is—other people!" And, finally, the metaphysical fables of, let us say, Robert Penn Warren, together with the moral fables of Sartre, are converted into political terms by a writer like George Orwell, so that in *1984* we are given still another abstract for a contemporary Inferno. Indeed, it is as if many of the representative writers of our time by an act of general consent had agreed to recreate "the myth of the land blighted by a curse, the land awaiting redemption by water." Toward the close of *The Waste Land* Eliot declares: "These fragments I have shored against my ruins," and this line might be given general application, for it is the image of "ruins" that is the residue in the mind after its encounter with a central strain in modern literature. And nowhere, perhaps, does the Myth of Hell have a more vivid and impressive life than in the novels of William Faulkner, whose greatness in the things of the imagination our generation is only beginning to discover.

An objection might, of course, be raised to the introduction of Faulkner into the pattern of our argument at this point, for it might be said that the literature with which we are dealing here is an international literature in the sense that the experience which it documents has become international, as we have become an international people. But, so the argument might run, on the other hand, there is no major figure in modern literature who has been more bound to a special locale than Faulkner. And in a sense this is true, for in the many wonderful books that have been coming from his pen during the past twenty years he has given us, first of all, as Malcolm Cowley has argued,[25] a connected story of the mythical kingdom that forms the landscape of his books and that he calls Yoknapa-

[25] *Vide* Malcolm Cowley, "An Introduction to William Faulkner," *Critiques and Essays on Modern Fiction: 1920–1951*, John W. Aldridge, editor, Ronald Press, New York, 1952, pp. 427–446.

tawpha County, Mississippi; and then he has gone on to offer this story as a legend not only of the patch of land in Mississippi in which he has his own familial roots but of all the Deep South. His myth has, in other words, been the Southern myth which has as its subject the fate of a ravaged land. In his recent book on Faulkner Irving Howe presents the following notation of this myth: he says:

The homeland—so the story goes—had proudly insisted that it alone should determine its destiny; provoked into a war impossible to win, it had nevertheless fought to its last strength, and had fought this war with a reckless gallantry and a superb heroism that, as Faulkner might say, made of its defeat not a shame but almost a vindication. But the homeland fell, and from this fall came misery and squalor: the ravaging by the conquerors, the loss of faith among the descendants of the defeated, and the rise of a new breed of faceless men who would batten on their neighbors' humiliation.[26]

And the old South, says Howe, over which the myth

chants in threnody is an ideal image—a buried city, Allen Tate has called it. Both the violence and the poignancy with which this ideal image have been employed suggest an awareness that the buried city can never be found.[27]

Faulkner's relation to this myth is, of course, highly complicated, and it can by no means be responsibly construed as having yielded, on his part, any simple program of Southern apologetics. And though the myth furnishes an excellent platform from which to launch into the world of *The Sound and the Fury, As I Lay Dying, Light in August,* and *Absalom, Absalom!*, we should not allow our preoccupation with it to betray us into an overemphasis upon the Southern elements in his writing. For, though his materials derive from the American South, his essential comment is upon issues of human existence that are common to the modern world.

The universe that Faulkner has created is, one feels, a world contaminated, fundamentally, by something like Original Sin. It is a

[26] Irving Howe, *William Faulkner: A Critical Study,* Random House, New York, 1952, pp. 21–22.
[27] *Ibid.,* p. 23.

world "peopled by young men like fallen angels, and of a meteoric violence like that of fallen angels, beyond heaven or hell and partaking of both: doomed immortality and immortal doom" (*Sartoris*). Indeed, the words to which he returns again and again for descriptive purposes, with a kind of desperate automatism, are "tragic," "inexorable," "intractable," and "outrage." He frequently speaks of "the tragic and inevitable land," "the ancient and tragic womb of the world," and one night, as Byron Bunch of *Light in August* enters the house of the Reverend Gail Hightower and notices the thick, musty smell of "the stale, mankept house," it occurs to him that this is "the odor of goodness. Of course," he reflects, "it would smell bad to us that are bad and sinful." Quentin McCaslin says to his sister in *The Sound and the Fury*: ". . . there's a curse on us it's not our fault," and thus he takes us directly to what is "the basic mold of life for Faulkner's characters." [28] And in this connection it is significant that Faulkner reminds us, in the Appendix which he prepared for the Modern Library edition of *The Sound and the Fury*, of Ikkemotubbe, the Indian chieftain who, when he went to New Orleans, was called *du Homme* but who, being "himself a man of wit and imagination as well as a shrewd judge of character, including his own, carried [it] one step further and anglicised it to 'Doom.'" The world, in fact, through which Faulkner's people move is a doomed and accursed place in which man has to bear heavy burdens and in which, as Hightower suggests, he has to perform, to engender, so much more than he can or should have to bear, in order to discover that he can bear anything at all.

All of this is, of course, written out in terms of the moral history of the South—which means that Faulkner, especially as he is at once a deeply committed and deeply skeptical member of that community, occupies an unusually favorable standpoint from which to view the larger community of the modern world. For it is the habit of the white Southerner who possesses a sense of history to look backward with regretful nostalgia toward "old ghost times" in which life was on occasion graced by a kind of honor, a kind of code, a kind of beauty and order, which it has not often attained in the subse-

[28] *Ibid.*, p. 104.

quent development of American society. But then, in the degree to which the conscience of the Southern white man is sensitive, he is also mindful of the sin by which those old times were accursed, of the tragic injustice inherent in them that assumed the form of Negro slavery, of the social tradition that has bequeathed to the children of the slaves such heavy burdens of deprivation and inequity. And so he looks forward to the community's expiation of its guilt, to the time when, as Faulkner says in *Intruder in the Dust,* the Negro can "shoot a white man in the back with the same impunity to lynch-rope or gasoline as a white man," when he can "vote anywhen and anywhere a white man can and send his children to the same school anywhere the white man's children go and travel anywhere the white man travels as the white man does it." But the present moment is suspended between the "old ghost times" and this desired future, and thus it becomes possible for the Southern artist to achieve, as Faulkner has done, a profound realization of the central predicament of modern man which is that of having to live, as Dr. Reinhold Niebuhr has said, in an "age between the ages" [29] in which a new era of justice and order awaits to be born but in which there is not strength to bring forth. "Thus saith Hezekiah, This day is a day of trouble, and of rebuke, and blasphemy: for the children are come to the birth, and there is not strength to bring forth" (II Kings 19:3).

Now the observations that we have been making have, essentially, been calculated to suggest that the modern writer has often wanted to lead us toward a deeper imaginative seizure of the infernal realities of our time, so that we might be brought nearer "New styles of architecture, a change of heart." [30] And in so doing he has often felt it necessary to use violence and melodrama as instruments for awakening his age out of its lethargies, for destroying its specious securities and revealing its underlying nightmare and tragedy. He has wanted to "prohibit sharply the rehearsed response" [31] and to exhibit the world itself, in all of its degradation, as the country wherein man's

[29] Reinhold Niebuhr, *Discerning the Signs of the Times,* Charles Scribner's Sons, New York, 1946. *Vide* Chapter III.

[30] W. H. Auden, "Petition," *The Collected Poetry,* Random House, New York, 1945, p. 111.

[31] *Ibid.,* p. 110.

spiritual origin is to be rediscovered. His purpose has, however, been sometimes misunderstood, and the complaint has been—very often, indeed, in the case of Faulkner—that his work is too negative in tone, that its excitation of terror is too radical, and we have sometimes even made the mistake of supposing that the sordid phenomena of dilapidation upon which he has focused have been simply analogues of his own spiritual condition, completely forgetting that more often than not the shape of his imagination has been a reflection of the tragically disordered world in which he has lived. But what we have always to remember is that modern literature, even in its most negative phases, need not be utterly spendthrift of hope and health. For, as men so different from each other as Aristotle and Jeremiah knew, the human heart may on occasion be resurrected through terror. And that is the noble aim which the artist of our day has often had in view. This is doubtless the explanation of the radically subversive quality in such modern texts as Ignazio Silone's *Bread and Wine,* Sartre's trilogy *Les Chemins de la Liberté,* W. H. Auden's *For the Time Being,* Robert Lowell's *Lord Weary's Castle,* and Ralph Ellison's *Invisible Man.* The writer has wanted, if I may paraphrase a line from Faulkner's Nobel Prize Award speech, to make our griefs grieve on universal bones, and to leave us with scars, for to be unscarred amidst the wreckage and castastrophe of our time is to be less than human. "The abyss destroys; the abyss exalts; descend that you may be saved. The enemy we conquer is the enemy we embrace and love." "Then one fine day," says the American writer Henry Miller, somewhere in his published correspondence, "we will burst the belt and we will be out—in a bright new realm, the unhistorical realm when art will have disappeared entirely because life itself will have become an art." And it is along the exposed and uncharted paths which lead to this "brave new world" that our great writers have sought to make us travel. They have wanted us, in other words, to undertake a journey—sometimes through the self and sometimes through the world—and thus it becomes possible to denominate as a third pattern of symbolic statement in contemporary literature what I have called the Myth of Voyage.

Auden, in an essay on Kafka, has discussed various versions in the history of literature of the Myth of Voyage or of what he calls "the Quest." He distinguishes there between the Fairy Story, whose hero goes out in quest of some sacred object and succeeds because he does not overestimate his gifts and because he is always willing to help even those who it would seem could not possibly assist him, yet, as it turns out, are precisely the ones who can; the Grail Story, in which the hero attains the sacred object because, being strengthened by the supernatural gift of grace, he withstands the temptation to give up the search for the sake of immediate pleasure; the Dream Quest, in which the purpose of the journey is not a sacred object but spiritual knowledge which the dreamer attains, if at all, by divine grace; and the "Pilgrim's Progress" which is, he says,

no longer a special journey within life, like the quest for the Grail or the Dream Journey, but earthly life itself from birth to death. The goal is salvation, and though this is a universal goal, for everyone has to take the journey, each journey is unique. . . . the Way may be difficult but it is not deceptive, so long as one keeps the goal clearly in mind and never stops willing to get there.[32]

Now it is this final type of voyage—"the journey of life itself which all must take, since its aim is salvation" [33]—that is a frequent symbol in modern literature. And since it is often "no journey to a land we know," the American poet Louise Bogan urges us:

> Bend to the chart, in the extinguished night
> Mariners! Make way slowly; stay from sleep;
> That we may have short respite from such light.
> And learn, with joy, the gulf, the vast, the deep.[34]

But however strange the country into which the pilgrim travels, it is, nevertheless, the pattern of pilgrimage, of voyage, which the modern writer has employed again and again by means of suggesting

[32] Auden, "K.'s Quest," *The Kafka Problem*, Angel Flores, editor, New Directions, New York, 1946, p. 49.

[33] Richard Hoggart, *Auden: An Introductory Essay*, Yale University Press, New Haven, 1951, p. 170.

[34] Louise Bogan, "Putting to Sea," *The Sleeping Fury*, Charles Scribner's Sons, New York, 1937, pp. 36–37.

the stratagem whereby Yeats's "bitter furies of complexity" [35] are to be broken. The voyage is, of course, as Stanley R. Hopper has reminded us, "not outward, but inward" [36]; and though Conrad's Razumov, Kafka's Joseph K., Joyce's Stephen Dedalus, and Sartre's Mathieu journey through the world, the world that contains them is the soulscape of contemporary man—which they explore, over all its devious terrain, in their search for "The Good Place." [37]

Toward the end of his life Thomas Wolfe came to realize that *You Can't Go Home Again,* and in the same year that Wolfe's book appeared posthumously (1940) Mr. Eliot was telling us in "The Dry Salvages" to "fare forward, voyagers." And it is to that version of the Myth of Voyage that is to be found in his later poetry that I want now briefly to turn. His delineation is perhaps not typical, as doubtless no Christian poet's could be in our present cultural situation; but he has seemed to so many of us today to be, as the Quakers say, "speaking to the human condition" as few modern writers have done, and so his is a good contemporary voice to listen to.

In setting forth the way by which the soul journeys toward "the completion of its partial ecstasy./The resolution of its partial horror," [38] Eliot's use of the sixteenth century Spanish mystic, St. John of the Cross, is decisive, for it is St. John's doctrine of the *via negativa* around which much of his later work is organized. St. John tells us in *The Ascent of Mt. Carmel* that

there are three reasons for which this journey made by the soul to union with God is called night. The first has to do with the point from which the soul goes forth, for it has gradually to deprive itself of desire for all the worldly things which it possessed, by denying them to itself; the which denial and deprivation are, as it were, night to all the senses of man.

[35] William Butler Yeats, "Byzantium," *The Collected Poems,* The Macmillan Company, New York, 1951, p. 244.

[36] Hopper, "The Problem of Moral Isolation in Contemporary Literature," *Spiritual Problems in Contemporary Literature,* Stanley R. Hopper, editor, The Institute for Religious and Social Studies, New York, 1952, p. 154.

[37] A frequently repeated phrase in the poetry of W. H. Auden: the poet's reference is to the precincts within which beatitude is to be had, to "the place of Love," but this "Place," perhaps inevitably, never gains sharp definition in Auden's writing.

[38] Eliot, "Burnt Norton," *Four Quartets,* Harcourt, Brace, & Company, New York, 1943, p. 5.

The second reason has to do with the mean, or the road along which the soul must travel to this union—that is, faith, which is likewise as dark as night to the understanding. The third has to do with the point to which it travels—namely God, Who, equally, is dark night to the soul in this life. These three nights must pass through the soul,—or rather, the soul must pass through them—in order that it may come to Divine union with God.[39]

And it is this Negative Way which is everywhere the presupposition of Eliot's poetry of the past twenty-five years. We find it adumbrated in the opening lines of "Ash Wednesday," as the speaker voices his recognition that the impotence and velleity must be suffered without lament; and Harry Monchensy in *The Family Reunion* comes finally to decide that "from a world of insanity" one can only go

> Somewhere on the other side of despair.
> To the worship in the desert, the thirst and deprivation,
> A stony sanctuary and a primitive altar,
> The heat of the sun and the icy vigil . . .[40]

It gains explicit statement in the opening lines of "Burnt Norton":

> Descend lower, descend only
> Into the world of perpetual solitude,
> World not world, but that which is not world,
> Internal darkness, deprivation
> And destitution of all property,
> Desiccation of the world of sense,
> Evacuation of the world of fancy,
> Inoperancy of the world of spirit;
> This is the one way, and the other
> Is the same . . .[41]

And in the second of the *Quartets,* "East Coker," the tourist who seeks the "strait way" of the "dark night of the spirit" is given "a list of guide-book maxims"[42]:

[39] "The Ascent of Mt. Carmel," *The Complete Works of Saint John of the Cross* (translated from the critical edition of P. Silverio de Santa Teresa, C. D., and edited by E. Allison Peers), Burns Oates & Washbourne, Ltd., London, 1934, I, pp. 19–20.
[40] Eliot, *The Family Reunion,* Harcourt, Brace, & Company, New York, 1939, p. 111.
[41] Eliot, "Burnt Norton," *op. cit.,* p. 6.
[42] Norman Nicholson, "T. S. Eliot," *Writers of Today,* Denys Val Baker, editor, Sidgwick & Jackson, London, 1946, p. 142.

> In order to arrive there,
> To arrive where you are, to get from where you are not,
>   You must go by a way wherein there is no ecstasy.
> In order to arrive at what you do not know
>   You must go by a way which is the way of ignorance.
> In order to possess what you do not possess
>   You must go by the way of dispossession.
> In order to arrive at what you are not
>   You must go through the way in which you are not.[43]

The way that leads toward health and blessedness involves, in other words, first of all, a descent into those dark and deep places of the soul which Dante, under Virgil's tutelage, takes us through in the first *cantica* of his poem. We must discover, yes, as Auden says, how,

> Ubiquitous within the bond
> Of one impoverishing sky,
> Vast spiritual disorders lie.[44]

But we must also discover what wretchedness there is within "Our parish of immediacy," [45] for the patient cannot be cured until he acknowledges that he is ill, and this acknowledgment becomes possible only after we have journeyed beyond the "hither" world of ignorant complacency into the "nether" world of dread and trembling. What is required is humility:

> The only wisdom we can hope to acquire
> Is the wisdom of humility . . .[46]

The necessary attitude is that of Rilke's "deeply-kneeling man," for thereby alone may the pilgrim behold the Blessed Face and hear the Voice. So

> Fare forward, you who think that you are voyaging;
> You are not those who saw the harbour
> Receding, or those who will disembark.
> Here between the hither and the farther shore

---

[43] Eliot, "East Coker," *Four Quartets,* Harcourt, Brace, & Company, New York, p. 15.

[44] Auden, "New Year Letter," *The Collected Poetry,* p. 272.

[45] *Ibid.*

[46] Eliot, *op. cit.,* p. 14.

> While time is withdrawn, consider the future
> And the past with an equal mind.
> At the moment which is not of action or inaction
> You can receive this: 'on whatever sphere of being
> The mind of a man may be intent
> At the time of death'—that is the one action
> Which shall fructify in the lives of others:
> And do not think of the fruit of action.
> Fare forward. . . .
> > > Not fare well,
> But fare forward, voyagers.[47]

"Our principal concern at the present moment," declared T. E. Hulme almost forty years ago, "should be the re-establishment of the temper or disposition of mind which can look at a *gap* or chasm without shuddering."[48] And it is this charismatic power that many of the great seers of our time have coveted for us and believed could be won only by a plunge into our "voided interiority."[49] Henry James told us many years ago: "In the destructive element immerse. That is the way"; and the psychologist-poet Carl Jung has spoken of the necessity of a descent into the "great waters" of the unconscious. Mr. Auden assures us that the "Pilgrim Way" leads to "the Abyss," and countless other modern writers might be cited who think of the contemporary hero as one who undertakes a voyage or journey into a "nether" world. But

As from true contemplation the soul inevitably returns to action, so from the "nether" she returns to a "hither" world regenerated in her regenerate vision.[50]

And so we must now finally turn to what I have called the Myth of Sanctity in contemporary literature.

Almost a quarter of a century ago Eliot, in his celebrated essay on Dante, told us that "It is apparently easier to accept damnation

[47] Eliot, "The Dry Salvages," *Four Quartets,* pp. 25–26.

[48] T. E. Hulme, *Speculations,* Herbert Read, editor, Kegan Paul, Trench, Trubner & Company, Ltd., London, 1936, p. 4.

[49] The phrase is Professor Stanley R. Hopper's, *op. cit.,* p. 162.

[50] Nicodemus, *Renascence: An Essay in Faith,* Faber & Faber, Ltd., London, 1943, p. 65.

as poetic material than purgation or beatitude; less is involved," he said, "that is strange to the modern mind." [51] And so, therefore, perhaps because of my own partial affliction with this modern insensibility, partly because of the paucity of descriptions of blessedness in contemporary writing, and partly because this paper requires termination at a reasonable length, I shall devote only the briefest word to this final pattern. It is, to be sure, a figure in the carpet of modern literature—though, unfortunately, perhaps for the reason Eliot suggests, it is a relatively minor figure. Thirty years ago the late Bernard Shaw, in the greatest play of his career, pondered the mystery of sanctity in *St. Joan,* and thirteen years earlier the French Catholic poet Charles Peguy was also meditating upon *Le Mystère de la charité de Jeanne d'Arc.* More recently in his play of 1935, *Murder in the Cathedral,* and in his latest work for the theatre, *The Cocktail Party,* Eliot himself has been coming to grips with this tremendous theme. Nor have the poets and dramatists been alone in this: the English novelist, Graham Greene, in two of his finest and most recent novels, *The Heart of the Matter* and *The End of the Affair,* has shared their preoccupation; and his fellow craftsman in the novel in France, the late Georges Bernanos, in such books as *Sous le Soleil de Satan* and *Journal d'un curé de campagne,* returned again and again to the mysteries of holiness and beatitude. But these writers, in their concern with this theme, have been a small minority, for the beauty of holiness has only rarely been exhibited by the principal artists of our period. This is not at all to say, however, that Joyce and Kafka and Faulkner have not taken us into the precincts of the world of love: it is only to say that it has been their more usual habit to reveal that world to us through the nocturnal glow of our own tragic time. They have wanted to give us myths and symbols of truth. And if they have succeeded, there may be coming a day not far hence when we may once again be given images of beauty.

[51] Eliot, "Dante," *Selected Essays: 1917–1932,* Harcourt, Brace & Company, New York, 1932, p. 214.

Bibliography

John Aldridge, *After the Lost Generation,* McGraw-Hill, New York, 1951.

Eric Bentley, *The Playwright as Thinker,* Harcourt, Brace & Company, New York, 1946.

Cleanth Brooks, *Modern Poetry and the Tradition,* University of North Carolina Press, Chapel Hill, 1939.

Brother George Every, *Christian Discrimination,* Sheldon Press, London, 1940 (Christian News-Letter Books No. 8).

—— *Poetry and Personal Responsibility,* SCM Press, Ltd., London, 1949 (Viewpoints No. 14).

Wallace Fowlie, *Clowns and Angels: Studies in Modern French Literature,* Sheed & Ward, New York, 1943.

—— *Jacob's Night: The Religious Renascence in France,* Sheed & Ward, New York, 1947.

Harold C. Gardiner, editor, *Fifty Years of the American Novel: A Christian Appraisal,* Scribner's, New York, 1951.

Stanley R. Hopper, editor, *Spiritual Problems in Contemporary Literature,* The Institute for Religious and Social Studies, New York, 1952.

J. Isaacs, *An Assessment of Twentieth-Century Literature,* Secker & Warburg, London, 1951.

Jacques Maritain, *Art and Scholasticism,* Scribner's, New York, 1943.

Norman Nicholson, *Man and Literature,* SCM Press, Ltd., London, 1943.

William Van O'Connor, *Sense and Sensibility in Modern Poetry,* University of Chicago Press, Chicago, 1948.

Donat O'Donnell, *Maria Cross: Imaginative Patterns in a Group of Modern Catholic Writers,* Oxford University Press, New York, 1952.

Nathan A. Scott, Jr., *Rehearsals of Discomposure: Alienation and Reconciliation in Modern Literature,* King's Crown Press, Columbia University, New York, 1952.

Lionel Trilling, *The Liberal Imagination,* Viking Press, New York, 1950.

Wladimir Weidlé, *The Dilemma of the Arts,* SCM Press, Ltd., London, 1948.

Amos Wilder, *Modern Poetry and the Christian Tradition,* Scribner's, New York, 1952.

Edmund Wilson, *Axel's Castle: A Study in the Imaginative Literature of 1870–1930,* Scribner's, New York, 1931.

XI

DEVELOPMENTS IN RELIGIOUS DRAMA
"O, Fabulous Wings Unused!"

MARION WEFER

*Associate Editor, "Players Magazine," American
Educational Theatre Association*

To tell the story of religious drama and follow its use down to the
present day is, in some measure, to retell the story of the Prodigal
Son, for drama was a child of the Church, cradled in the chancel,
and it grew into a lusty, wayward youth who left his Father's house
and wandered into a strange secular country. It was some hundreds
of years ago that he walked away from the chancel into the body of
the church, lingered for a while on the steps, tarried in the churchyard, and finally went his way down the village streets. Today the
wanderer appears ready to establish a visiting acquaintance, at least,
in his Father's house and puts a tentative foot across the threshold.
Who will let him in? The Roman Catholic Church with its admirable organization of Catholic Theatre Conference, Catholic Theatre Guild, and Catholic college and university drama groups would
seem to play the father's part and fall on the prodigal's neck and
kiss him. The Jews, who have made such a rich contribution to his
secular growth in all its aspects, extend a welcoming hand. The
Protestants, for lack of a united voice to greet the rover, present a
picture of varying degrees of hospitality. Some are eager to draw
him in with a hearty welcome, others salute him conditionally, and
a few would bar the door against him and set the dogs at his heels.

The parallel is not a perfect one. Drama was not so much a sinfully rebellious son of the Church as an exuberant child of promise who needed room to grow, an establishment of his own to grow in, and an unhampered opportunity to develop his powers happily and freely. He was not born to be a tool of sectarian propaganda alone. If, on his experimental return, there is a disposition to wrap swaddling bands about him and exact childish docility of him after he has attained a vigorous majority in the outer world, he will be off and the Church will be the poorer.

Suppose we go back through history and consider drama "as it was in the beginning." From the Old Testament we learn that God was praised "with timbrels and with dances" and we read the poetic dialogues of the Song of Solomon and the Book of Job, but theatre begins with the Greeks. And theatre to the Greeks was worship. The gods and the legendary heroes of Greece; men against the gods, conflicts of will between the greater and lesser gods; these were the subject matter of the great Greek tragedies with their conception of theatre as a religious institution. Greek tragedy is that which W. H. Auden defines as "the tragedy of necessity; that is, the feeling aroused in the spectator is 'What a pity it had to be this way.'" Imagine the Grecian multitude turning homeward after a performance of Oedipus! While Christian tragedy, continues Mr. Auden, "Is the tragedy of possibility, 'What a pity it was this way when it might have been otherwise.'" Thus we, today, after seeing Willie Loman die the Death of a Salesman.

Then Greece fell and the conquering Romans took over the theatre and somewhat improved it physically. They roofed the stage, devised a curtain which rose from a slot in about the place where footlights were to glow on stages hundreds of years later, and spread an awning for the comfort of the customers; for such the spectators had become—no longer worshipers. But the Romans, who could drill armies, build straight roads and codify laws, could not provide plays for the people. They offered them stupendous spectacles. Among these was the execution of hundreds of members of a strange, subversive sect who worshiped an unknown God and called themselves "Christians." The faith of these Christians who died submissively and heroically in the arena grew in power and it is small wonder that they regarded the theatre, scene of martyrdom, with abhorrent disgust. A Church Council of the fourth century declares that "an actor who mounts upon the stage follows the worship of the old, false gods." Tertullian thundered that the stage was "the Devil's Church": while St. Augustine confesses that in his wild youth he dearly loved a play (we dearly love him for so confessing), and in his "City of God" he makes a distinction between "high drama," and "low drama," and even advocates the use of "high drama" as an aid in education. Then Rome fell and the Dark Ages rolled over the face of the known world.

With the coming of the Middle Ages drama was reborn in a religious setting. In the tenth century some priest, yearning over his unlettered people and longing to make divine truth more plain to them, wrote a four line dialogue to be inserted in the liturgy at Eastertime. In the simplest of forms he employed action, impersonation, costume and "stage properties." A wooden box covered with a cloth represents a tomb and is placed in the chancel. Beside it sits a priest robed in white. Three figures approach him in evident search of something and he chants, "Whom seek ye in the tomb, O Christian women?" The three make chanted reply, "Jesus of Nazareth, the crucified, O holy one." The angel then lifts the cloth from the tomb showing its emptiness and announces to them that He is risen and they must go and tell abroad that Christ is risen from the dead. The seekers turn to the choir singing, "Alleluia!" The angel lifts the cloth, triumphantly urging, *"Venite et vidite locum!"* The anthem swells and all the bells ring out for joy that the Lord is risen.

This was the beginning of a stream of mystery and miracle plays and formed the germ of the Passion Play which survives to this day both in Europe and in America. At present several Passion Plays are enacted annually in the United States. One is at Spearfish, South Dakota, another in Oklahoma, two are in Illinois, while in the Hollywood Bowl a "Pilgrimage Play" is presented which depicts the life of Christ as well as His Passion.

As more and more episodes were added to the original playlets, small "vignette sets" were built here and there in the body of the church and the players moved from one to the other as the script indicated. Presently the church steps were tried. as a playing place, next the churchyard. Here arose a question of the desecration of the graves by the crowds that flocked to the sacred dramas. Finally drama was enacted on the streets on the movable stages of the pageant wagons. They trundled away from the church toward the homes where the people lived and the marketplaces and crossroads where they moved and had their being. The clergy were no longer the actors but the trade guilds took over the roles. They assigned them with a quaint fitness that would suggest an early attempt at "type casting." Thus the Shipwrights appear in "The order of the Pagents of the play of Corpus Christi in the third year of the reign of King Henry V," as responsible for "God warning Noah to make an Ark of floatable wood," and the Goldsmiths and "monemakers" portray the three Kings offering gifts to "Mary with the Child, a star above."

But in time the old plays were played out and the pageant wagons creaked away into obscurity. A vigorous secular theatre was coming into being and the age of the first Elizabeth, second only to Greece in the glory of its theatre, brought forth playwrights richly furnished with ability whose names will endure "to the last syllable of recorded time." The child of the Church came to full stature and was housed in his own home, "The Theatre," the "Curtain," the "Globe," the "Blackfriars." Against him stood the Puritans blasting him with the terrible sincerity of convinced righteousness. "Whosoever shall visit that Chapel of Satan, I mean the Theatre, shall find there no want of young ruffians, utterly past all shame!" They might also have found young William Shakespeare acting and writing plays.

Meanwhile ships were sailing from the Old World to the New and Protestant, Catholic, and Jew shared the shaping of a diverse civilization in the wilderness. The theatre crossed the waters, too, when cities began to stud the Eastern coast of the New World. Theatre men came over with church men, but they did not come hand in hand.

The Puritan spirit toward the theatre in America was a phenomenon of which Fanny Kemble writes in her *Records of a Girl-hood*. She visited New York with her famous father in 1832 and they chanced to meet the Rector of "the most fashionable Church in New York City" when he was calling upon English friends at their hotel. "He can neither call upon us or invite us to his house," she writes with amazement, "much less set his foot in the theatre. The probable consequences of any of these enormities, it seems, would be deserted pews next Sunday and perhaps eventually the forced resignation of his cure of souls." [1]

In the early years of 1860, Henry Ward Beecher certainly used the techniques of the theatre in his slave auctions held in the church, yet he blistered the institution. He wound up a series of indictments with the ringing peroration, "If you would become infected with each particular vice in the catalogue of human depravity—go to the theatre!" And a great many people did. For the theatre kept pace with the growing population and wherever people went, the players went also. There were resident stock companies in the cities, traveling companies covering the face of the nation under conditions of hardship and actual danger, and there were showboats on the rivers. There was even a "Temple of the Muses" on the Hudson. The Far West opened capacious arms to the theatre for, as Thomas Wood Stevens records it, "The West was so splendidly eager!" The greatest stars of the day took the road from New York to Chicago to San Francisco. The Mormons built a Community Theatre in Salt Lake City and for a long time the performances were opened with prayer. Channing Pollock, the playwright, played there as an extra when he was a boy. To read his memoirs, *Harvest of My Years,* is to get an excellent survey of American theatre. The history of his play, *The Fool,* shows clearly that the hostile attitude of the Church toward the theatre was fully reciprocated. Manager after manager refused to produce it. They wanted no "religious buncombe."

A great opportunity for reconciliation was missed in 1879 when David Belasco directed a Passion Play which was produced at the

[1] Frances Ann Kemble, *Records of a Girlhood,* H. Holt & Company, New York, 1879, p. 544.

Grand Opera House in San Francisco. It was soon closed because of religious opposition. The role of Christ was briefly presented by James O'Neill, father of our greatest American dramatist, Eugene O'Neill.

In the late nineties and early nineteen hundreds there comes what might be dimly seen as the entering wedge of religious drama. Quaintly enough, it comes as did the medieval beckoning to drama, at Eastertime and Christmas. At these seasons of Christian festival special service material began to be arranged for many of the denominations which included bits of poetry, recitations, drills, and dialogues. Sometimes costumes were suggested and the use of "hand props." Little girls in white would spell out a text each holding up a gilded letter or there would be tableaux in what was conceived to be biblical dress. As a proof of the lasting impression that this thin entering wedge of the dramatic method made upon myself I could still sing the song I sang carrying a candle and wearing a long nightgown on a far away Christmas.

> Little candle lit tonight,
> Shed abroad your shining light,
> Up and down the darksome street . . .

And I well remember my child's vision of the "Christ Child sweet," wandering the streets of my hometown companioned by the rays of my candle.

This was the beginning, but it was deplorably feeble. The use of special material—"exercises" they were called—increased, but the quality of the exercises did not improve. They were, in the words of St. Paul, exercises that profited little. Ruth Suckow, distinguished novelist and child of the manse, writes of this period in her memoir *Some Others and Myself,* and says forthrightly:

I had little expectation of finding what was fresh and creative in the arts in anything connected with the churches. . . . Programs, "exercises," pieces for church and Sunday School use were poorer in quality than most of those used in school . . . again, as if in that artistic mediocrity lay moral safety. I enjoyed the exercises when I was a child because I craved anything that would give a chance for acting and speaking; but later, how

I came to despise them! . . . "Religious people" it seemed were somehow withheld from appreciating high quality in any work of art, at least when it pertained to "religion." [2]

Nevertheless the "exercises" continued to be published and became increasingly ambitious. Dialogues lengthened into short plays and publishers began to be interested in the church trade. One act biblical plays began to appear in the catalogs of play publishers and were listed as "religious." Churches began to use them with the comfortable feeling that as long as they were biblical they were safe. The production of the plays generally fell to well intentioned individuals who were perfectly guiltless of any knowledge of dramatic art. Altogether it was much as a contemporary theatre critic described the performance of a certain actress, "Shining innocence, devoid of technique." Percy Mackaye, the poet and playwright whose ideal for drama was to make it a recreational and cultural activity for whole communities, castigated the commercial theatre of the time for recognizing art and debasing it for profit, then turned upon the schools and churches and blistered them for "ignoring art completely while seeking to uplift the public without it."

Admitting the palpable hit and revolting against the poor quality of the plays offered them, patrons of the secular theatre sought to circumvent the rising power of the Theatrical Syndicate which deprived them of the drama they desired. The Drama League of America organized and spread its gospel in as many towns and cities as possible. Their policy was to encourage good professional theatre and discourage the inferior by non-attendance. The Little Theatre movement which set footlights twinkling across the face of the nation adopted a more vigorous plan of creating drama nearer to their heart's desire. The Theatrical Syndicate might pipe, they decided, but they need not dance to its tune. They would open their own theatres and do their own playing! This they did. They might be satirized in *The Torchbearers* but the movement was wholesome and creative. The cultural influence was carried into the church where it helped to lift standards of play selection and production. Christopher

[2] Ruth Suckow, *Some Others and Myself*, Rinehart & Company, New York, 1952, p. 236.

Fry in his religious drama, *A Sleep of Prisoners* characterizes the latent powers of the soul as "fabulous wings unused, folded within the heart." Thus the fabulous wings of a great art hitherto unused, although religious in origin and essence, began to stir. Mrs. A. Starr Best of Evanston, Illinois, the first president of the Drama League of America, was one of the first directors of drama in a local church. The Federal Council of the Churches of Christ in America, working through a Committee on Religious Drama headed by Dr. Fred Eastman, sought to improve drama in the church and extend its use. Dr. Eastman, a prolific playwright, taught dramatic writing in Chicago Theological Seminary, compiled lists of plays, edited anthologies, and together with Louis Wilson, published a textbook, *Drama in the Church,* which is indispensable to the student of religious drama.

In New York City a Religious Drama Council was established under the Greater New York Federation of Churches. It held several national playwriting contests, conducted institutes to stimulate interest and teach techniques of production, issued play lists, and tried to maintain an advisory service by mail. The response was wide. One drama group from Texas asked for guidance in staging *The Eternal Road*. But the Drama Council had the tiniest of budgets and was largely dependent on the work of devoted volunteers. Dr. Elliot Field, playwright, was the first president of the Religious Drama Council and the gifted Mrs. Robert W. Searle gave abundantly of her time and the benefit of her own professional training, but the aim of the Religious Drama Council was an idea whose time had not yet come to the churches of Greater New York. The fabulous wings were forced to fold.

With the recent merging of the Federal Council into the National Council of the Churches of Christ in the United States of America, the concern of the churches for worship, drama, and the other arts was recognized by the establishment of a Department of Worship and the Arts. It was intended that the interests of the former Committee on Religious Drama should be continued and developed through the Department's Commission on Drama. It is devoutly to be hoped that it will work out a way to coordinate the scattered drama interests of the various denominations into a unified whole. That is the way toward development. A free interchange of experience is needed, a clearing house for scripts, a training ground for playwrights, and the advice of the professional theatre. Consider the potential wingspread of the American National Theatre and Academy. Mr. Clarence Derwent, recently elected president of ANTA, past president of Actor's Equity, was a guest star in *A Sleep of Prisoners* when presented at the Pacific Lutheran College at Parkland, Washington. It is entirely logical to expect sympathetic cooperation from him in the use of the resources of his organization. Besides what but good could come of a more amicable understanding between men of the theatre and men of theology? There might be far fewer feeble plays and fumbling productions and possibly the exit of that fatuous figure of fun, the "stage clergyman."

The Roman Catholic Church has fully realized the opportunities afforded by such a joining of forces. In 1937 the Catholic Theatre Conference was organized with the objective of providing a means of exchange of information between groups and individuals concerned with dramatic arts in the church. The Conference has headquarters in New York where it maintains a Service Bureau for its members. It issues a monthly newsletter telling of events in professional and non-professional theatre and also publishes an annual Catholic Theatre magazine for its members. They have a lending library of over 2,000 published and manuscript plays which are available for examination. The Catholic Theatre Conference is a member of the National Theatre Conference whose membership is limited to one hundred organizations which comply with certain standards. It had representation in the National Theatre Assembly called in 1951 and the Rev. Gilbert Hartke of Catholic University, Washington, D.C., was recently elected a member of the Board of Directors of ANTA. The Blackfriars Guild whose object is to "study, present, and encourage the presentation of plays based on philosophy, sociology, and psychology in accordance with the teachings of the Roman Catholic Church," maintains an experimental theatre in New York City. The Guild has many chapters in other cities across the country. The Rev. Urban Nagle, playwright, was one of the founders of the Blackfriars Guild. It is constantly reading scripts and holds frequent playwriting contests. Its theatre in New York is just entering its twelfth season.

The Jewish-American Theatre was organized as a Drama Department among the activities of the Young Men's Hebrew Association. It aims to encourage the production of plays which show the present condition of the Jew in a changing social environment. Its ideal play is one which illumines the present in relation to the past and looks prophetically toward the future. Such plays are hard to come by and so the Jewish-American Theatre is concerned with stimulating playwriting and furnishes incentive to playwrights by means of frequent contests. The dramatic groups of the YMHA produce only plays written in English, because their aim is to educate the younger. Jews in their own racial culture, and yet not to hark back too nostalgically and endanger their growth by getting "stuck fast in yesterday."

The sole effort to correlate the drama interests among Protestant churches appear to be a ten day "Religious Drama Workshop" which has been held annually at Green Lake, Wisconsin, for the past four years. This comes late and the enrollment, in consideration of its potential, is small. Nevertheless, the "fabulous wings" are agitated. They need support if their flight is to be sustained. In 1952, the Workshop was sponsored by the Division of Christian Education of the National Council of Churches and the American Baptist Assembly, which owns the conference ground with its theatre. As a brochure states, "The Religious Drama Workshop is designed for adults with lay or professional interest in the use of religious drama in the local church, church school, or college." Miss Amy Goodhue Loomis is the Director and brings to the venture a background of training for the professional theatre and many years of experience in the "Ministry of Drama" in the Fountain Street Baptist Church of Grand Rapids, Michigan. She gathered many specialists in the field into her faculty. It included Dr. Fred Eastman, pioneer playwright of religious drama; Miss Hulda Niebuhr, author of *Ventures in Dramatics* and professor of Christian education at McCormick Theological Seminary; Miss Mildred Hahn, specialist in the production of pageants and compiler of an excellent analytical list of *Best Plays for the Church;* and Harold A. Ehrensperger, author of *Conscience Onstage,* formerly head of the Department of Plays and Pageants of the Methodist Church, founder of a Department of Religious Drama in Garrett Biblical Institute, and promoter of the Wesley Players. In the summer of 1952 the Workshop's major production was Henri de Gheon's *Christmas in the Village Square,* presented in true medieval style.

The National Society of Wesley Players, a Methodist student organization, was founded in 1924 at the University of Illinois where its three original chapters drew up a constitution and bylaws. The Society has forty chapters today with a prospect of becoming international by including clubs that have been started by former Wesley Players in foreign countries. The Wesley Players publish a monthly called *Footlight* which was, at one time, the only magazine devoted to religious drama in the country. Wesley Players have sponsored playwriting contests and given experimental productions of manuscripts. They are interested in making film strips and have presented some homemade movies. A chapter in Tallahassee, Florida, emphasized liturgical drama and one at the University of Minnesota has been working with the related interest of interpretive dance. Wesley Players in Stillwater, Oklahoma, are especially community conscious and take their plays to local churches where they report a very good response. The West has lost none of its splendid eagerness for drama. Much of the well knit organization of the Wesley Players and the formation of their standards of dramatic excellence is due to the experienced guidance of Mr. Ehrensperger during the years of his work among college students. The Methodist student magazine, *Motive,* of which he was the first editor, is one of the few, the very few, religious publications which recognize the very existence of drama. An issue of February, 1948, contained an article by Sheldon Cheyney and a survey, "The Quintessence of Drama," to which Clifford Odets, Owen Dodson, Elmer Rice, Thornton Wilder, Eric Bentley, Judith Anderson, George Jean Nathan, and others of like stature contributed. John Mason Brown appeared in *Motive* and time fails me to tell the complete roster which Editor Ehrensperger marshaled on his pages. While drama has had consistent recognition in *Motive,* Protestant religious journalism as a rule ignores drama entirely. On the other hand, the Roman Catholic publication, *Commonweal,* makes a feature of its expert dramatic criticism.

It is the lack of regularly published information about religious drama activities on an interdenominational, interfaith scale that makes the discovery of a great deal of excellent work by groups and individuals a matter of pure chance. It was by sheer accident that I learned of the production of an experimental chancel drama, *Saraband for a Saint,* by Gordon Langley Hall. This is believed to be the first interracial play to be given in the chancel of a New York City church. An interracial cast performed it in the very beautiful chancel of St. Martin's Protestant Episcopal Church on Lenox Avenue. Mr. Hall, the playwright, tells me that *Saraband for a Saint* will be published and available for dramatic groups in the near future.

It was chance also that made me acquainted with the work of the Pilgrim Players under the leadership of Mrs. Edgar A. Walton, formerly professor of English and drama at Manchester College, Indiana. The Pilgrim Players produced *They Came to a City* by J. B. Priestley as a feature of a Christian Youth Conference held at Purdue University and attended by more than a thousand delegates. Four of the cast were members of the Manchester College Players who, under Mrs. Walton's direction, played *They Came to a City* in North Manchester, Elkhart, Chicago, and Dubuque, in 1950. Favorable comments were received at that time from Bethany Theological Seminary in Chicago and the Wartburg Theological Seminary in Dubuque. A professor of Missions with a background of familiarity with the Goodman Theatre wrote, "I came away with a clean feeling, because in an age of fear and frustration, some young people found a way to clarity of thought and life."

Mrs. Walton's dream is to gather a troupe of student actors at her farm home in Colon, Michigan, where a big red barn is available for rehearsals, and take them on a tour of twelve towns with significant plays. She attempted to make this a united church effort in these towns in her first valiant essay at making her dream come true and visited many ministerial associations and spoke with many pastors. There was gratifying enthusiasm at first and then with one consent they began to make excuses. Mrs. Walton with her background of past successful performances and her vision for the future was obliged to fold her fabulous wings. They do not droop, however, and she intends to try flight again. More power to her!

It was a picture in a secular magazine that set me in quest of information about the Mount Vernon Players of Mount Vernon Place Methodist Church in Washington, D.C. This group, whose excellent work has received notice in *Theatre Arts* and *Players Magazine,* was organized in 1936 by a small group of enthusiasts into whose midst came a tall Texan, Edward P. Mangum. The growth and development of the Players became his special concern and for twelve years he directed them, becoming a full time paid worker in 1944, with the responsibility of maintaining an overall drama program for the church. Starting with no more support from the church than permission to use a stageless auditorium, the Players proved their worth and, being importunate as the widow of old, gradually acquired a stage, lighting equipment, dressing rooms, a workshop, and an office. With wisdom they were organized under a constitution providing for a council of officers, a monthly business meeting, rules for membership, dues, and a clear statement of their aims. Membership in the Mount Vernon Players is open to all comers without barriers of creed or color. They have never charged for tickets but prefer a free will offering. They have been producing steadily for sixteen years. *The Terrible Meek, The Little Shepherd Play, Family Portrait,* have been presented in the church sanctuary. Plays such as *The Importance of Being Ernest, The Late Christopher Bean,* and *The Taming of the Shrew,* were given in the auditorium. With the establishment of a Department of Drama in the church program, Mr. Mangum set up a school with courses in playwriting, directing, and technicians' crafts. There was even an instructor in fencing. When their original director left them for a university post, the Players proved the vitality of their organization by continuing, though on a somewhat smaller scale. There is a significant sentence in the detailed letter with which my query about the Players was answered. "More plays would have been produced if they could have been found." This places a diagnostic finger upon an ailing spot in the development of religious drama. It is also significant that a group whose work was of a quality to be recognized in *Theatre Arts* did not know about the existence of the four year old Interdenominational Religious Drama Workshop. Nor are they the only group which I have found thus uninformed. This suggests either that the fabulous wings of planned publicity have been clipped by a limited budget or that their hovering is concentrated over workers for the denominational Boards of Education whose attitude toward drama is less of love than duty. Did not someone once say that a fault of the ministry is not that the sheep are not fed, but that the wrong sheep showed up at the feeding place?

Chance—or perhaps predestination is a more appropriate word for Presbyterian—led my eye to a short paragraph reporting a play among the notes of a Californian correspondent of *The Christian Century*. *The Christian Century* very, but very, occasionally publishes an article on religious drama, and one must turn all stones. Had it been movies I was hunting for the stones would have been all turned for me and the celluloid dramas sorted for size. This was a brief report about the Council of Churches of Redlands, California, sponsoring the production of a trilogy called *Paul at Corinth* which was presented in the Redlands bowl and reached an audience of 3,000. Correspondence with the dramatist, Edward Longstreth, developed the fact that the play, written to be used in the manner of the "drama quartet" was also adaptable to chancel use. It had been given effectively in the First Presbyterian Church of La Jolla, California, which holds about 400 people. This represents a most interesting development of the latest technique in drama peculiarly suitable to the purposes of drama in the church.[3]

[3] To make *Paul at Corinth* better known when the medium of publicity is largely chance and a grapevine transmission among a few enthusiasts, let me say that churches wishing to use this play should obtain permission from Mr. Edward Longstreth, P.O. Box 736, La Jolla, California. The playwright has included full and detailed production notes with his script.

It may be that effort which might have been expended in the promotion of living religious drama is now preening its fabulous wings for flight among the mass media of communication, motion pictures, radio, and television. There has been a good deal of accomplishment in these fields, though some of it has been ineffective because of the lack of a basic knowledge of drama. In general, Protestantism has contributed little that is outstanding, and nothing of the calibre of *Monsieur Vincent* in which Pierre Fresnay played the role of St. Vincent De Paul so compellingly, or the radio scripts of Morton Wishengrad for *The Eternal Light* and *Frontiers of Faith,* produced by The Jewish Theological Seminary of America, or the television classic *Amahl and the Night Visitors,* which could wring the tribute from John Crosby that one was the better Christian for seeing it. While I am aware that this last was not televised under religious sponsorship, I contend it is the kind of work that should be so sponsored. Work of such compelling beauty that it arrests not only the convinced sheep safely grazing, but the black sheep and wanderers from the fold.

Does this trend to other media mean the scrapping of live religious drama? There is a straw in the wind, if nothing more, in a headline from *Variety* which reads, with the elegant terseness of that bible of show business, "Fordham lops legit." Which, being interpreted, means that Fordham University, which has made fine theatre under distinguished leadership, has now discontinued operation of the Fordham University Theatre and dropped its theatre course in the Communications Arts Department. Yet it seems to me significant that the National Association for Mental Health chooses living theatre as the vehicle to convey its message of the whole mental health movement to forty cities in fifteen states. A play called, *My Name Is Legion,* a dramatization of the autobiography, *The Mind That Found Itself,* is on tour with an Equity cast from the American Theatre Wing to teach the American people the real nature of mental illness. These experts know what impact living drama has upon the mind and they prefer to use it in their crusade. Incidentally, church drama groups can do their "young marrieds"

no greater service than by producing the trilogy on family relationships known as *Temperate Zone* and published, with discussion
guides, by the National Health Association.

With the drama interests of the Roman Catholic Church and the
Jewish-American Theatre developing individually and needing only
to continue with "more of the same," it appears to be the Protestants
who need to take an all inclusive wing count and practise flying
in mass formation. There is a tremendous need of understanding
between dramatists and those who would use their skill. This would
prevent such an absurdity as the request once made in good faith to
a playwright to produce an Easter play and include in it a few
timely statistics on the narcotic traffic. Or the miscalling of bright
little conversation pieces of obvious propaganda "religious drama."
While Christopher Frys are not created out of hand, a climate
favorable to the growth of competent dramatists can be induced if
church folk and writers can meet in an atmosphere of mutual respect. As Philip Clark, director of the Dock Street Theatre in Charles-
ton, South Carolina, writes in *Motive*, "There are a lot of fine views
from the lower slopes of Olympus. . . . We do have to find playwrights who at least want to climb. For better or worse they are
the lead-men on the rope."

Unless the child of the church is to remain in a state of arrested
development, with a few fixations that are doing him no good, we
must get rid of the idea that there is something slightly immoral in
being expert. We need the precision, the patience, the high pride
in perfection of the professional, but as long as we remain in isolated little groups here and there and yonder, we can hardly claim
either the attention of the experts or the privilege of coming into
association with them to learn of them. What is needed is a united
approach by the Protestant denominations toward availing themselves of the dramatic means of grace.

A study of "Appendix A," by Amy Goodhue Loomis in Mr.
Ehrensperger's *Conscience Onstage,* shows what the ministry of
drama meant to one church and could mean, with necessary local
adaptation, to any church. Then, too, there must be the learning
to apply Christian standards of criticism to the study of drama so

that we can separate that which is harmful to us and extract the good for our own growth. Thus we go to see Tennessee Williams's pitiful Blanche Du Bois who could never bear the light of reality, Arthur Miller's Willie Loman, the man who never knew who he was, the futile folk who walk in Lillian Hellman's *Autumn Garden,* or the groping pair in William Inge's *Come Back, Little Sheba.* But we dare to take account of something that does not seem to have been dreamed of in the philosophy of the dramatists: we know that, by the grace of God, it might have been otherwise!

The Protestant denominations would do well if they would give serious, concerted study to the enriching of the lives and deepening of the faith of their followers through the means of religious drama. It is not too difficult for the willing. "Turn but a stone, and start a wing." A wing count of the congregation or the community might discover a wealth of fabulous, folded pinions. But,

> 'Tis ye, 'tis your estrangèd faces.
> That miss the many-splendored thing.

Bibliography

Katherine Lee Bates, *The English Religious Drama,* Macmillan & Company, New York and London, 1893. (Out of print, consult library.)

Eric Bentley, *The Playwright as Thinker,* Reynal & Hitchcock, New York, 1946.

Sheldon Cheyney, *The Theatre,* Longmans, Green Company.

Alfred W. Pollard, *English Miracle Plays,* Clarendon Press, Oxford, 1927.

Glenn Hughes, *A History of the American Theatre, 1700–1950,* Samuel French Company, New York, 1951.

Channing Pollack, *Harvest of My Years,* Bobbs Merrill Company.

Marian Gallaway, *Constructing a Play,* Prentice-Hall Company, New York, 1950.

Fred Eastman and Louis Wilson, *Drama in the Church,* Samuel French Company, New York and Los Angeles; Samuel French, Ltd., London, 1933.

Harold A. Ehrensperger, *Conscience Onstage,* Abingdon-Cokesbury Press, Nashville, 1947.

Mildred B. Hahn, *Best Plays for the Church,* Heidelberg Press.

J. L. Moreno, *Psychodrama,* Beacon House, New York, 1946.

Temperate Zone & Other Plays, National Association for Mental Health, Inc., New York.

George and Fannie R. Shaftel, *Role Playing the Problem Story,* National Conference of Christians and Jews.

The Commonweal (Weekly edited by Roman Catholic laymen—features expert coverage of stage and screen.)

Motive (Interested in drama but not as articulate as formerly. See back numbers February, 1948, March, 1952, March, 1950, April, 1950. Methodist Student Magazine.)

Players Magazine, Religious Drama Department Editor, Doctor Elliot Field.

Theatre Arts Monthly (Publishes scripts and has back-number department.)

XII

THE FUTURE OF RELIGIOUS SYMBOLISM—
A JEWISH VIEW

BY

MORDECAI M. KAPLAN, D.H.L.

*Professor of Philosophies of Religion, The Jewish
Theological Seminary of America*

Only what happens in the heavens above or in the laboratories beneath is predictable. In the heavens above nature displays forces like those of gravitation and light uncomplicated by other forces. In the laboratories man artificially creates situations in which he whittles away as much as possible from the complexities of the world about and studies the workings of highly simplified states of reality. That is why astronomy, physics, and chemistry lend themselves to prediction. With regard to all else, prediction, unless some supernatural claim be made for it, can amount only to stating the conditions that have to be met, if a certain desired result is to be obtained, or a feared result is to be averted.

Those of us who are interested in the future of religious symbolism generally wish to see religion flourish, and associate vital religion with a rich and meaningful symbolism. A concern for the future of religious symbolism, I take it, implies a worried realization, that religion, in the best sense of that term, is at present far from flourishing, and that religious symbolism is being crowded out by other symbolisms as well as by matter of fact realities. Instead, however, of asking in a general way what can be done to reawaken men's interest in religion, we prefer to be more specific and center the problem on the most visible manifestation of religion—its rites and ceremonies. We assume that they are intended to make us aware of our relation to the Divine, but that for some reason they are falling into neglect. This method of attacking the problem of growing religious indifference is as good as any other, provided we keep close to the facts involved. By asking what is wrong with the rites and observances which form part of the Judeo-Christian tradition, we might get at the root of the prevailing religious apathy, and learn what has to be done to overcome it.

I shall confine myself to the rites and observances of the Jewish religion, although I believe that *pari passu* the same condition obtains in the Christian religion as in the Jewish. The trouble with the traditional rites and observances is that they are not uniformly and unequivocally symbolic. Instead, they are to some extent theurgic, authoritatively, and to a far larger extent, popularly. Moreover, those which are definitely symbolic point to referents that are in need of being reinterpreted and revalued in keeping with the modern world outlook.

I.

To get at the heart of the problem of religious symbolism, we must learn to distinguish it from theurgy. Genuine religious symbolism is a late development in religion. It obtains when rites and observances are practised for what they do to stir the mind and the heart religiously. They are a means of enabling man to commune with himself or with his fellowmen about things divine. On the other hand, if they are supposed to influence directly any supernatural being to extend help or to withhold from doing harm, they are theurgic.

Theurgy is the display of objects or the performance of actions with a view to setting in motion superhuman forces assumed to reside in animate or inanimate beings, or in the environment generally, so that they come to one's aid or are prevented from doing harm. Those forces, whether regarded as invisible or as residing in visible objects, are of a demonic character. They lack the kind of divine personality that came to figure in the more developed religions of the pre-Christian civilizations. They act, as it were, automatically, in response to the theurgic object or action, just as the electric lamp lights up or the bell rings when an electric button is pressed.

Actually there is as much difference between symbolism and theurgy as there is between astronomy and astrology. By this time, nearly everyone recognizes the difference between astronomy and astrology, but most fail to draw any distinction between symbolism and theurgy. Theurgy is part of man's primitive efforts to adjust himself to his environment and to acquire sufficient control of it to counter the dangers that lurk everywhere. Out of these efforts arose various procedures in connection with hunting, fishing, shepherding, farming, fighting, and other pursuits, intended to bring under control the unpredictable elements in them. They arose with as much spontaneity and with as little planning as speech. Associated with those procedures were some very loosely and vaguely held notions, about spirits, demons, ghosts, or about power in general which was identified by such terms as mana, wakanda, orenda, beraka, etc. There was nothing symbolic to those procedures.

But there comes a time when together with the growing complexity of human life and culture, the human mind acquires the intellectual capacity to distinguish between impersonal forces acting blindly or automatically and personal forces such as arise in human relations: hate, love, jealousy, anger, or pity. It is then that the vaguely conceived spirits, demons, etc., acquire in the mind of man humanlike traits and are regarded as entering into personal relations analogous to those of parents to their children, masters to their servants, or kings to their subjects. The inherited rites and observances are no longer merely theurgic, but begin to take on meaning of some kind, usually as part of some mythology. The now divinized spirits and demons are thought of as playing a role which grows out of their presumed interest in man. That is the beginning, or promise, of genuine religious symbolism.

That development, however, has to go a long way before the rites and observances actually come to be practised purely for what they can do or say to man's own mind and soul. The momentum of theurgy accompanies them far down through the ages long after man has achieved a high order of civilization. That is the history of religious practises in the traditions of Jewish, Christian, and Islamic religions. In Judaism, for example—and the same fact obtains, in Christianity and Islam—the religious practices are considered *"mitzvot,"* *i.e.,* divine commandments which have to be adhered to scrupulously. I shall have occasion later to point out that many of them are associated with symbolic meanings which are actually stressed in the course of the observance; nevertheless the emphasis on their being commanded by God, to be performed in the manner prescribed, is such as to render their symbolic function entirely secondary.

Before the advent of modern science and technology, it was difficult even for thinkers of note to abandon the theurgic habit of mind. They could not reconcile themselves to the fact that man's will could have no direct influence upon his surroundings. They noted how language, which articulates man's will, effects changes in the human and physical environment. Therefore, words were to them not merely symbols that enabled the mind to think, remember, and imagine, but actual realities or forces that could put other forces into motion. The tendency of the human mind to reify (to treat as a thing) whatever it has a name for, grew so strong that it gave rise in the Middle Ages to a type of thinking known as realism, in contrast with the view held by those who refused to reify words or concepts, the view known as nominalism. That philosophical quarrel had an important bearing on the idea of God, and especially on the ritual practises. The "realists" regarded the nominalists as heretics, and the nominalists regarded the "realists" as idolaters.

It was among the "realists," both Jewish and Christian, that mysticism had a great vogue in the Middle Ages. The reason for that is quite understandable. Medieval mysticism is, to a large extent, a survival of the prehistoric theurgic approach to reality. It sought to discover ways of utilizing the traditional ritual and the various names by which men identified God as means of acquiring potency over the environmental forces. Jewish mysticism expressed itself through astrology and Kabbalah. Christian mysticism added alchemy.

The foregoing indicates how deeply the momentum of primitive theurgy penetrated revealed religion which deemed it as its mission to combat pagan religions, largely because of their theurgic practises. An objective description of revealed religion, however, would have to ascribe to it an ambivalence or a vacillation between the theurgic and the symbolic approach to ritual practises. So long as that ambivalence persists, more of the historic religions will make any headway with those who have so absorbed the spirit of modernism as to be unable to come to terms with theurgy in any form whatever. How far traditional Jewish religion suffers from that ambivalence becomes apparent even in a rapid survey of its ritual system.

II.

In ancient Jewish religion, divine worship took the form of animal and food offerings. In that respect the Jews merely followed the practise that prevailed among all the peoples they had come in contact with. Maimonides was the only Jewish authoritative thinker who recognized this fact, and dared to publish it, though he drew no logical consequences from it, when he formulated his Code. There he treats the sacrificial system as a divine institution which is bound to be reinstated with the advent of the Messiah.

The institution of sacrificial offerings in the Torah probably dates back to prehistoric times when religion—if it may be called such —was still in its theurgic stage. But by the time that institution became part of the divine code, or Torah, by which all Israelites were expected to regulate their lives, it began to possess an ambivalent character. In some of the prescribed sacrifices the element of religious symbolism stands out strongly, but, for the most part, the theurgic tendency is quite unmistakable.

The paschal sacrifice is a clear case of a theurgic practice being given symbolic meaning. It probably dates back to the nomadic stage of the Israelites. When the yeaning season arrived, they would offer the first born sheep to the local spirit of the oasis in the wilderness. It was a way of ensuring the fecundity of the flocks. By the time the Israelites took possession of Canaan and turned largely to agriculture, the old practise of offering the first born sheep continued. By then, too, they no longer worshiped some vague local spirit, but the God Yahweh Who had redeemed them from Egypt. Had they regarded Yahweh mainly as a nature deity, the way the natives regarded the *baalim,* they would simply have transferred to Him the offering they had made to the local oasis spirit. But Yahweh's main attribute was that of redeemer from Egyptian bondage. The paschal sacrifice was therefore transformed from a theurgic act to a religious symbol, reminding those who offered it of what Yahweh had done for their ancestors. In order to serve as such a symbol, it had to be supplied with a rationale which took the form of a saga in which the paschal sacrifice was said to have been offered in Egypt the night before the redemption took place. That saga started an intricate system of religious rites of a symbolic character, as part of the Passover ritual which is one of the most beautiful and inspiring observances in the Jewish home to this day.

At the other extreme, we have in the sacrificial system of the Torah prescribed offerings that were carried out in a purely theurgic spirit, devoid of all symbolic significance. That is particularly the case with offerings brought for unwitting sins and as part of purification ritual. None of the ideas, attitudes, or values that enter into personal relationship with Deity had a part in those offerings. In the Rabbinic era, the theurgic approach had been outgrown, especially on the part of the spiritual elite, but they did not get to the point of symbolizing the sacrificial system beyond what the Torah itself had done.

An interesting illustration is the story concerning Rabbi Yohanan ben Zakkai who was asked by a Gentile the reason for the practise of ritual purification by means of the ashes of the red heifer. Rabbi Yohanan replied by comparing that ritual to the practise of exorcising evil spirits. When the Gentile left him, the Rabbi's disciples said to him in effect: "That kind of an answer might satisfy a Gentile, but what is actually the reason for that law?" He might have explained that practise, as another Rabbinic authority explained later, namely, as a symbol of atonement for the sin of the Golden Calf. Instead, he merely replied: "That practise is a divine decree, which has to be implicitly obeyed, regardless of any reason or purpose." In other words, while rejecting his own theurgic explanation, he refused to give it symbolic significance.

The Pharisaic authorities also displayed an ambivalence toward the sacrificial system during the last century of its existence. An illustration of their maintaining the theurgic approach is their insistence upon the ritual of water libation at the Feast of Tabernacles. There is no provision in the Torah for such an offering. In all likelihood it was a holdover which persisted from early days when "sympathetic magic" was still in vogue, and the act of pouring water on the ground was part of an elaborate ritual to produce rain. Or the Jewish "peasant folk" (*amē ha-arazoth*) might have picked up that practice more recently from their pagan neighbors. In the face of strong opposition on the part of the Sadducees, the Pharisees succeeded in having that rite made an integral part of the offerings during the Feast of Tabernacles.

On the other hand, the Pharisees made an issue of having the prescribed daily offerings, morning and evening, defrayed from funds of half shekels collected from all Jews both in and outside Palestine. Their intent was clear. They wanted to have those offerings serve as a symbol of the nearness of God to the entire people of Israel, regardless of difference of station or piety. This measure was resisted by the Sadducees, who maintained that the daily offerings should be brought in accordance with the prescribed rule which makes no mention of their being defrayed from public funds.

The fact that ritual practises had to be meticulously observed may also be used as an indication of the element of theurgy. Were the prescribed rule assigned a meaning, the observance of the rule would lend itself to symbolic interpretation. Because that is not the case, a prescribed rule indicates a theurgic approach. For, being a primitive way of acting on the intuition of cause and effect relationship, theurgy or magic would naturally tend to be very punctilious in following whatever procedure seemed to have proved effective.

So eminent a poet and thinker as Rabbi Judah Halevi explained the numerous minutiae which had to be observed in the sacrificial rites, by means of an analogy taken from chemistry. He makes the point that, just as in mixing chemicals, one has to follow definite formulas as to the proportion of each that has to be put into the mixture to obtain specific results, so the satisfactory observance of any of the rites is conditional upon due regard to the prescribed minutiae. To be sure, any symbol, in order to serve as such, has to conform to some established convention, else it cannot convey any meaning to others. But it is a far cry, *e.g.,* from the death meted out to the two sons of Aaron for using "strange fire" in the performance of the initiation ritual in the consecration of the Sacred Tabernacle in the Wilderness to insistence upon uniform procedure as a means of rendering a ritual symbolically intelligible.

In traditional Judaism the sacrificial system is regarded not as having been abolished, but as having been suspended when the Temple was destroyed in the year seventy. That is emphasized not only by the prayers thrice daily for its restoration, but by the fact that those prayers themselves are considered a temporary substitute for the sacrificial system. As such a substitute, they constitute a religious symbol, in that they are intended to act as a reminder of a spiritual lack in the life of the Jew, owing to his being deprived of the opportunity to approach God by means of offerings at the Temple. They, too, however, are partly theurgic, in that they have to be recited at specific times and in a certain order if they are to be valid or effective; otherwise the Jew does not discharge his religious duty.

The other religious duties, besides prayer, which in the main constitute the religious routine of the Jew are the following: observance of the dietary laws, Sabbaths, and festivals; fringes on the garments; frontlets; and inscribed parchment on the doorposts. The outstanding fact is their function as religious symbols and not as theurgic practises (*cf.* Genesis 17:21; Leviticus 11:45; Exodus 33:13; 20:41; Deuteronomy 5:15).

They are commanded in the Torah for the purpose of recalling one or the other of the following facts concerning the Jews in their relation to God: 1) that Jews are covenanted to God, 2) that they are a dedicated priestly caste among the nations of mankind, 3) that God is the creator of the world, 4) that He redeemed the Israelites from bondage, 5) that He is the protector of Israel. The one festival which is not given a symbolic significance in the Torah is Pentecost. It is to be observed solely as the festival of the first fruits which had to be given to the Deity, in recognition of His lordship and munificence. Though that is no longer strictly a theurgic act, as the Deity to whom such a debt of gratitude is rendered is assumed to stand in personal relationship to His people, it is still far from being a symbolic act in which the content of the act is entirely of secondary importance, and all that counts is the state of mind or meaning accompanying it. In the Rabbinic era, however, the agricultural character of the Pentecost was eclipsed by the interpretation of it as the "Day of the giving of our Torah."

It is quite evident that every one of the foregoing ritual observances had its origin in the prehistoric nature religion which existed in the Near East, and began its career as a theurgic performance. Every one of those observances has its analogue in ancient and primitive religion. In a theurgic ritual the content of the action is all important, so the manner in which it is performed plays an essential role. Hence the legalistic spirit in which ritual observances were carried on in all ancient religions and are still carried on in existing primitive religions. To the extent that legalism still marks the observances of Jewish religious tradition, they still retain the effects of their early theurgic origin. Thus, as with the sacrificial system, the ambivalent character of Jewish ritual practise comes out also in those that constitute in the main the religious routine of the Jew. That routine is both theurgic and symbolic.

On the other hand, perhaps nothing so indicates how Jewish religion, whether consciously or unconsciously, has sought to break with theurgic practises as the fact that it is the first religion in the world to dispense with them at the turning points in the life of the individual, such as birth, initiation, marriage, and death. Those turning points have always been felt as transitions from one stage of existence to another, and therefore aroused fears of the unknown which man was always wont to meet with some kind of magic or theurgy. In that way man hoped to acquire the potency that would help him to effect the transition without sinister consequences to himself. Christian sacraments, like baptism, confirmation, marriage, and extreme unction, retain to a large extent the original theurgic mood and attitude. Neither the Torah nor Rabbinic law, however, prescribes rites that are equivalent to those sacraments.

Only Jewish folk religion has surrounded some of these turning points in the life of the individual with rites that have a theurgic character, but it has not succeeded in transforming them into occasions for sacraments which are authoritatively prescribed. The rite of circumcision is purely a symbolic act. The *Bar Mitzvah* ceremony is optional. The marriage rite is mainly contractual, and the confession of the dying carries with it no theurgic effects. The recital of the *Kaddish* for the dead is simply a prayer for the advent of God's Kingdom. It was taken over by the Jewish folk spirit as a potent means of saving the departed from the tortures of *Gehinnom,* but it never acquired anything more than a symbolic status in authoritative Jewish practice.

The foregoing sketch of the ambivalent character of religious practises provides the background against which we have to view the problem of religious symbolism, particularly as it affects Jewish religion. I venture to assume that the situation is not different in other religions. Ever since modern science and technology enabled man to achieve progressive control of the forces of nature, he has been veering away from traditional religion, because to the average person religion is synonymous with theurgy, or with the resort to the supernatural to help him in meeting the crises and turning points of life. Religious symbolism, or that aspect of it which is intended to direct his thinking, to bring his emotions under control, and, in general, to mold his personality, is for the most part beyond his grasp.

The so-called conflict of religion with science is actually a conflict only between religion, conceived as theurgy, and science, conceived as a method based upon experience and experiment. There can be no quarrel between religion, conceived as a source of values and meanings, and science, as a description of what actually exists. It will be a long time before those who have broken with religion are able to see that. Their contention is that religion is to be judged not by what it means to the few who are adept in the interpretation of its symbolism, but by the way it functions among the masses.

As far as Jewish religion is concerned, the resistance to it on the part of those Jews who have become secularized is based largely on their refusal to see it as anything but a form of theurgy. In verification of that view they point to the numerous legal details and the legalistic spirit as a whole in which the Jewish ritual practises are steeped. The situation with non-Jews, who find themselves at odds with their ancestral religion whether it be Christianity, or Islam, is to a large extent similar.

III.

From the preceding summary of Jewish ritual practise it becomes evident what is wrong with it, and why so many Jews have become alienated from traditional religion. It is the fact that traditional Jewish religion is ambivalent. While definitely applying the symbolic approach to a large section of its ritual practise, it also maintains to a considerable extent the theurgic approach.

We shall not get very far, however, with any attempt to win back the secularized Jew to Jewish religion, if all that we do is to eliminate the theurgic element in its ritual observances. To reinstate Jewish ritual observance, it is not enough to make every element in it significant. The question is: significant for what? In other words, if Jewish religion is to be revitalized through its ritual observances, those observances must not only have a symbolic meaning, but the meaning itself has to be such as to activate the better part of us, our latent potentialities for what is fully human. The referents of the symbolism have to be intrinsically worthwhile, to say nothing of their being objectively acceptable.

What is involved in this affirmative aspect of the task of retrieving Jewish ritual practise becomes clear when we note what, in the main, are the referents in all ritual practise, viewed symbolically. Religious symbols are objects displayed, or actions performed, as a means of evoking helpful attitudes, ideas, and values pertaining to God. Because symbols are a means of communication, their very existence implies that those states of mind pertaining to God are regarded as helpful to a number of people who, by virtue of their common approval of those states of mind and their use of those symbols, form a religious fellowship or community. Those symbols, therefore, perform the additional function of articulating the collective mind or soul of some people, church, or religious fellowship. And, finally, as all relationship to God is assumed, by those who wish to abide in it, to be essential to their salvation or fulfilment as human beings, the religious symbol, by making them aware of that relationship, functions normally as a means to their salvation. Thus the three referents to which religious symbolism points are: Divinity, community, and salvation.

In traditional Jewish religion, those three referents have been conceived in terms of theurgy. One meaning *e.g.,* to which the Sabbath points, according to the Torah, is that God created the world in six days and rested on the seventh. That anthropomorphic conception of divinity belongs to the antiquated notion of an earth-and-man-centered universe, with God intervening in the world order at any time He chooses to help or to hinder human beings in their pursuits, in accordance with their obedience or disobedience to the laws said to emanate from Him. Or, take for example the dietary laws as symbolizing the chosenness and special priestly function which the Torah assigns to Israel, a function that demands keeping aloof from other peoples, something which Jews nowadays repudiate both in theory and in practise. Moreover, take the salvation to which the performance of the ritual acts is a means according to traditional religion, of a share in the world to come, or bliss in the hereafter. How can that kind of salvation be sought after by those whose conception of a worthwhile human life has come to be essentially one which contributes toward making this world a better and happier place to live in? Why should they want to look forward to that kind of otherworldly salvation to such an extent as to practise acts that would remind them of the need of striving for it?

It thus becomes evident that the future of Jewish religious symbolism depends not alone upon the elimination from it of its theurgic element, but also upon reinterpretation or revaluation of the three main referents of that symbolism. Divinity, community, and salvation as indispensable elements in the pattern of our lives as human beings cannot form an integral part of the modern mind if they have to be conceived in such a way as to flout scientifically verified experience. They have to be reinterpreted and revalued if they are to vitalize the religious practises which symbolize them.

It would be going beyond the scope of this paper to do more than indicate some of the principles that have to be reckoned with in such a process of reinterpretation. It will not do to start out in the manner of a Descartes by doubting everything and then arrive at some metaphysical conception of God. Even if we were to arrive at some intellectually satisfying idea of God, it would hardly be conducive to the resumption of long abandoned religious ritual. It certainly is not the function of religious ritual to have us reflect on the metaphysical reality of God. Religion as such never originated from philosophical reflection about being. To have religious ritual function as a means to such reflection is like putting a square peg in a round hole.

In religion the conception of God has always been a correlate of the destiny which human beings ascribed to the community of which they were an organic part, and of the salvation which they hoped to achieve as members of that community. Consequently the problems to be dealt with in the revitalization of ritual practise are: 1) How shall we conceive the religious community so that we may count on it to help us achieve our salvation? 2) How shall we conceive salvation so as to find membership in our community indispensable to it? When we have answered these questions to our satisfaction, we have ready to hand the substance of that religious conception of God which should serve as the main referent in religious symbolism.

God, not merely as a metaphysical being but as the referent in worship and prayer is the Power that makes for salvation of man through the community that *organizes its entire social order around the purpose of man's salvation.* As the Power that makes for salvation, God will figure in the symbolism of ritual practise as the source of all moral and spiritual values. That makes an important difference in the way those values are regarded. Detached from their source in God, they are all too likely to be reduced to arbitrary rules which the group in power sets up for the furtherance of its own interests. Related to God, they are seen to be groping attempts which human nature, under all conditions, makes to approximate those ways of human living that are certain not only to perpetuate the human race but to help it fulfil the highest potentialities that inhere in all of its members.

The normal procedure, therefore, in the process of reinterpretation of traditional referents of religious symbolism is to begin with a study of the role played by the religious community in laying the foundation of the human person. For Jews, that community is the Jewish people; for Christians, it is the Church. The community provides that historic orientation to the life of mankind which gives direction and purpose to the life of the individual. Man's self-consciousness tends to individualize or separate him out of his human context. As an individual, the human being tends to experience a sense of aloneness and anomie unless he feels that he is organically related to some permanent group.

On the other hand, those who are born into a religious community with a long history and a great tradition behind it generally experience a sense of oneness with members of it, no matter where they happen to be. That sense of oneness has to find an outlet in moral and spiritual activity of a high order. It is the function of the community to provide such an outlet. Jews can raise the level of their historic people without necessarily regarding it as mankind's chosen people. Christians can do likewise with their Church, without regarding it as a *corpus mysticum* endowed with supernatural potency. Neither religious community is in need of claiming sole possession of the key to salvation.

It thus appears that before we can even wish to reinterpret the referents of the religious practises of any people or church we must experience a sense of active oneness with it. That provides the indispensable motive to translate its traditional and theurgy-laden conceptions of salvation and divinity into natural and spiritual terms.

There is no problem more difficult and more urgent than that of knowing in what direction man should develop and utilize his unique urge for salvation. Religious ritual, freed of theurgy and interpreted symbolically, can help to keep alive that urge. Even if it cannot advance, it can intensify the desire to attain, the knowledge of what salvation consists in and how it can be achieved. That is how we can come to know God, in the only way it is possible for man to know Him, as the Power that makes for salvation.

How the referents of the symbolic trend in ritual practise—God, the community, and salvation—can be reinterpreted along lines entirely free from theurgy may be exemplified by means of what can be done with the Jewish Sabbath. The Sabbath is the most sacred of all observances in the religious routine of the Jew. Tradition assigns to it four meanings: 1) God as the Creator of the world, 2) Israel as covenanted to God, 3) God as Israel's redeemer, and 4) a foretaste of the bliss in the hereafter.

In the tradition, every one of these meanings carries with it theurgic implications. By substituting for those implications moral and spiritual values which are essential to the realization of our human potential, the Sabbath comes to symbolize the following: 1) creativity as a manifestation of the Divine in nature and in man; 2) realization, on the part of the Jewish people, of that organic unity which is essential to its living with a sense of destiny as every people should; 3) man's creativity, which is a manifestation of the Divine, and which cannot be released unless man is free from coercion both individually and collectively; 4) concern with salvation, which should permeate all human endeavors.

The same method of reinterpretation can be applied to the other religious practises. Given the desire on the part of the Jew to belong to the Jewish people, or on the part of the Christian to belong to his Church, most of the traditional practises in their respective religions can be made to symbolize those compelling and inspiring truths that are certain to revitalize the Judeo-Christian tradition.

XIII

THE FUTURE OF RELIGIOUS SYMBOLISM— A CATHOLIC VIEW

BY

JOHN LaFARGE, S.J., M.A.

Associate Editor, "America"

The future of religious symbolism is I believe very bright. My reason for hopefulness is a confluence of impulses encouraging such a development. The astounding growth of commercial symbolism seen in the advertising industry and in various forms of public relations is balanced by the decommercializing in recent times of religious art, or at least the steady movement to free religious art from the bondage of commercial production. This means a release of creativeness. The creation may often be of a not very high order, some of it juvenile, some of it fumbling or bizarre. But the upsurge around the country of such creativeness in religious art points to the liberation of church art from the bonds which have so long disgraced it.

In such a matter generalizations are difficult. Nevertheless, it can be safely said that the tremendous use of symbols by the totalitarian movements has stimulated the feeling that they must be offset not by mere ridicule but by positive constructive symbolism on the part of the democratic world. In other words, the quest for effective symbols of democracy goes hand in hand with the quest for a more perfect symbolic statement of religion itself.

Solicitude for a greater dignity of the liturgy in the various religious groups is also a natural encouragement to developing of symbolism. In the Catholic liturgical movement stress on certain doctrines such as the Mystical Body of Christ, the social significance of the Sacraments, the mystical interpretation of the marriage ceremony, and particularly the wide development of congregational participation in the Eucharistic Sacrifice have enormously stimulated the quest for more perfect symbolic expression.

At the present day, indeed, it is inconceivable that any religious group, certainly of the Judeo-Christian tradition, can divest itself completely of symbolic expression. Even one of the most non-symbolic of cults, that of the Society of Friends, or Quakers, is sustained in the sense of worship and religious activity by the powerful symbolic expression inherent in the practise of silence and in certain restrictions or plainness of dress. A complete abandonment of all symbolism, or attempt at its abandonment, could only result in a sort of bizarre rationalism, as was the case with the odd character of medieval legend, Till Eulenspiegel, half clown and half sage. Till's aim was to mock all human pretense by taking every allegorical or figurative expression in an absolutely literal sense, and to treat every symbol in the same spirit. In this way he held up the "mirror" (*Spiegel*) to human pretense, but in so doing drove himself into an arid and sterile spiritual desert.

Certain responses to the age appear in this rather universal revival. Religious symbolism did not originate in a vacuum but grew out of the imaginative and occupational concepts of the period and its prevailing sense. We sense today the universality of human interests, the problem of adapting the individual to the exigencies of the world organization; so through religious symbolism those elements are most likely to be developed which stress the universal and link the individual to the world.

On the other hand, linking the individual to the entire world means also linking the individual to past time. As we penetrate the significance of symbolism itself we understand the deeper significance of ancient and traditional symbolic forms; we desire to revive and cultivate them and to stress those elements which are imperishable. To take an instance out of many: in recent times we have come to understand more clearly the symbolic character of one of the least symbolic forms of religious art, that of the baroque period in the seventeenth century. Through its very literalness this type of art symbolizes the existential battle of the soul striving to liberate itself from the impurities of life and unite itself with the eternal.

A third great response to the age is the development in religious art of an appreciation of what is native and cultural. The very attention paid today to the universality of the human race has also opened our eyes to the individual gifts of particular races and regions. We prize the dignity of aboriginal art with its competent use of materials and its fidelity to the world as the native artist sees it. In any collection of so-called primitive art you are impressed by the skillful use made of the form and gestures of the human body as a means of expressing a mood or an idea.

A particularly difficult problem in religious symbolism arises from the change that has taken place in recent times. How far must it draw on new imaginative sources in order to adapt itself to the contemporary urban dweller's? The most beautiful and appealing elements in traditional religious symbolism are drawn from a life which moved at a different rhythm from that of the modern world. Liturgy and art drew their images from the cycle of seasons, seedtime, harvest, crops, the movements of the sun and the moon, the world of familiar natural objects. In an agrarian culture change of season aroused much greater emotional response than it does in our well regulated modern suburban or industrial existence. The modern American's life rhythm is that of a person taking the train or speedway to his place of work and back, the rhythm of the lunch hour and the evening motion picture, of the summer vacation and the forty hour week. Much of the modern rhythm can be expressed graphically through language, but it is difficult for the eye and ear to draw from it inspiring images.

At the same time, in the modern world we are susceptible to wider rhythms than were felt in former periods. We sense the world rhythm, the march of events through whole continents and cycles. At New Year's we do not simply recall our personal household affairs of the past year or those of our immediate neighbors; we review the preceding year and speculate as to what may happen during the coming twelve months in the nation, in the world.

Again, there are new rhythms of human relations. When vast but highly ordered and highly organized multitudes meet together for intellectual discourse or community organization of prayer and worship they challenge the symbolic imagination.

Here indeed is a twofold challenge. Challenge number one is obvious: richer creativeness; concepts of new forms that will be fundamentally in line with religious tradition, yet will express it in language more adapted to the modern mind and modern psychological experience. But we also need to emphasize those elements of religious symbolism which preserve the steadying influence of ancient rhythms amidst the monotony and confusion of modern life. This is the second challenge. It is not without significance that the most perfectly run museum in the City of New York and possibly in the whole country is that of the Cloisters at the northern end of Manhattan Island. Religious symbolism will not merely interpret the age but it will also enable men to escape from the age's tyranny, for that tyranny is a violation of the essential dignity and rhythmic harmony of human life.

I see, therefore, in the future a kind of dialectic: a creative adaptation, a creative preservation, and a creative innovation in the matter of religious symbolism, and along with that an interpretation of this creation through language itself. A certain rivalry will always prevail between symbolism and language, language which interprets and explains discursively that which the symbol conveys in its own inimitable fashion. Symbolism without language becomes stale and superstitious; language without symbolism is devoid of emotional appeal and deprives man of one of his noblest sources of religious intuition. Contrary to some views, I hold that genuine religious symbolism can be interpreted in terms of language. I do not know whether all language can be interpreted in terms of religious symbolism, but at any rate there is a noble contest between the two.

History repeats itself, and we may expect in the future some elements of a contest which has colored the history of Christian art and is bound to influence all other forms of religious art as well, a contest which reached its most acute form in the iconoclast battles of the eighth century of the Christian era. Today, in the field of religious representations, we see a revolt against an overnaturalistic and sweetly human type of pictorial or plastic expression. The revolt takes the form of non-figurative decorations, or in a preference for the stark and tragic rather than the gentle and pleasing in the depicting of religious personalities and events. Yet this tendency in turn produces its own reaction, as medieval art was not content with the solemn and hieratical splendors of the early basilicas. The Church, ever on guard against the aberrations of the idolater with his appeal to sensuality and superstition, remembers also from bitter experience, that the one-track-minded image smasher can be as religiously destructive in his own fanatical way as the idolater. In their own sphere symbolic rites and gestures steer a course between the two extremes of loose individualism, leading to a virtual denial of the communitarian nature of worship, and a rigid petrification of ritualistic minutiae.

I personally believe that no set of formulas, however adroitly limited and conceived, can serve as a perfect guide in the age long journey between the two extremes: midway between the pious hedonist and the blazing angel of iconoclastic righteousness. Only the Spirit of God can point the way, working in the creative minds of Heavenward-struggling generations. My confidence in the future of religious symbolism reflects my trust in the abiding presence of the Holy Spirit Himself.

XIV

THE FUTURE OF RELIGIOUS SYMBOLISM—
A PROTESTANT VIEW

BY

STANLEY ROMAINE HOPPER, PH.D.

Professor of Christian Ethics, Drew Theological Seminary

Protestantism is frequently charged with being esthetically barren, and so without enduring appeal either to the "people of taste"
or to "the masses." The first part of this statement is to a great extent
true, though less so, perhaps, than is generally supposed. At the
same time, it is doubtless better, as Jung remarks, "to confess strong-
mindedly to the spiritual poverty of a want of symbols than to feign
a possession of which we can in no case be the spiritual heirs." [1]

In making such a confession, however, it ought to be noted that
the plight of Protestantism, in this regard, is but one side of the
coin of Christendom; for we experience today a sort of Kantian
antinomy (if the paraphrase may be allowed): symbols without concepts are empty (the priestly excess); concepts without symbols are
blind (the legalistic excess).

The true Protestant principle, however, is prophetic, and belongs
to neither of these extremes, though constantly tempted by both.
In its actual development it has succumbed to the "Puritan" barrenness, the legalistic extreme; and today there is a strong movement
within the Protestant church to correct this excess by resort to the
other—to a reinstatement of the medieval matrix of images. Thus,
like Luther's intoxicated man on the horse—you prop him up on one

---

[1] C. G. Jung, *The Integration of the Personality*, Farrar & Rinehart, Inc., New
York, 1939, p. 63.

side and he topples on the other. This is a pathetic move, dramatizing the failure of Protestantism since the time of the Reformation to grasp its own principle and to elaborate it creatively. We are left in the awkward position of going after strange gods, of seeking ready-made symbols wherewith to clothe our nakedness; but (to quote Jung again) "are we not commanded, somewhere, to hold no masquerade, but perhaps even to make our own garment ourselves?"

Jung's views on Protestantism are useful for a variety of reasons. They state a position bluntly and clearly:

> The history of the development of Protestantism is one of chronic iconoclasm. One wall after another fell. And the work of destruction was not too difficult, either, when once the authority of the church had been shattered. We all know how, in large things as in small, in general as well as in particular, piece after piece collapsed, and how the alarming impoverishment of symbolism that is now the condition of life came about. The power of the church has gone with that loss of symbolism, too. . . .[2]

The iconoclasm—the shattering of icons, images—is not necessarily a bad thing.

> That the gods die from time to time is due to man's discovery that they do not mean anything, that they are good-for-nothings made by human hands, fashioned out of wood and stone. In reality, man has thus discovered only this: that up till then he had not achieved one thought concerning these images.[3]

Dogmas, based upon authority, are also a protection against thoughts such as these, which lead the thinker into the precincts of what Paul J. Tillich calls our "ultimate concern." The dogmatic symbol "protects a person from a direct experience of God as long as he does not mischievously expose himself."[4] But again, the shattering is not necessarily a bad thing:

> Though properly speaking it is a pitiful collapse which offends our sense of history, the disintegration of Protestantism into nearly four hundred denominations is yet an infallible sign of life, and shows that the

[2] *Ibid.*, p. 61.
[3] *Ibid.*, p. 60.
[4] *Ibid.*, p. 52.

restlessness is growing. The Protestant with nothing left but the historical figure of Christ, a much-debated idea of God, and a compulsive faith, in which—Heaven knows!—he has very poor success, is actually thrust forth into a state of defencelessness. . . .[5]

I am convinced that Protestant man has not in vain been despoiled of his own development, and made to go naked. This development has an inner consistency. . . . It is dangerous to confess to spiritual poverty, for whoever is poor has cravings and whoever craves draws his fate upon himself . . . spiritual poverty seeks to renounce the false riches of the spirit. . . . Whoever has chosen the state of spiritual poverty, the true heritage of a Protestantism lived out consistently to the end, goes the way of the soul that leads to the water. . . . Water is the commonest symbol for . . . spirit that has become unconscious.[6]

Certainly this is an impoverished view of an impoverished Protestantism; but the point is (for whatever causes) that with the failure of the symbols of Christendom to contain the experience of Western man, we have been thrust increasingly upon ourselves, and in our ambiguous experience of our "dreadful freedom" we have had to experience that confrontation with the unconscious—one of the "more unpleasant things that may be avoided as long as we possess living symbol-figures in which all that is inner and unknown is projected." [7]

Jung feels that this condition is something new in the history of the race; that heretofore all peoples believed in gods of some kind. "Only an unparalleled impoverishment in symbolism could enable us to rediscover the gods as psychic factors, which is to say, as archetypes of the unconscious." [8] Here the way swings off into his own special answer, the development of the archetypal symbols of the unconscious, which it is not our present purpose to pursue. We are interested only in this blunt appraisal of our situation, and in this oblique recognition of the Protestant dialectic, the very genius of which (as with Scripture generally) is to confront man with himself at the point of his God-relation (or his ultimate concern). It also suggests that Christendom's alliance with Neo-Platonism and the sub-

[5] *Ibid.,* p. 61.
[6] *Ibid.,* pp. 63–68, *passim.*
[7] *Ibid.,* p. 69.
[8] *Ibid.,* p. 72.

stantialistic world view generally, was itself an alliance with a world picture, susceptible of indefinite symbolic expansion, and of such a sort that the confrontation symbols of the New Testament were accommodated to a sacramental system which floated the symbols in the protective suspension of estheticomystical archetypes—themselves preceded by "the Greco-Roman mysteries" which in turn "reached back into the grey mists of neolithic prehistory." "Mankind has never lacked powerful images to lend magic aid against the uncanny, living depths of the world and of the psyche." [9] The biblical realism was certain to break through this unstable "synthesis": that it did so in the "Reformation" is only the external (historical) evidence of what was latent from the beginning. This is the "historical" factor which Christian symbolism must take into account in the future. In short, the confrontation-redemption events of Scripture are the genuine paradigms of the "symbols of transformation" so dramatically pursued today by the depth psychologist. Otto Rank comes nearer to this perspective when he remarks that "the modern type of psychotherapist who gradually succeeds the priest, has to thank this same ideology of redemption-of-the-other for his origin and steady growth." [10]

Before pursuing this point further—full development of which would require a closer definition of the "Protestant principle," as well as a further amplification of the symbolic virtues of the Scripture paradigms—it is desirable to broaden the setting of the Jungian assault: for it (1) channels the analysis too preclusively within the psychologist's perspective (though we shall perforce return to this); and (2) it takes too parochial a view of Protestantism. For while the Protestant principle is a principle of protest, it is also a protest against "Protestantism"—if viewed parochially, or statically: for Protestantism is itself a protest—a protest against both ecclesiolatry and metaphysical compromise, and a protest for (*pro*) the biblical *kerygma,* the core of the teaching, and the prophetic-biblical-existential *koinonia,* the open fellowship in the Spirit of *all* those who are "called." We must note more closely, however, the several ways in which this

[9] *Ibid.*, p. 60.
[10] Otto Rank, *Will Therapy and Truth and Reality,* Alfred A. Knopf, New York, 1945, p. 303.

consciousness is today being precipitated, almost fortuitously, by the inner dialectic of the pervasive "impoverishment of symbols."

A useful instance, for example, is that of Brice Parain,[11] who discovered through difficult personal experience that words are intrinsically ambiguous, partly expressing and partly constricting (and so falsifying) our meanings. He discovered further that all communication is based upon systems of agreement and social norms. Words, symbols, images, are thus a protection and structure of order, up to a point. "I have learnt," he said, "after much spiritual abandon, that the mediating forms exist to prevent us from escaping from ourselves, and raise against our excesses barriers beyond which we are threatened with destruction." But when these mediating forms become diseased, or lose their relevance, or become morally ambiguous, or are emptied from within when the life of man moves out from under them and passes on to a deeper need, then they become oppressive and vicious in their restraining and enslaving power. Parain discovered this to be true of the language of 1940: it was full of diseased words, in which "Peace" meant aggression, "Liberty" oppression, and "Socialism" a regime of social inequality. This perception had a disintegrating effect upon Parain, and led Sartre to say of him, "He was word-sick, and he wants to become cured." This is a dramatic instance of the way in which the deterioration of the very words of a culture—themselves derivative from metaphor, from the more primitive sign and symbol—may help to bring about the deterioration of the ordered consciousness, both culturally and individually. This is true equally, and in much the same manner, of the mediating forms and symbols of religion.

This is a point, however, which we may grasp too easily. We may be tempted to accept it superficially, and so unwittingly insulate ourselves against its implications. Or we may argue defensively that we have here an uncriticized instance of putting the effect for the cause, that the *real* cause for the deterioration of words and symbols is in the antecedent moral deterioration of the people who use them. Which is undoubtedly true in the foreshortened perspective of the observer

[11] Brice Parain, *Essays on Language and Literature,* J. L. Hevesi, editor, Allen Wingate Publishers, London, first published 1947.

who still (either consciously or unconsciously) accepts the presuppositions which the experience of deterioration has (at bottom) called
into question. This irrational fact of inner conflict challenges the
adequacy of the classical postulates, with its analogies of "logic" and
"mathematics" and "being," and the concomitant supposition that
"truth" is something "objective" and "absolute" in this same analogical context. "Words should be left to rot where they lie," urges Parain.
No doubt they do this slowly, once their original living (metaphori-
cal) properties have died. But the difficulty is similar to that which
every great thinker learns in relation to his followers: droves of disciples will hive in the carcass of a philosopher's system long after the
philosopher himself has moved on to another position. In other words,
there is a primary practical setting in which or out of which the
symbols of communication (of meaning) are wrought: we strive to
maintain the stabilities of meaning through sanctifying, and so making rigid, the setting which contains the meanings. But as we *must*
keep meaning alive, every such indurated setting becomes a chrysalis
from which transformed flights of meaning must emerge.

Parain comes near to saying this in a passage which he quotes from
Karl Marx:

The question of finding out whether human thought can lead to an objective truth is a practical, not a theoretical, question. It is by action, that
is to say, by its reality, its objectivity, that the truth of a thought must be
proved . . . . so far the philosophers have done nothing but interpret the
world in different ways. Now it is a matter of transforming it.

This is clearly a dangerous extension of the insight; but the very
danger in it points up the importance (1) of not taking the insight
superficially; and (2) of recognizing that truth is not, as Hegel remarked, a "minted coin which can be freely given and received."

The allusion to Sartre above will serve to indicate how easily this
experience of Parain, with its implications, finds an easy rapport with
the existentialist's "dreadful freedom." Sartre's point of view puts the
primary freedom always in the foreground of his work:

Il s'agit censément de ruiner l'idée d'une nécessité qui nous serait
extérieure et dériverait d'une stabilité des choses ou d'un ordre moral ob-

jectif. . . . Au contraire, le principe premier de leur existence concrète, est à situer dans une *option profonde, absolument gratuite,* par laquelle ils se choisissent absolument.[12]

The flaw in Sartre does not appear to me to lie in his situating the individual at the point of his primary option (absolutely gratuitous), by which he must choose himself absolutely; nor does it lie at the point of the *psychanalyse existentielle* whereby the individual is forced dialectically upon this choosing. It lies rather in his nihilistic begging of the religious question. The Nietzschean proposition of the "death of God" may apply to particular gods, to particular symbolizations of the ultimate, in line with Jung's notation that the gods die from time to time due to man's discovery that they do not mean anything: *i.e.,* that they have ceased to symbolize adequately the nature of reality and thus have ceased to satisfy the demand which present experience lays upon them. No doubt these symbolizations were in some part "projections" (as Jung implies), like projections upon a screen, to use Tillich's figure; but this is not the *whole* story, for, as Tillich observes, they are projections upon something. The screen is there, as an Unconditional somewhat other than ourselves; and, at the very least, this otherness conditions us into an awareness of the boundaries, or "limit-situations," of the human predicament. This also is in line with the Protestant principle, save that the Protestant principle would carry the imperative of the primary option over into the context of Pauline freedom and the indicative of love (*agape*). It is not true, therefore, as François Mauriac has remarked of Sartre's liberty [13] that it is an "absurd liberty" (though Sartre, on nihilistic grounds, may hold it absurdly); but it is profoundly true, as Mauriac concludes, that "we know that a creature loved as much as we are has no other liberty than that of refusing that love, to the degree to which it has made itself known to him and under the appearances it has been pleased to assume." [14] This again is the Protestant principle (relative

[12] Regis Jolivet, *Les Doctrines Existentialistes de Kierkegaard à J.-P. Sartre, Éditions de Fontenelle,* Paris, 1948, p. 145.

[13] François Mauriac, *Men I Hold Great,* Philosophical Library, New York, 1951, p. 127.

[14] *Ibid.,* p. 128.

to freedom and *agape*) though enunciated by the French Catholic winner of the Nobel Prize; that is, it is the Christian principle stated within the categories of its biblical setting, showing no refracting dependence on the alien metaphysic of Hellenic intellectualism.

This latter point we must now consider with some care, not from the standpoint of philosophical system, but from the standpoint of *Weltanschauungsphilosophie*—especially with regard to the revision of the philosopher's starting point going on about us, and the bearing of this upon symbolic representation.

Let us note first that the cosmological setting of our basic images, or symbols, has been altered radically; secondly, how this gives rise to what Susanne K. Langer has called "philosophy in a new key"; and thirdly, how clearly the semantic implications emerge from this.

The first is easily stated, though not, perhaps, easily grasped. We are today well aware of the movement of the Western consciousness from a variety of primitive world pictures through the well articulated Ptolemaic and Copernican "systems" and into our radically altered "expanding universe" picture of the present time. Nevertheless, the present world of relativity and quantum hypotheses cannot be pictured as were the older world views. It is now pictured through the abstract symbols of mathematics. These are offered in the form of hypotheses awaiting verification of the statistical and probable kind. Assertions made within the context of a given hypothesis are relative to the practical validity of the hypothesis. The hypothesis itself is "a symbolic representation" of the world as seen from a unique vantage point—a symbolic structure built up on what Eddington described so graphically as "pointer readings." "Our knowledge of objects treated in physics consists solely of readings of pointers and other indicators." [15] Which scrutiny leads "not to a concrete reality but to a shadow world of symbols." [16] This blunt recognition of the subjective and symbolic features of the "world building" of contemporary science illustrates graphically the radical nature of the changing world

[15] Sir Arthur S. Eddington, *The Nature of the Physical World,* University Press, Cambridge, England, 1928, p. 258.

[16] Eddington, *Science and the Unseen World,* The Macmillan Company, New York, 1929, p. 73.

view through which we are moving. "It appears," writes Émile Cailliet, ". . . that Western man has been·thinking thus far within two great cosmological frames of reference, namely, the Aristotelian and the Newtonian. Further, it would seem that from the second one he is now slowly proceeding into a third, that is, the framework of relativity and quanta. It should also be pointed out that each transition involved a cultural crisis." [17] This forced upon Eddington, *qua* philosopher, a "return to our starting point in human consciousness" —which meant, for him, a return upon philosophical idealism. For others it has meant a return upon themselves desperately; unable any more to picture themselves in their ordered place in the world they fall prey to a floating insecurity, fear, and "metaphysical anxiety."

In yet another way men have been despoiled of the symbolic order of philosophical systems, in so far as these systems were expressions of the world picture become obsolete. "Each philosophical creed petrified the state of physics that prevailed at the time," says Philipp G. Frank [18] on which Cailliet comments: "And so, in a way, comprehensive philosophical views prove to be in part abandoned rationalizations of an obsolete science." [19] Mrs. Langer, however, puts this differently, by shifting the focus from the obsolete world picture to the philosophical form in itself. "A philosophy is characterized more by the *formulation* of its problems than by its solution of them." [20] These questions "make the frame in which its picture of facts is plotted." [21]

It is quite impossible to present here an outline of the full implications of this claim. We may note, nevertheless, that what these questions articulate is a backlying attitude of mind, a *Weltanschauung:* and though there may be a number of variant philosophical systems which expound a limited number of basic assumptions underlying a given philosophical epoch, there are only "a certain limited number

[17] Émile Cailliet, *The Christian Approach to Culture,* Abingdon-Cokesbury Press, Nashville, 1953, p. 168.
[18] Philipp G. Frank, *Modern Science and Its Philosophy,* Harvard University Press, Cambridge, 1949, p. 23.
[19] *Op. cit.,* p. 174.
[20] Susanne K. Langer, *Philosophy in a New Key: A Study in the Symbolism of Reason, Rite, and Art,* Penguin Books, Inc., New York, 1942 p. 2.
[21] *Ibid.*

of types of philosophic systems . . . possible" within such an epoch. From which it follows that when the implications of the basic questions are fully explored a given philosophical epoch is terminated, and when a new basic question is raised a new epoch begins.

Today, Mrs. Langer holds, "the springs of philosophical thought have run dry once more . . . (and) a new generative idea has dawned." [22] This new idea for philosophy will be found "in the fundamental notion of symbolization" which has become the keynote of all our present problems.[23]

Practically, this means that we do not all of us inhabit the same world, as T. S. Eliot once remarked. Some continue to project the medieval world view upon reality, and weave increasingly complex metaphysical and authoritarian defenses wherewith to secure the attitude; others are still (perhaps unconsciously) Copernicans, or Deists of the Enlightenment, or primitives by one resort or another. The psychological factor in all this is clearly recognized by Mrs. Langer. "The driving force in human minds is fear, which begets an imperious demand for a world-picture that fills all experience and gives each individual a definite *orientation* amid the terrifying forces of nature and society." [24] From which it may easily be seen how, when our master images, or generative ideas, or basic symbols are threatened with radically new perspectives which require of us the courage to venture into an uncharted realm of fresh concepts and more adequate symbols, the unconscious security-demand will drive us into all manner of reactionary efforts. The "neo"-movements will usually be found to conceal unconscious security interests seeking the comfort of earlier formulas at the precise moment when the life-demand is in the call to construe creatively the symbolic structure of the new epoch.

Mrs. Langer's own world picture owes much to Whitehead and to Cassirer who had much to say concerning the symbol:

No longer in a merely physical universe, man lives in a symbolic universe. Language, myth, art, and religion are parts of this universe. They are the varied threads which weave the symbolic net, the tangled web of

[22] *Ibid.*, pp. 9, 16.
[23] *Ibid.*, p. 19.
[24] *Ibid.*, p. 128.

human experience. . . . [Man] has so enveloped himself in linguistic forms, in artistic images, in mythical symbols or religious rites that he cannot see or know anything except by the interposition of this artificial medium. . . . Hence, instead of defining man as an *animal rationale,* we should define him as an *animal symbolicum.*[25]

We should note, in all of this, a transposition of the place and function of logic, as well as a rejection of the "classical" orientation generally. The traditional "logic of terms," says Mrs. Langer, is "really a metaphysic of meaning; the new philosophy of meaning is first of all a logic of terms—of signs and symbols—an analysis of the relational patterns in which 'meaning' may be sought." . . . "The Aristotelian metaphysic of substance and attribute is a counterpart of the Aristotelian logic of subject and predicate." The new view recognizes that "a proposition is a picture of a structure—the picture of a state of affairs," and that such a picture "is essentially a symbol, not a duplicate, of what it represents." [26]

The bearing of all of this upon the semantic problem may be illustrated quite briefly. Two instances will suffice. In a recent volume dealing with the problem of communication, it is held that "truth" is relative to the context in which it is held; and that "context is determined by the questions which we ask of events." [27] Again, Alfred Korzybski remarked in 1924:

All human knowledge is conditioned and limited, at present, by the properties of light and human symbolism. . . . Einstein's theory is a fundamental inquiry and *application* of the known properties of light; the *irrefutable minimum* of his theory results in an entirely new world conception, as beautiful and cheerful as the old ones were gloomy and despairing.[28]

Such an irrefutable minimum must be made the starting point for an inquiry into the structure of human knowledge and symbolism.

[25] Ernst Cassirer, *Essay on Man,* Yale University Press, New Haven, 1944, pp. 25–26.
[26] *Op. cit.,* pp. 54–55.
[27] Gregory Bateson in *Communication, the Social Matrix of Psychiatry,* by Jurgen Ruesch and Gregory Bateson, W. W. Norton & Company, New York, 1951, p. 236.
[28] Alfred Korzybski, *Time-Binding: The General Theory,* abstract, E. P. Dutton & Company, New York, 1924, p. 5.

Enough has now been said to make it clear that the future of symbolism in Protestantism (or elsewhere) has nothing to do with esthetics primarily. The question of "esthetic barrenness" is almost purely secondary. The problem of the future of Protestant symbolism has to do with the primary context of the Christian faith, from which esthetic factors should emerge as functional means definable with reference to the objects of belief. First comes, Christianly speaking, the Event—at the intersection of contexts, meanings, symbols; gathering them up, so to speak, "absolutely," in order to invest them with new context, new meaning, new (and infinite) implication. This is the Event which "recapitulates" (Irenaeus) the whole, qualifies radically all previous signification, and disposes the future of meanings in so far as the Event is *seen*. It *opens* the universe of meanings infinitely, bursting the hardened forms of finitized beliefs, and requiring the creative construction of its infinite implication. But at once the Event is converted into an object of belief: Jesus as manifesting the Christ, defines and finitizes the Event in its soteriological significance. This is already a first abstraction from the Event in its infinite implication. Then comes the label—the "Christ"—itself a symbol of the first abstraction, and the point of primary danger in the symbolization of further meanings.

The Christian is persuaded, in other words, that the Event of Christ brought about what Austin Farrer has so well described as a "crisis of images." Behind the general images of a culture (*e.g.*, that of the Hebrew people), there are certain "master images" which not only reflect the backlying world picture of the people, but also inform and control the subordinate images through which the people of that community interpret their experience and formulate their meanings. The master images of the Hebrews included "the image of the God who is as man and not as man: the image of the divine word . . . : the image of the covenant . . . : the image of the divine indwelling in the hill of Zion. . . ." These were "the unalterable images, the axiomatic images of faith, which stand behind all the prophet's particular oracles." [29] But the Event of Jesus as manifesting the Christ

[29] Austin Farrer, *The Glass of Vision*, Dacre Press, Westminster (London), 1948, p. 133.

brought about a crisis of these master images: "The appearance of a new religion (which the apostles were publishing), and the transformation of basic images, are not simply connected things: they are one and the same thing. There was a crisis of images in the experience of the witnesses to the incarnation. . . ." [30] But the danger point came when the Event which was seen passed over into the symbols of communication—especially as these were constrained by contexts (Hebrew and Hellenic) which bent the Event into the restrictive arc of antique world views. And here again (the temptation which assails all symbols), the symbols were themselves objectivized and to a degree substituted for the living and infinite properties of the Event. Thus the Event, with its infinite opening into the life abundant, becomes closed in the coercive attempt to make it revolve about the pseudo-centers of contention between the competing claims of objectivized symbols.

The Protestant protest is against this conversion of symbols from means of communication to false centers of objectivization, even when it occurs within Protestantism. The efficacy of the symbol, that is, must lie in its power to draw the one to whom it communicates its meaning not into itself, nor into an accommodation of itself to an alien context, but into the infinite and living realism of the Event it partially represents. The symbol must not stand between, blocking the way, but must *point to* and, at the same time, communicate the Event. Which is again a part of the Protestant protest, and of its doctrine of the Word. For symbols we have with us always; and even Korzybski concedes that "man is ultimately a doctrinal being." [31] But there is a difference between those symbols and doctrines which close upon themselves as coercive centers of control, and those which forbid such foreclosure and open the way to the Event and to the place of meeting.

Because a full application of this difference is out of the question in so brief a treatment, we shall focus briefly upon three aspects of Protestant symbolism as they relate to this requirement.

[30] *Ibid.*, p. 134.
[31] *Op. cit.*, p. 23.

(1) *The question of the context, whether it is hierarchical or dramatic.*

This question has to do with the way in which Christian symbols are held, and with the two predominating or competing contexts within which they now appear. The hierarchical context appropriates the Heraclitean formula of the "upward and the downward way," compounds it metaphysically with Platonic, Aristotelian, Plotinian and Neo-Platonic principles, and characterizes the Hellenic periods in Christian history through the medieval period. It is prominent in the tradition of medieval mysticism; its soteriological principle is that of ascent to union with God. This is the "Catholic" context within which ecclesiastical symbols have acquired their form and definition. It is this "universe of discourse" which consciously or unconsciously dominates the interpretation of symbols and their meanings in the Christian community today. It is foolish to discuss the future of symbolism in Protestantism as long as this hierarchical context remains unchallenged; just as it is foolish for Protestants to attempt to overcome the "barrenness" of their orders of worship by importing "symbols" which attach, by definition, to this hierarchical context. Such attempts represent a failure to understand the prophetic import of the Reformation "protest."

The other context is the dramatic one. As over against the Heraclitean "upward and downward way," its motif is that of "journey and return" after the pattern, the redemptive pattern, of the Prodigal Son. It implies a theological displacement of the entire "primacy of Being" orientation. As against the scholastic analogy of logic and mathematics (in which the esthetic principle is confined after Pythagoras), its analogy is that of existence culminating in the *analogia crucis*—the analogy of the Cross. Instead of mystical withdrawal and otherworldly absorption, its movement is one of engagement in the world; instead of union its goal is communion, instead of mediation of the priest, the Christ of the Gospels becomes the Paradigm. Its tradition begins with God's creative act, but moves through Abraham (the covenant image), Hosea, Jeremiah, the Suffering Servant, Job, Irenaeus, Clement's recognition of the "drama," Athanasius's view of sin as "moral phthisis," or wasting away, together with the later work of Augustine and Luther's renewal of the dramatic view of the work of Christ.

One must hasten to add that this view has never yet become normative for Protestantism; for the obvious reason that this dimension was not grasped by those who came after Luther. The Reformation protest congealed quickly around the Institutes of Calvin and the work of Melancthon: too quickly for the radical rejection of the classical categories to take hold, with the result that classical rational theology, without benefit of the mystical hierarchical metaphysic, flowed through—a scholasticism necessarily "barren" esthetically, ameliorated only by the belated appeal to the "feeling" principle in Schleiermacher (which does not shift the contextual axis), and by the immeasurable grandeur of music, which essentially dramatic, not hierarchical in its nature, responded joyously to this prophetic move to oratorio and praise.

It is for this reason that the effective symbols in Protestantism, up to the present time, have been largely musical, though art and letters bear witness to it, too. But the recovery of this context is going forward apace both philosophically and theologically today, chiefly in those centers where existentialism has taken hold. "The Protestant formative power is at work wherever reality is transformed into an active expression of a *Gestalt* of Grace." [32] Or, to repeat in Tillich's form what we have said above:

The Protestant principle . . . is not to be confused with the "Absolute" of German idealism or with the "Being" of ancient and recent philosophy. It is not the highest ontological concept derived from an analysis of the whole of being; it is the theological expression of the true relation between the unconditional and the conditioned or, religiously speaking, between God and man.[33]

One may go further and say that, due to the failure of the early Protestant theologians to grasp this principle in its dramatic form, the principle itself had necessarily to go underground—that is, to

[32] Paul Tillich, *The Protestant Era,* The University of Chicago Press, Chicago, 1951, p. 219. This essay, and the others in Section IV of that volume are highly relevant to this entire discussion.
[33] *Ibid.,* p. 163.

disclose itself through the extra-ecclesiastical ventures of secular enterprise. It is for this reason that the Protestant protest exhibits itself with such vitality today in contemporary literature, where, working outside the sanction of the Church in unconscious protest against the rationalistic Protestant scholasticism, it probes from within the sense of alienation the very secrets of alienation, and so moves increasingly into the moment of recognition. "We are approaching it the hard way, through an unparalleled period of dissidence. . . . The new substance must be reached through the battlefield of alienation." It is the moment of "transfiguration by estrangement." [34] Which again is a part of the Protestant principle, which leads one not out of the world but into it, not out of our condition but into it, in order that the reversal may take place at the core and not at the periphery of authentic self-hood.

The dramatic principle, in short, contains the initial opposition between protagonist and antagonist; it is bound to the time factor which moves dialectically toward the catastrophe; here must take place the peripety, or discovery, with the recapitulation and catharsis of the whole *in an event* which brings about the reversal of fortunes or the reconciliation ethically of the principles at issue. It is for this reason that the Protestant principle revives philosophy of history, brings the teleology of the Kingdom into prominence, and renews the dimension of eschatology. But this is a prophetic, and not a priestly context; just as it is a dramatic and not an hierarchical one. As Austin Farrer puts it when speaking of the prophet Jeremiah:

If we grant that the self-will of the creature can be experienced by the creature as a straining of its bond with the creative act, then we can say that the prophet dramatizes the ineluctable hold of the creator, and the self-punishment of our rebellions; he casts into personal and mythological form the ever varying revenges of Eternal Truth upon our restless infidelities.[35]

But that is the Protestant *Gestalt*, derived redemptively from the work of Christ.

[34] Harry Slochower, *No Voice is Wholly Lost*, Creative Age Press, New York, 1945, p. 380.
[35] *Op. cit.*, p. 125.

(2) *The question as to the mode of deliverance, whether it is by repression and sublimation, or by grace and the spirit.*

Both the Hellenic psychology and its intellectualistic metaphysic impose an ethic of repression, later ameliorated by the Church into one of sublimation. Protestantism, with no place for the Virgin Mary, is perpetually running the risk of an overmasculinized world view tending toward a tyrannical and overbearing theology—Calvin, Barth, Kafka, etc. The doctrine of the Holy Spirit has never succeeded in becoming a compensating feminine principle, though the claim that the Holy Spirit is the feminine person of the Trinity has not been without its devotees.

Jung has recognized this problem, and feels that the strength of Protestantism consists in its power to draw the worshiper into the precincts of his inner self, to expose him to the real abyss, where those persons with sufficient strength and courage may be brought through to a mature religious consciousness. In this consists the immense power of Protestantism; but its weakness appears here also. Its prophetic call is highly individualistic; and, from Jeremiah down, it must stand against sacrifices and ceremonies in its attempt to call the people into a sense of themselves as God intended them to be in the world. But there is risk in this, and many people resist, shy from, or pervert this understanding, preferring not to expose themselves either to God or to themselves. Also many who respond and "come to themselves" experience the institutional church as a restriction, dispense with it, and carry their vocations individually into the surrounding world.

Conversely, the weakness of Catholicism becomes its strength, in Jung's view. It retains perforce the moment of encounter with the abyss, as in Gerard Manley Hopkins's beleaguered cry, "I am gall, I am heartburn." [36] But through its retention of the worship of Mary it sublimates this encounter: at the moment of the individual's need for individuation it supplies a mother substitute, a mystical security whereby the worshiper may be protected from the agonistic question.

[36] Gerard Manley Hopkins, *Poems*, edited by Robert Bridges with appendix of additional poems, and a critical introduction by Charles Williams, Oxford University Press, London and New York, 1935, no. 45, p. 65.

So far Jung. At a much deeper level Martin Buber protests (as against Max Scheler's adoption of the Freudian principle of sublimation) that "the drama of a great life cannot be reduced to the duality of spirit and instinct"; that it is misleading to "identify the daemons with the instincts; they often have a purely spiritual face." [37] It is rather the passionate coincidence of these in creative vocation which is the sign of the spirit. One may experience, truly enough, what Scheler calls the "contrary-ness" of things, of contradiction in the "essence" of things. But over against this is the experience of "the grace of things"—"for example when the ploughshare has sunk softly and deeply into the soil as though the furrow were deliberately opening to receive it." "Certainly the experience of grace is only made possible by the experience of contrariness and in contrast to it. But here too it holds true that the spirit arises from concord with things and in concord with instincts." Or better:

> There is no other spirit but that which is nourished by the unity of life and by the unity with the world. Certainly it experiences being separated from the unity of life and being thrown into abysmal contradiction to the world. But even in the martyrdom of spiritual existence true spirit does not deny its primal community with the whole of being; rather it asserts it against the false representatives of being who deny it.[38]

But probably there is no finer formulation of this truth than that contained in the Protestant protest of "justification by grace through faith"—once the formula is deprived of its scholastic use as an antischolastic prejudice; that is, once it is as experience of the Event, and not merely a form of a doctrine about the Event.

Which brings us to the third question: (3) *the question of the will-guilt problem, and the creative Gestalt of Grace.*

This is a problem whose complications arise on the difficult terrain of the psychological even before they pass into the ravines of theological difference. We must be content, therefore, with observing simply that we appear to be called, to be required, to create, to produce what is latent within us as our authentic selves; but the

---

[37] Martin Buber, *Between Man and Man,* K. Paul, London, 1947, p. 191.
[38] *Ibid.,* pp. 194, 195–196.

moment we become conscious of this self-consciousness and begin to express the *own* will, we discover the *counter*-will (whether in parents, civic officials, society, or wherever), and guilt attaches to our authentic affirmations. Religiously we have been led too often into the negative denial of will; either by projecting the counter-will upon God producing thus a Jahvistic father-God whose will requires obeisance and obedience (as in Kafka); or, we have attempted the sublimation of the guilt through a Dantesque feminizing of the erotic principle. But the Protestant principle is a principle of calling, a vocational principle in which we are called to create as God creates, to form on the finite level as He forms infinitely, in which the guilt arises not from willing or creating, but from not creating, or from willing against one's calling, or creating outside the *Gestalt* of grace.

This phrase, the *Gestalt* of grace, is Tillich's phrase.[39] "Protestantism asserts," he holds, "that grace appears *through* a living *Gestalt* which remains in itself what it is. The divine appears *through* the humanity of Christ, *through* the historical weakness of the church, *through* the finite material of the sacrament. The divine appears through the finite realities as their transcendent meaning. Forms of grace are finite forms, pointing beyond themselves." And then he adds, "The Protestant protest prohibits the appearance of grace through finite forms from becoming an identification of grace with finite forms. Such an identification is, according to the Protestant principle, demonic *hybris*." [40]

From this it follows that Protestant symbols and Protestant forms must take their foothold in a "present situation"; they must represent what the existentialist calls "engagement"; but this is an engagement in depth: "The depth of every present is its power to transform the past into a future"—which can be creatively managed only by risk, venture, daring and courage. "Venturing without obedience to reality is wilful. But, without venturing, reality cannot be discovered. . . . A daring act is demanded, an act that penetrates to the deepest level of reality, to its transcendent ground. Such an act is what in the

[39] *Cf. op. cit.*, pp. 206 ff.
[40] *Ibid.*, p. 212,

religious tradition is called 'faith' . . ." It is for this reason that "Protestantism denies the security of sacramental systems with inviolable forms, sacred laws, eternal structures. It questions every claim of absoluteness; it remains dynamic even if it tried to become conservative." [41] And it is for this reason also that Protestant symbols, or Protestant formative power, are "at work wherever reality is transformed into an active expression of a *Gestalt* of grace." [42]

We may conclude, then, so far as the future of religious symbolism from the Protestant viewpoint is concerned, that the *notion* of symbolism itself needs to be freed from the classical substantialistic context in which it has been strait-jacketed. Here it has been subordinated to the analogy of classical logic, in which context it has had but two metiers in which to work—either the hierarchical one of Plato, which supports and informs the "sacramental" system; or the "romantic" reaction therefrom in which "esthetics" becomes an escape, or a form of play, or (as Delmore Schwartz puts it) "merely a Sunday with the beautiful." The term, "esthetics," is in either case controlled by the context; whereas in the dramatic context "esthetics" comes into its own, occupying at once the heart of the call to vocation and creativity which the prophetic-Christian context requires.

This means that the future of symbolism in Protestantism is completely open. For the subject until recently has moved within the confines of the classical hierarchical context, and the "barrenness" of Protestant symbols has been due entirely to the fact that Catholic symbols (quite rightly, as a matter of fact) were not richly in evidence. Protestantism has now to enter esthetically into possession of its own master images—the Covenant, the Word, the Cross, the Kingdom—and to expound them in the patterns suitable to its prophetic and dramatic *Gestalt*. We begin to see this in music, poetry, and art. The fact that it has not appeared to any great extent in liturgical change is not necessarily a fault. It is possible that we still think the term, "liturgical," within the substantialistic context;

[41] *Ibid.*, p. 215.
[42] *Ibid.*, p. 219.

thus the celebration of the Eucharist may be received without external change by the Protestant who, while rejecting the magical formulas which the substantialist theology requires, is at once released into his own *Gestalt* of communion and fellowship where the celebration takes on dimensions of meaning.

A word of warning must be added. The Protestant principle is a paradox. Its primary aim is not to build the cultus, nor to adorn the rite, nor to amplify the forms. It may be possible to speak of a "Catholic art"; but a "Protestant art" would necessarily be a contradiction in terms. For the Protestant principle aims not to make art but to make men who as Christians are artists. It aims to make men who will live in the world as God intended them to live and work in it—men called to co-creativity with God in the infinite and perpetual producing of the really new. Its symbols, in short, will be the old ones and the new, symbols of journey and return, symbols which symbolize the dangers of symbolism, symbols which draw men upon the ultimate *crux* of the human predicament in such a way as to effect there a *trans*formation and deliverance into the open and the new.

INDEX